CHINESE
STREET
FOOD

CHINESE
STREET FOOD

SMALL BITES, CLASSIC RECIPES, AND HARROWING TALES
ACROSS THE MIDDLE KINGDOM

Howie Southworth and Greg Matza

Skyhorse Publishing

Skyhorse Publishing books may be purchased in bulk at special discounts for sales promotion, corporate gifts, fund-raising, or educational purposes. Special editions can also be created to specifications. For details, contact the Special Sales Department, Skyhorse Publishing, 307 West 36th Street, 11th Floor, New York, NY 10018 or info@skyhorsepublishing.com.

Skyhorse® and Skyhorse Publishing® are registered trademarks of Skyhorse Publishing, Inc.®, a Delaware corporation.

Visit our website at www.skyhorsepublishing.com.

10 9 8 7 6 5 4 3 2 1

Library of Congress Cataloging-in-Publication Data

Names: Southworth, Howie, author. | Matza, Greg, author.
Title: Chinese street food : small bites, classic recipes, and harrowing tales across the Middle Kingdom / Howie Southworth and Greg Matza.
Description: New York, NY: Skyhorse Publishing, [2018]
Identifiers: LCCN 2018007371 | ISBN 9781510728158 (print) | ISBN 9781510728172 (ebook)
Subjects: LCSH: Cooking, Chinese. | Street food. | LCGFT: Cookbooks.
Classification: LCC TX724.5.C5 S634 2018 | DDC 641.5951—dc23 LC record available at https://lccn.loc.gov/2018007371

Cover design by Mona Lin
Cover photograph by Howie Southworth

Print ISBN: 978-1-5107-2815-8
Ebook ISBN: 978-1-5107-2817-2

Printed in China

TABLE OF CONTENTS

热搅团 6元/份

凉拌搅团 6元/份

酸菜鱼鱼 6元/份

INTRODUCTION

Chinese cuisine has a rich history dating back more than three millennia. Increasingly, those of us living outside of China are getting a clearer picture of the complexity that has developed over the duration. Thankfully, regional specialties, beyond your typical Cantonese, Sichuan, and Hunan dishes, are beginning to arrive on US shores, and a contemporary Chinese meal is no longer the egg foo yung of yesteryear. Still, one element of Chinese cookery that remains rare throughout the Western world is the most popular style of cuisine across China: *street food*! Every day, nearly one-fifth of humanity sustains itself on conveniently placed bites and cheap alfresco meals. In China, one's home is often small, kitchens are cramped, and time is short. So, a walkable nosh on the way to the office, a quick, cheap lunch, or an evening spent hopping from snack stand to snack stand with friends is an everyday occurrence.

We have been traveling to China for the past twenty-two years. Essentially, we go to China to eat. From the summits of temple-dotted mountains and the banks of picturesque river valleys to the sidewalks of frenetic, crowded, honking mega-cities, the names of which you've likely never heard, we've never had to look very far to find our next indulgence. Where restaurants are exquisite, numerous, and undeniably welcoming to foreign friends, we have a special place in our hearts for street food. It's relatively simple, filling, kind to the ol' wallet, and perhaps most importantly, it satisfies our need to be impulsive. *What's he cooking? That looks incredible! Did you smell that? We'd like three, please.* Since our objective has always been to eat well and we've been surrounded by the right stuff, it just makes sense to follow our five senses rather than a restaurant guide. We're also avid cooks, so it helps that with street food, we can eat, watch, and chat with cooks on this block, then the next, then the next. Endless fun.

Over the years, we've noticed the street food scene in China slowly changing. Some larger city governments, concerned about sanitation and pollution, have forced vendors to head indoors, or in some unfortunate cases, have closed stalls and makeshift cooking operations altogether. Some cities have gone the more creative route of collecting street cooks into dedicated snack halls, and formalizing the affair as an evening entertainment option. In cities and towns where vendors are unmoved and still thriving, popular food streets have become bucket-list entries for social media-leaning traveling foodies, for better or worse, making the crowds and queues we must endure longer and longer. Though the placement and context of *xiao chi*, or "small eats," may be shifting to accommodate a rapidly modernizing China, the cuisine itself is enjoying a renaissance.

On a recent visit to Beijing, we had the opportunity to sit down and chat with notable filmmaker Chen Xiaoqing. A few years ago, he produced two seasons of a madly popular documentary series for China Central Television entitled *The Tip of China's Tongue*, or known to the English-speaking world as *A Bite of China*. A natural storyteller, Chen gave us an elegant and succinct course in Chinese street food that was in step with what we've been able to witness firsthand, as well as hope for its future.

When I was young, I had no chance to study real street food. There was none. In the era of Communism, the streets were cleared, no restaurants, no shops, no stalls. It was years before I saw any snacks to buy. But, post-Mao, especially in the last thirty years, street food has become more and more popular [again]. It has become a very important part of our common lifestyle. In Beijing, recently, they have been closing down a lot of street stalls. They want cleaner streets and smoother traffic, so food, actually on the street, is fighting to survive. But, I believe it's also forcing traditional street food preparation to become more refined. Interestingly, this cuisine also holds an archive of any time period. Records of diet, social status, and how people relate to one another can all be reflected in street food. More important than the snacks themselves are the consumers and how they evolve over time. China's society is undergoing big changes. As the migration of people around the country picks up, so does diversity in cooking. From an evolutionary standpoint, the future of street food is very bright.

We wrote *Chinese Street Food* to celebrate a culinary culture that is quickly changing yet deeply rooted in tradition. We wanted to simultaneously preserve the feeling of a misty morning along a cobbled alleyway lined with billowing bamboo steamers, and shamelessly evangelize for a style of cooking that we feel should be better known. Our aim is to share a bit of culinary history as well as our personal relationship to the food, the vendors, the cooks, and to our fellow gastronomes. At times, we revel in the fantastical origin stories of superhero snacks, and at others, highlight the accessibility of timeless recipes that give a whole new meaning to *Chinese takeout*. The dishes throughout *Chinese Street Food* are simple, delicious, and far from top-of-mind when you consider the cuisine of the Middle Kingdom.

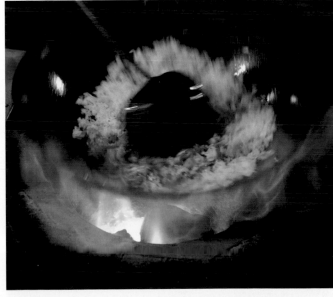

牛肉饼 Burgers ¥12.00元/个
土豆饼 Potato latkes ¥10.00元/个
煎饼火腿 HamPancakes ¥15.00元/张
煎饼肉松 PorkFlossPancakes ¥17.00元/张
绿豆沙冰 MungBeansmoothie ¥10.00元/杯
椰果凉茶 Coconut herbal tea ¥10.00元/杯

锦里移动支付

米米豆汤粥粥粥
浆
4 35   3 3

CHAPTER 1: WHAT'S IN A NAME?

WE HAVE A WONDERFULLY ENTERTAINING Chinese buddy named Qu Feng. He is an archaeologist and our go-to guy for historical perspective on Chinese cuisine. Some years ago, we had a lengthy discussion about food nomenclature, and it all started with the ubiquitous, fluffy white bun called a *mantou*. Mantou, according to Qu Feng, was originally *yemantou*, or "head of the barbarian!" Sounds delicious, no?

The story goes that the famous general and statesman during the Three Kingdoms period, Zhuge Liang, was leading his troops away from battle with many prisoners of war. They came across a raging river that they found improbable to cross. The general came up with a gruesomely simple way to appease the river gods and calm the waters. "What if we decapitated our prisoners and tossed just the heads into the horrendous current," pondered Zhuge Liang. "That's sure to ease the angry flow." Seems a weird gamble, right?

As legend has it, it worked. The only trouble was, eventually they reached a mad torrent with not a prisoner in sight. "Let's fool the river gods by replacing the real heads with bread heads, filled with meat, like brains!" Again, it worked, and *mantou* were born! As the Chinese have a tendency toward linguistic gymnastics, filled buns were replaced by the term *baozi* (see page 49) and *mantou* morphed into simple steamed white bread.

At some point, after hundreds of years, a political correctness wave hit the Chinese language and the term "barbarian heads" was just too gross for the name of a scrumptious food. So, move a line here, change a tone there, tack on the strokes meaning "food" and they were left with something close to "beautiful heads to eat." Still, one has to wonder about them leaving the word "head" in there . . .

So, we asked Qu Feng, of course. He simply shook his head and said, "Sometimes the individual parts of Chinese words, like in many other languages, lose their meaning. There's an entire school of Chinese linguistics dedicated to figuring out why words change and why some remain the same. People just get used to it, say what feels right, and don't mind so much." In other words, sometimes a head is just a bread.

The Chinese have a knack for naming foods in two distinct ways: brutally descriptive or metaphorical. Whether the goal is to be ironic, clever, or funny, the memorable names of several street foods abound. Just as with many restaurant dishes, these names are good for a chuckle, and offer endless dinner table conversation. Ask us sometime about "Water-Boiled Fish," or "Ants Climbing a Tree"! The former has very little to do with water, in fact it has the opposite effect on the palate, and the for the latter, not one ant was harmed.

Before we delve into more fun names and their recipes, we'd be remiss not to mention a physics professor named Anthony Zee from Howie's alma mater, UC–Santa Barbara. He wrote a wonderful book titled *Swallowing Clouds*, in which he takes readers through Chinese food names, their history, and their cultural roots. By the way, "swallowing clouds" is English for *wonton* (more on that later)!

Mantou
馒头
(Steamed "Barbarian Head" Buns)

If you're in New York City on any given weekday morning, on any given street, someone is walking with bagel in hand. If you're in Paris, it's a baguette. In Beijing, you can bet it's going to be *mantou*, that ubiquitous fluffy white bun and most simple of the street foods. Seldom eaten on its own, mantou is often enjoyed as a starchy staple in the company of warm soy milk, a steamy cup of green tea, or a hearty rice porridge (page 65). At times, particularly later in the morning to early afternoon, mantou meets the grill, is sliced open, and is filled with all kinds of goodies as in the Paocai Kaomantou (page 79). That's one popular barbarian head!

One winter's morning in Beijing, the winds out of the north were brutal, as we were venturing out to show a filmmaker friend of ours, Tim, a good time on the Great Wall. "It's not cold enough, let's go up a mountain!" Crazy. We were shooting a web series we produced for Asia Society called *China in Plain English*. Look it up. Anyway, before heading out, we decided to carbo-load and sat for a wonderful warming breakfast of Mantou, Egg-Drop Soup (page 278), Tofu "Brains" (page 29), and crispy, thick Fried Dough Sticks (page 67). We highly suggest it . . . and the Great Wall in winter. Brrr.

Total Time: 2 hours, 45 minutes | Serves: 4–6

3½ cups all-purpose flour, plus more for dusting
2 tsp rapid rise yeast
½ tsp salt

2 Tbsp granulated sugar
1 cup warm water, plus more for steaming
1 Tbsp vegetable oil

In a large mixing bowl or the bowl of stand mixer, whisk together flour, yeast, salt, and sugar. Using clean hands or the dough hook of the stand mixer, incorporate water and oil until a smooth dough forms.

Dust the countertop or work surface with additional flour and transfer the dough onto the flour. Dust the top of the dough, knead, and form the dough into a ball. Transfer the dough to a large, clean, lightly oiled bowl and cover with plastic wrap. Allow the dough to double in size, about one hour to 90 minutes.

continued on page 12

Uncover the dough, dust the work surface with flour, transfer the dough atop the flour, and evenly hand-roll it into a 2-inch-thick log. Cut the dough into 2-inch pieces. Roll each dough piece into a ball. Prepare steamer baskets by lining them with cheesecloth or parchment paper. (We prefer to cut individual 3-inch x 3-inch squares of parchment paper for individual buns.) Place the dough balls atop the lining, about 2 inches apart. Cover the steamer basket(s) with their matching lid. Let the dough balls rest for 20 minutes.

Place a skillet or pot over medium heat, fill with 2 inches of water, and bring to a boil. Carefully place the steamer baskets atop the pot of boiling water, cover, and steam the buns for 12 minutes.

This dough and a similar process is used for a variety of recipes in this book, including Steamed Eggplant or Pork Buns on page 49 and Pan-Fried Buns on page 245.

Jiandan Guokui
煎蛋锅盔
(Fried "Pan Helmet" Egg Sandwiches)

The history and naming of *guokui* can vary depending on who you ask. Every story involves some ancient Chinese military squadron, lack of armor and/or lack of cookware, stale pastry being used as the former, and shields being used as the latter. We thank our archaeologist friend Qu Feng for providing our favorite among them. In Han Dynasty China, as legend has it, guokui were fried so large, so hard, and so thick, that leftover specimens were often used to protect soldiers from falling arrows. Today, we wouldn't recommend this type of protection. Modern guokui are delicate, comparatively diminutive, and dangerously delicious. Progress.

Though we've enjoyed guokui in dozens of forms from Beijing to Kunming, there's one experience from last year that stands out as the guokui to put others to shame. While pedaling our Ofo bikes around the Muslim Quarter of Xi'an, tucked up in the northwest corner in the shadow of the city wall, we met a man who ruined other breakfast sandwiches forever. The kindly yet devious Mr. Guan took his seventeen years of guokui-making experience and changed the rules of breakfast, entirely. Imagine an impossibly crispy, thin, buttery bun, with a creamy, peppery, simple fried egg nestled within. No ham, no bacon, no avocado! Just egg. Stop imagining and cook.

Total Time: 1 hour, 15 minutes | Serves: 5–6

DOUGH:
3 cups all-purpose flour, plus more
   for dusting
½ tsp salt
1 cup hot water
1 tsp vegetable or canola oil, plus
   more for brushing

FILLING:
6 eggs
½ tsp salt
½ tsp ground black pepper

½ cup vegetable or canola oil for frying

Whisk together flour and salt in a large mixing bowl or the bowl of a stand mixer. Using clean hands in a mixing bowl or the dough hook in a stand mixer, slowly incorporate the water and 1 teaspoon of oil and knead until a single mass of dough forms.

continued on page 15

Dust the work surface with flour and transfer the dough on top. Knead and form the dough into a smooth ball. Transfer the dough to a lightly oiled, clean bowl, and cover with plastic wrap. Allow the dough to rest for 30 minutes.

Preheat the oven to 475°F. Brush a thin layer of oil across the work surface. Uncover the dough, transfer the dough atop the oil and evenly hand-roll it onto a 2-inch-thick log. Cut the dough into 2-inch pieces. Knead and roll each of the dough pieces into a ball. Hand-roll one ball into a 1-inch log. Using a rolling pin, roll the dough into a long oval, ¼-inch or thinner is best. Using a clean fingertip, dipped into oil, rub the surface of the dough, leaving the edges untouched.

Starting from one narrow end, roll it up as you would a poster. Stand the roll on its end and gently flatten and roll it into a 4- to 5-inch disc. If an outer edge sticks out, fold it under the bottom of the disc as you roll it. Set aside and continue to make discs with the remaining dough balls.

Add ½ cup of oil in a skillet over medium heat. When the oil begins to shimmer, place a few discs comfortably in the skillet, and work in batches. Fry the discs on one side for 2–3 minutes, or until the bottom is golden brown. Flip the discs over and continue cooking for 2 minutes. Remove the partially cooked discs from the skillet and place on a rack over one or more sheet pans. Finish browning the remaining dough discs.

Transfer the sheet pan(s) to the oven and bake the dough until the guokui are cooked through, about another 6–8 minutes. Remove the guokui from the oven and let them cool for 2 minutes. Fry each egg and sprinkle with salt and pepper. Cut open a guokui and fill it with one egg. Serve hot. Best breakfast sandwich *ever*.

Bangbang Ji / Guaiwei Ji
棒棒鸡/怪味鸡
("Strange-Flavored" Chicken)

Sometimes food in China is named for what it looks like (see "Barbarian Heads," page 11), sometimes for what the dude selling it looks like (see "Pole" Noodles, page 32), and sometimes it carries several fun names. In the case of "Strange-Flavored" Chicken, it's obviously named for an eating experience that can't be easily explained, but also for the sound made when a cooked chicken is being pounded with a big baton, busting the meat into serving portions. (Wow, that was a mouthful.) *Bang!* *Bang!* Where those days are largely gone and this delectable chicken dish has mostly gone to citywide, less noisy shops, the name still conjures up mouthwatering anticipation for anyone waiting in the inevitable line.

   "Strange-flavored" bears some need for explanation, no? Traditionally, the five flavors in Chinese cookery are salty, sour, sweet, spicy, and bitter. When a dish comes along that embodies all five, it's difficult to nail the overall sensation other than to call it *guai*, or "strange." The first time we tried bang bang chicken was in Chengdu, capital of Sichuan Province, seventeen years back. Friends had already introduced us to Sichuan's penchant for strong flavors. Thanks a ton, Dave Fan! But, one bite of this dish sent our tongues and minds reeling. It was as if our palates had suddenly graduated from Chengdu elementary school and gone straight to Sichuan University.

Total Time: 50 minutes | Serves: 6–8

¾ cup sesame paste or creamy
   peanut butter
1 cup soy sauce
⅓ cup Chinese black vinegar
⅓ cup toasted sesame oil
⅓ cup sugar
2 tsp Sichuan peppercorn, ground

6 chicken pieces, boneless, cooked, diced or shredded, *or* roasted chicken from Kaoji (Roasted Chicken) on page 191
⅓ cup red chile oil with sediment *or* Lajiao You (Chile Oil) on page 132
2 Tbsp white sesame seeds

In a mixing bowl, thoroughly whisk together sesame paste, soy sauce, vinegar, sesame oil, sugar, and peppercorns. Be sure that the sugar dissolves completely.

To serve the bang bang ji like they do on the streets of Chengdu, pour the sesame mixture into individual bowls, followed by some pieces of chicken and some lajiao, and finally sprinkle on some sesame seeds. Suggest that guests mix everything together before enjoying this rather piquant snack or appetizer.

Zhajiang Mian
炸酱面
("Deep-Fried Sauce" Noodles)

The name of this dish, *zhajiang mian*, causes us great distress. Who would want to eat noodles with a sauce that was deep-fried? Is it even possible to deep-fry a sauce? Even if it were physically plausible, would it be very appetizing after you somehow got a sauce out of scaldingly hot oil? "Deep-fried sauce" is just plain wrong and simply misleading. Perhaps it was used to elicit shock? It worked. The sauce is actually stir-fried and delicious. So, why not call it "Stir-Fried Sauce" or chaojiang? It's curious and a little more than hilarious.

We've asked many an expert on food etymology this very set of questions. A while back in Beijing, we were fortunate enough to meet with Chen Xiaoqing, the Director of the award-winning documentary series called *A Bite of China*, which appeared on China Central Television. If you're into food on film, *watch this series*. It will change the way you think about going out for Chinese. But, we digress. Mr. Chen brought us to a well-known Michelin-starred duck restaurant and ordered the chef's take on traditional street foods.

We had the perfect opportunity to ask our *deep-fried question* when zhajiang noodles came to the table! Mr. Chen, when we inquired about the naming oddity, echoed what our archaeologist buddy Qu Feng always says about Chinese food etymology: "Most people don't see individual characters anymore. They just know the dish name and forget that it sounds weird, and it does when you think about it too much." We do think about things too much. This dish is divine.

Total Time: 1 hour | Serves: 6–8

SAUCE:
½ lb ground pork
½ teaspoon salt
½ tsp white pepper
1 inch ginger, peeled, minced
3 cloves garlic, minced
1 Tbsp vegetable or canola oil
4 Tbsp sweet bean sauce
  (tianmianjiang) or hoisin sauce

1 tsp Chinese black vinegar
2 Tbsp mushroom or other dark soy
  sauce
2 tsp cornstarch
1¼ cup chicken broth *or* broth from
  Jirou Tang (Chicken Soup) on
  page 189

continued on page 20

NOODLES:
½ lb Chinese wheat noodles,
  spaghetti, or other long noodle

GARNISH:
2 cucumbers, shredded
5 red radishes, shredded
1 large carrot, shredded
6 oz edamame, blanched, shelled
4 scallions, thinly sliced

In a mixing bowl, thoroughly mix pork, salt, pepper, ginger, and garlic. Set aside and cook the noodles according to package directions. Drain and rinse the noodles and set aside.

Add oil to a skillet over medium heat. When the oil begins to shimmer, add the marinated pork mixture and sauté for 4–5 minutes, or until all of the meat is cooked through. Stir in sweet bean or hoisin, vinegar, and soy sauce, and continue to sauté for 3 minutes. In a small bowl, whisk together cornstarch and chicken broth or water. Stir this mixture into the skillet, bring to a boil, reduce the heat to low and simmer for 20 minutes.

Evenly distribute noodles into bowls. Then top with some sauce from the skillet, followed by the garnishes. Suggest that guests mix it all together before enjoying.

Huixiang Jiubing
茴香韭饼
(Fennel Frond "Garlic Chive" Pancakes)

As you can see by browsing through this book, there is a dizzying array of stuffed dough within the Chinese culinary pantheon. Some are rolled, some are coiled, some are beautifully pleated, and some are simply pinched. But, in the case of *jiubing*, the filling is just sandwiched between two thin pieces of dough before the whole package is fried. This is the simplest among the pancakes and the oldest format found across China.

When we first met jiubing, it was a late summer evening on a roadside somewhere in Shaanxi Province. We were on our way back to our hotel after a long day of temple spotting and of course, eating too much. Seeing the unmistakable pancake griddle at 100 yards, we were naturally drawn in to examine what was on offer. "What's another meal?" we said to ourselves. In talking to the vendor, we learned that these gems are what he calls "garlic chive pancakes," but only one of his fillings is garlic chives. We asked, "Are these *all* garlic chive pancakes?" "Of course," he responded. "Even the ones with no garlic chives?" we follow on. "Yep." So, we picked the one with fennel fronds, since it was pretty unique. When the order came up, he approached us and said, "Here's your fennel frond garlic chive pancake with no garlic chives!" What's in a name, indeed!

Total Time: 1 hour | *Serves: 4–6*

WRAPPERS:
3 cups all-purpose flour, plus more
for dusting
½ tsp salt
1 cup hot water
1 tsp vegetable or canola oil

FILLING:
1 tsp vegetable or canola oil
2 cups fennel fronds, finely chopped
4 scallions, minced
½ tsp salt

¼ cup vegetable or canola oil for frying

Whisk together flour and salt in a large mixing bowl or the bowl of a stand mixer. Using clean hands in a mixing bowl or the dough hook in a stand mixer, slowly incorporate the water and 1 teaspoon of oil and knead until a single mass of dough forms.

Dust the work surface with flour and transfer the dough on top. Knead and form the dough into a smooth ball. Transfer the dough to a lightly oiled, clean bowl, and cover with plastic wrap. Allow the dough to rest for 30 minutes.

Heat oil in a skillet over medium heat. When the oil begins to shimmer, add fennel fronds, scallions, and salt to the skillet. Sauté for 2 minutes, or until all of the contents are wilted. Remove from the heat, transfer the filling to a bowl and set aside. Wipe out the skillet.

Dust the work surface with flour. Uncover the dough, transfer the dough atop the oil and evenly hand-roll it onto a 1-inch-thick log. Cut the dough into 1-inch pieces. Roll the dough pieces into balls. Flatten each dough ball by hand, then use a rolling pin to create very thin 4-inch rounds.

Spread 2 tablespoons of filling onto the center of half of the dough rounds, leaving a ½-inch gap at the edges. Place the remaining half of dough rounds atop the halves with filling. Press to seal the edges of the filled dough.

Add 2 tablespoons of oil into a skillet (with a matching lid) and heat over medium. When the oil begins to shimmer, place a few filled dough discs into the skillet. Don't crowd the pan. Work in batches if necessary. Fry for 2–3 minutes or until the bottoms are golden brown. Flip the pancakes, cover with a lid, and fry for another 2–3 minutes. Remove the pancake to a paper towel-lined plate and repeat for the remaining dough discs.

Serve hot as a quick snack.

Huntun Tang

馄饨汤

("Swallowing Clouds" Soup)

There are a number of ways that the Chinese refer to what we've come to know as the *huntun*, or "wonton," which is close to the Cantonese pronunciation. Even though written Chinese is common between Mandarin and Cantonese speakers, in this case, they surprisingly use different characters for the same food. In Mandarin, *huntun* can mean "chaos," and in Cantonese, *wonton* means "swallowing clouds," which we find to be more fun. Where most of this book is based upon Mandarin names for street food, this is an exception that's impossible to pass up.

You see, *wonton* is one of the most poetic names for a Chinese dish we've ever encountered, and as a bonus, it's a double entendre! Cloud-like pillows of pasta, swallowing a tiny bit of ground meat filling? Or, is the diner swallowing these clouds as they enjoy a delicately delicious bowl? In reality, wontons in the US often are actually *tangjiao*, or dumplings in soup under a more recognizable name. They typically have meatball-volumed filling inside a thick skin. In China, huntun are a study in minimalism. Very thin pasta sheets, with a tiny bit of meat filling, such that when they are cooked, they float gently atop the clear soup, like, well, clouds. Swallow them.

Total Time: 45 minutes | Serves: 6–8

14–16 cups salted chicken stock *or* broth from Jirou Tang (Chicken Soup) on page 189
1 recipe Pork Filling from Zhurou Jiaozi (Steamed Pork Dumplings) on page 53

1 16-oz package wonton or gyoza skins, square preferred
1 gallon plus 1 cup water for boiling, plus more for sealing the dumplings
4 scallions, thinly sliced

Bring the broth to a boil over medium heat, then reduce the heat to low to maintain a simmer. In a large mixing bowl, thoroughly combine all of the Pork Filling ingredients.

In the middle of one wrapper, place 1 teaspoon of filling. With a wet finger, moisten the edges of the wrapper. Fold the wrapper in half into a triangle around the filling and seal by pinching the edges completely. Repeat with the remaining filling and wrappers.

Bring 1 gallon of water to a boil over high heat. Stir the pot to create a current such that as you drop the individual wontons into the water, they are not likely to stick together. When the water comes to a boil again, add 1 cup of cold water and continue to cook for an additional 7–8 minutes. Remove wontons from the water to a plate using a slotted spoon or sieve.

Evenly distribute cooked wontons to bowls, then add 1–2 cups of hot broth to each bowl. Top with scallions and serve hot.

WHAT'S IN A NAME?

25

Niurou Guokui

牛肉锅盔

(Fried "Pan Helmet" Beef Pastries)

Over the last two millennia, buns in China have undergone invention, deconstruction, reconstruction, reinvention, and innovation. Pancakes with the fillings evenly embedded into the body of the dough, like a cyclone hit a farmers' market next to a bakery, such as the Scallion Pancakes on page 272, Baked Sesame Buns on page 197, and *guokui*, or "Pan Helmets," are among the most advanced examples of pastry the world has seen. Take that, cronut! We kid. Guokui are more of a technique than a recipe. The unique method of flattening, filling, rolling, and re-flattening into a spiral boggles the mind and pleases the palate. By the way, if you've missed our entertaining explanation of the "pan helmet" name, see the introduction for Jiandan Guokui on page 13.

Throughout this book, we frequently mention the city of Xi'an, as it is a food mecca and has been for us for two decades. You should really visit. Within the Muslim Quarter, there are a ton of guokui vendors. But one of our favorites is offered by the Wu family, who are fifty years deep (fried?). Their finesse and rolling expertise is second to none, but what makes them unique is a super thin, crackly outer shell, almost shatteringly crisp, followed by a tender, flaky chewy interior. Their biggest seller is a beef and scallion masterpiece that features the humble green onion with a mere hint of meat. We meet them in the middle with this recipe, and allow both to shine.

Total Time: 1 hour, 25 minutes | Serves: 6–8

DOUGH:

3 cups all-purpose flour, plus more
    for dusting

½ tsp salt

1 cup hot water

1 tsp vegetable or canola oil, plus
    more for brushing

½ cup vegetable or canola oil
    for frying

FILLING:

½ lb ground beef

1 tsp Lajiao You (Chile Oil), page 132

1 tsp soy sauce

1 clove garlic, minced

½ inch ginger, peeled, minced

2 scallions, thinly sliced

1 tsp ground cumin

1 tsp dried red chile flakes

½ tsp ground Sichuan peppercorn

½ tsp salt

1 tsp vegetable or canola oil

Whisk together flour and salt in a large mixing bowl or the bowl of stand mixer. Using clean hands in a mixing bowl or the dough hook in a stand mixer, slowly incorporate the water and 1 teaspoon of oil and knead until a single mass of dough forms.

Dust the work surface with flour and transfer the dough on top. Knead and form the dough into a smooth ball. Transfer the dough to a lightly oiled, clean bowl, and cover with plastic wrap. Allow the dough to rest for 30 minutes.

In a mixing bowl, thoroughly combine the filling ingredients. Preheat the oven to 475°F. Brush a thin layer of oil across the work surface. Uncover the dough, transfer the dough atop the oil and evenly hand-roll it onto a 2-inch-thick log. Cut the dough into 2-inch pieces. Knead and roll each of the dough pieces into a ball. Hand-roll one ball into a 1-inch log. Using a rolling pin, roll the dough into a long oval, ¼-inch or thinner is best.

Smear a thin layer of the filling, about 1–2 tablespoons, across the long center of the dough. Be sure that the filling does not reach the edges. Starting from one narrow end, roll it up as you would a poster. It's okay to stretch the dough as you roll it to completely surround the filling. Stand the roll on its end and gently flatten and roll it into a 4- to 5-inch disc. If an outer edge sticks out, fold it under the bottom of the disc as you flatten it. If some of the filling pops through the disc as you roll it, dust the exposed filling with flour and continue. Set aside and continue to make discs with the remaining dough balls.

Add ½ cup of oil in a skillet over medium heat. When the oil begins to shimmer, place a few discs comfortably in the skillet, and work in batches. Fry the discs on one side for 2–3 minutes, or until the bottom is golden brown. Flip the discs over and continue cooking for 2 minutes. Remove the partially cooked discs from the skillet and place on a rack over a sheet pan or a few. Finish browning the remaining dough discs.

Transfer the sheet pan(s) to the oven and bake the dough until the guokui are cooked through, about another 6–8 minutes. Remove the guokui from the oven and serve hot.

Doufunao
豆腐脑
(Tofu "Brains")

For the last 2000 years, give or take a few, freshly made tofu could be found across China. In days past, it was common to find walking *douhua* hawkers with a pole across their shoulders, a barrel of tofu hanging from one end and a bucket full of toppings dangling from the other, selling to hungry passersby. Some toppings favor the sweet: cinnamon, sugar syrup, aged soy sauce, and dried fruits, while others tend toward the savory and/or spicy: soy sauce, black vinegar, red chile oil, Sichuan peppercorn, and herbs. At times, crackers, fried beans, and/or nuts are added for texture.

Where Southerners are likely to simply refer to the snack as *douhua*, Northerners call it *doufunao*, or tofu "brains"! This rather descriptive name comes from the textural/visual likeness to brains after you break soft tofu up in a bowl along with colorful ingredients. Swerving away from the name, did we tell you that we'd always kept an eye out for the pole guy as long as we've been visiting China? This was our white whale. Last Summer in Chengdu, it finally happened! We enjoyed a quick chat with Mr. Ding, and of course, ate his tofu. "I'll carry this pole as long people are buying my food," he exclaimed! Enjoy Mr. Ding's brains

Total Time: 1 hour | Serves: 4–6

1 Tbsp vegetable or canola oil, plus more for frying

6 scallions, separated into white and green parts, thinly sliced

10 oz shiitake mushrooms, thinly sliced

5 oz Chinese dried black wood ear mushrooms, rehydrated, drained, thinly sliced

4 cups chicken broth, *or* broth from Jirou Tang (Chicken Soup) on page 189

¼ cup soy sauce

1 Tbsp Chinese black vinegar

12 wonton wrappers, ½-inch strips

2 lb fresh or silken tofu

Add 1 tablespoon of oil to a pot over medium-high heat. When the oil begins to shimmer, add the scallion whites and mushrooms. Sauté for 5–6 minutes or until the scallions are translucent and the mushrooms have begun to brown.

continued on page 31

Add broth, soy sauce, and vinegar to the pot and bring it to a boil. Reduce the heat to low and maintain a simmer for 20 minutes while you fry the wonton strips.

In a separate pot over medium heat, add oil to a depth of 1 inch, and heat to 360°F.

Fry the wonton strips in batches until golden brown. Remove to a paper towel–lined plate.

Evenly hand-crumble tofu into 4–6 bowls. Ladle broth over the tofu, top with scallion greens and wonton strips, and serve hot. Optionally, you may also garnish it with Lajiao You (Chile Oil) on page 132.

Handy Trick: No thermometer? No problem! To test the readiness of the oil for frying, use a wooden chopstick. Dip the chopstick into the oil at an angle and touch the bottom of the pot. When the submerged part of the chopstick is surrounded completely by little bubbles, the oil is ready.

Dandan Mian
担担面
(Spicy Sesame "Pole" Noodles)

Just like Tofu "Brains" on page 29, vendors of *dandan* noodles walked the streets, notably in Sichuan Province, with a pole across their shoulders, barrels of noodles and sauce dangling from opposite ends. But this dish actually retained the name of the pole, the *biandan*. I guess we know who won that popularity contest. Noodles! Dandan noodles are a Sichuan classic, made up of all of the southwestern Chinese celebrities: chile oil, sesame, Sichuan peppercorns, and salty preserved mustard tubers. Some say that it carries the same appeal of "Strange-Flavored" Chicken (page 16) by hitting all of the notes: sour, salty, sweet, spicy, and bitter. But, we disagree.

Dandan noodles are exquisitely unique, if only for the textural adventure it presents. Slippery noodles, crunchy peanuts, crispy herbs, creamy cold sauce, chewy meat, and the prerequisite red chile oil burn! Going further, there's a bit of a competition across Chengdu for who can fine tune dandan noodles while remaining traditional. We prefer the standard, but one thing that sets a noodle joint apart for us is the hospitality. In particular, the Hexin Mianzhuang (noodle house), in the Wenshufang neighborhood of Chengdu at 27 Silver Street, is simply the best, warmest, kindest that we've encountered.

Where else in the world would we be able to set up a photo-shoot of beautiful noodles in a gorgeous bowl, *in the middle of a busy street*? Nowhere else but here. That was a fun afternoon of people gathering around to see what we were up to, giving suggestions of bowl placement on the pavement or in the air, and keeping cars from crushing us. You know, just normal travelers. At one point, a local cop started to approach what was becoming a pretty big crowd of gawkers with us at the center. We thought, *oh well, the jig is up*, as we braced ourselves to quickly pack up the gear. The cop walked up to us, leered at the camera's LCD screen, and said, "Hey, that looks great!" Patted us on the back and walked away. China.

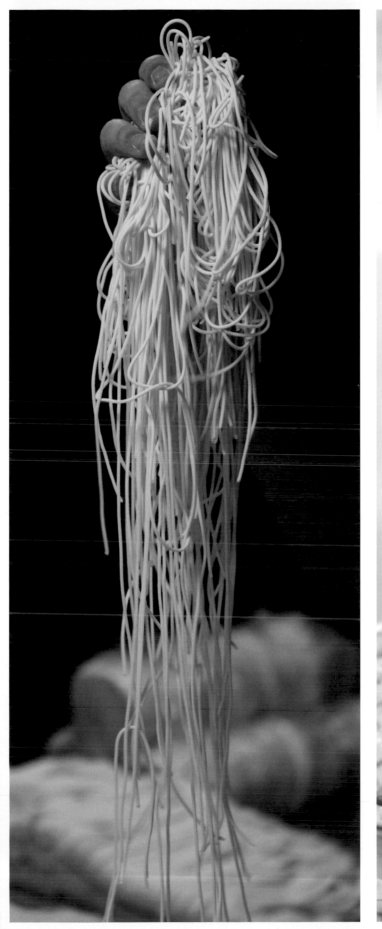

HOT SAUCE:
1 Tbsp vegetable or canola oil
1 lb ground pork
½ tsp salt
2 tsp five-spice powder
3 cloves garlic, minced
2 Tbsp Chinese rice wine or dry
    sherry
2 Tbsp sweet bean sauce
    (tianmianjiang) or hoisin sauce
4 tsp mushroom or other dark soy
    sauce
½ cup preserved Sichuan vegetables
    (yacai), pickled cabbage or mild
    kimchi, drained, minced

NOODLES:
1 gallon water
2 Tbsp salt
1 lb Chinese long wheat noodles or
    thin spaghetti

COLD SAUCE:
½ cup Chinese sesame paste or tahini
½ cup soy sauce
2 tsp sugar
2 tsp Sichuan peppercorn, ground
    (optional)

GARNISH:
¾ cup red chile oil with sediment *or*
    Lajiao You (Chile Oil) on page 132
1 cup roasted peanuts, crushed
4 scallions, thinly sliced
¾ cup yellow soybeans, crispy fried
    (optional)

Add oil to a skillet over medium heat. When the oil begins to shimmer, add pork, salt, and five-spice powder, and sauté until the pork is cooked through, about 5 minutes. Add garlic, rice wine, sweet bean or hoisin sauce, soy sauce, and preserved vegetables, and continue to sauté until the liquid has mostly dried, about an additional 5 minutes. Keep warm.

Cook the noodles according to package directions. Drain the noodles, and keep the cooking water.

In a mixing bowl, whisk together the cold sauce ingredients, plus ½ cup of the noodle cooking water. Distribute this mixture evenly into bowls. Then, spoon on some Lajiao to each diner's taste. Equally distribute noodles into the bowls. Top with meat sauce, then peanuts, scallions, and optionally, soybeans. Suggest that guests mix it all together before enjoying.

Pugai Mian
铺盖面
("Bedspread" Noodles)

There's no other way to put it—as noodles go, pugai mian are gigantic, well, like a bedspread, hence the name. Eating them is unlike any other noodle slurping experience in China, since it's not a noodle slurping experience at all. It's a noodle biting event, to be sure. Lift up the edible bedspread, chomp, lower the bedspread, sip some soup. These things are so big, a single bowl may only present one or maybe two monster pasta sheets for your eating pleasure. They're big, that's all we're saying.

One day, lost somewhere in Sichuan Province, we pulled up to a stand while the smiley staff were freshly fashioning some bedspread noodles next to a huge wok of boiling water. Take a hunk of dough, pull, stretch, stretch, pull until it's deemed huge enough, then lower the appropriately harassed dough into the bubbles for a minute or two. Accordingly, every single noodle has its own shape, size, and personality. All of a sudden, it dawned on us. Rather than *this* bowl of noodles being a quick bite, pugai mian is a slow-you-down kind of meal, just like the laid-back nature of Sichuan. Eating them takes time, intentionality, and mindfulness to fairly notice the love that went into making each tasty, steaming bowl.

Total Time: 1 hour, 35 minutes | Serves: 6–8

SAUCE:
2 tsp vegetable or canola oil
1 lb ground pork
½ tsp salt
½ tsp ground black pepper
1 Tbsp soy sauce
½ tsp Chinese black vinegar

NOODLES:
1 lb dried lasagna noodles (not oven-ready) *or*
   1½ cup high-gluten flour
   1½ cup all-purpose flour, plus more for dusting
   ½ tsp salt
   1 cup water
2 Tbsp salt for boiling

GARNISH:
⅓ cup red chile oil with sediment *or* Lajiao You (Chile Oil) on page 132
⅓ cup soy sauce
⅓ cup Chinese black vinegar
4 scallions, thinly sliced
1 bunch cilantro, roughly chopped

To make the sauce, add oil to a skillet over medium heat. When the oil begins to shimmer, add pork, salt, and pepper, and sauté until the pork is cooked through, about 5 minutes. Add soy sauce and vinegar and continue to sauté until the liquid has mostly dried. Keep warm.

If using lasagna noodles, cook them according to package directions and skip the next two paragraphs.

If making noodles from scratch, in a large mixing bowl or the bowl of a stand mixer, whisk together flours and ½ teaspoon of salt. With clean hands or the dough hook of the stand mixer, slowly incorporate 1 cup of water and knead until a single mass of dough forms. Cut the dough in half. By hand, knead each half into a ball, cover with plastic wrap and let them rest for 1 hour.

Bring 1 gallon of water and 2 tablespoons of salt to a boil over high heat as you cut the noodles. Dust the work surface with flour. Starting with one dough ball, roll it into a 12 x 12-inch wide square. Cut into 3-inch strips. Dust the strips with flour to keep them from sticking. Repeat with the other ball of dough. Pick up one strip by grasping either end between four fingers and a palm. Try to keep a 3-inch width as you stretch the dough strip a few more inches long. Then, lower it into the boiling water. Repeat with the remaining dough strips. Noodles are cooked when they reach a pleasantly chewy consistency, 2½–3 minutes.

Carefully remove the noodles from the water using a slotted spoon or a sieve. Evenly distribute noodles into bowls. Ladle some of the pasta water into each bowl, then top with some sauce from the skillet, followed by the guest-selected garnishes. Suggest that guests mix it all together before enjoying.

Biangbiang Mian
("Table Slap" Noodles with House Sauce)

If "Barbarian Heads," or *mantou,* were the inspiration for this chapter, certainly *biangbiang* noodles take a close second place. Not only is the very complex visual character made up, but the word *biang* is not even a Chinese word! Notice the lack of Chinese script above! According to a Chinese gastronome friend, Jiao Erqiang (English name "Joe"), though many origin stories exist, the most touching is that many moons ago, a student who happily filled up on this whimsically-titled dish couldn't pay his bill. Uh oh. So, in exchange, the shop owner took him up on the offer to invent a visual character to represent this style of noodle. Would this humble shopkeep soon be the *only* one in town with a legit brand? Not on your life. It caught on *in a big way* across central and southwestern China.

The "word" biang itself is very cool. It's onomatopoeiaic! But, exactly how? We'd never actually gone for biangbiang noodles with the expressed interest in *listening* to the experience. Curious upon hearing the story from Joe, we grabbed a few stools at a little shop in Xi'an and ordered up. We were determined to identify the exact sound that led to the name. Theories abound in literature. Was it the sound of someone chewing the noodle? Can't be, as there's nothing terribly unique to the sound of chomping on one pasta vs. another. Maybe it's the shop owner's call to gather a crowd? Nope, he was a pretty quiet dude. Just then, as if someone knew our intent, *biang, biang, biang*! Joe was the first to zoom in on the noise. It's surely the sound of the dough, after being stretched, getting whacked with gusto on the wooden worktable just before being launched into boiling water. Biang! You can play the home version!

There is one other standout aspect of this dish: fresh vegetables! Though every restaurant that serves biangbiang noodles serves up their own proprietary formula for sauce, it's also not unusual to see this noisy pasta keeping company with whatever looked best at the farm market on any given morning. The world of biangbiang is simply special. Here is a great combo that we enjoyed on that auspicious day with Joe.

Total Time: 1 hour, 45 minutes | Serves: 6–8

VEGETABLES:
8 cups water
2 tsp salt
1 head cauliflower, small florets
½ lb green beans, 1-inch segments
3 stalks celery, julienned
4 Roma tomatoes, small wedges

GARNISH:
⅓ cup soy sauce
⅓ cup Chinese black vinegar
1 bunch cilantro, roughly chopped,
    including stems
⅓ cup red chile oil with sediment *or*
    Lajiao You (Chile Oil) on page 132

NOODLES:
1 lb pappardelle or other wide, flat
    noodles *or*
    1½ cup high-gluten flour
    1½ cup all-purpose flour, plus
        more for dusting
    ½ tsp salt
    1 cup water
1 gallon water for boiling
2 Tbsp salt for boiling

To prepare the vegetables, in a pot over high heat, bring water to a boil. Add salt, cauliflower, green beans, and celery, and boil for 5 minutes. Add tomato and cook for one additional minute. Using a slotted spoon or a sieve, remove the vegetables from the water and keep warm.

If using prepared noodles, cook them according to package directions and skip the next two paragraphs.

If making noodles from scratch, in a large mixing bowl or the bowl of a stand mixer, whisk together flours and ½ teaspoon of salt. With clean hands or the dough hook of the stand mixer, slowly incorporate 1 cup of water and knead until a single mass of dough forms. Cut the dough in half. By hand, knead each half into a ball, cover with plastic wrap and let them rest for 1 hour.

Bring 1 gallon of water and 2 tablespoons of salt to a boil over high heat as you cut the noodles. Dust the work surface with flour. Starting with one dough ball, roll it into a 12 x 12-inch wide rectangle. Cut into 1-inch strips. Lightly dust the strips with flour to keep them from sticking. Repeat with the other half of dough. Pick up one strip by grasping either end between two fingers and a thumb. Try to keep a 1-inch width as you stretch the dough strip a few more inches long. As one is stretched, give it a good slap against the work surface and see if you can produce the *biang*! Then, lower it into the boiling water. Repeat with the remaining dough strips. Noodles are cooked when they reach a pleasantly chewy consistency, 2½–3 minutes.

Carefully remove the noodles from the water using a slotted spoon or a sieve. Evenly distribute noodles into bowls. Ladle 3 tablespoons of the pasta water into each bowl, then top with a balanced amount of vegetables, followed by a tablespoon each of soy sauce and vinegar and some cilantro and chile oil to taste. Suggest that guests mix it all together before enjoying.

Tianshui Mian
甜水面
("Sweet Water" Noodles)

Tian means sweet. *Shui* means water. *Mian* means noodles. So, which is sweet, the water or the noodles? Or are the noodles cooked in sweet water? Is the dough blended with water from an ancient spring? Confusing, no? Truth be told, tianshui mian is another example of Chinese linguistic trickery. Not unlike a Sichuanese restaurant classic, *shuizhu niurou*, or "water-boiled beef," you think you're going in for something boring, tame, and frankly, a little lame. Au contraire. This sauce is dense, rich, complex, a little sweet and a tad spicy, and the noodle itself is a true adventure.

They are thick, irregularly shaped, pleasantly chewy, and soak up a rather unique sauce like nobody's business. There is a small, typically crowded (to the rafters) joint across the street from a huge Buddhist temple in Chengdu. They have kept a laser focus on tianshui noodles for the last century and have perfected the dish. Also noteworthy is their efficiency at getting people in and out quickly while remaining filled to the brim. Once we managed to get our butts onto a wooden stool, we tucked into what turned out to be quite a worthwhile workout, as these noodles were deliciously toothsome. We made a little friend at the next table. She was about five years old. She had no such look of exhaustion on her face after eating tianshui mian. Jealous.

Total Time: 1 hour, 35 minutes | Serves: 6–8

SAUCE:
- ¾ cup mushroom or other dark soy sauce
- ¼ cup Chinese black vinegar
- 8 oz brown sugar
- 1 stick cinnamon
- 2 star anise
- ¼ cup water
- 4 Tbsp sesame paste or tahini
- 3 Tbsp toasted sesame oil
- ¼ cup red chile oil with sediment *or* Lajiao You (Chile Oil) on page 132
- ½ cup vegetable or canola oil
- 1 Tbsp Sichuan peppercorn, ground
- 1 Tbsp white sesame seeds

NOODLES:
- 1½ cup high-gluten flour
- 1½ cup all-purpose flour, plus more for dusting
- ½ tsp salt, plus 2 Tbsp for boiling
- 1 cup water, plus 1 gallon for boiling

To prepare the sauce, stir together soy sauce, vinegar, and sugar in a skillet over medium heat. Stir in cinnamon, star anise, and water, and bring to a simmer. Reduce the heat to medium-low and continue to simmer for 10 minutes. In a small mixing bowl, whisk together sesame paste, sesame oil, chile oil, vegetable oil, peppercorn, and sesame seeds. Add this mixture to the skillet and whisk thoroughly. Remove the cinnamon stick and star anise, reduce heat to low and keep warm while you make the noodles.

In a large mixing bowl or the bowl of a stand mixer, whisk together flours and ½ teaspoon of salt. With clean hands or the dough hook of the stand mixer, slowly incorporate 1 cup of water and knead until a single mass of dough forms. Cut the dough into 4 quarters. By hand, knead each quarter into a ball, cover with plastic wrap and let them rest for 1 hour.

Bring 1 gallon of water and 2 tablespoons of salt to a boil over high heat as you cut the noodles. Dust the work surface with flour. Starting with one dough ball, roll it into a 12 x 5-inch wide rectangle. Cut into 5 x ½-inch strips and lightly dust them with flour to keep them from sticking. Repeat rolling and cutting noodles from the other balls of dough. Lower them into the boiling water and cook until they reach a pleasantly chewy consistency, 3–3½ minutes.

Carefully remove the noodles from the water using a slotted spoon or a sieve. Evenly distribute noodles into bowls. Spoon a few tablespoons of sauce over the noodles. Suggest that guests mix it all together before enjoying.

CHAPTER 2:
GOOD MORNING, CHINA

8:00 A.M. BEIJING. The morning commute is in full swing. Bicyclists deftly navigating throngs of pedestrians through narrow alleys. Broad avenues teeming with old folks and young, en route to the schoolhouse, the tea house, the shop, and the farmers market. The bright Eastern sun, gleaming through the haze of a dusty construction site, strategically surrounded by bamboo scaffolding. Billows of steam rising from tiny, sidewalk kitchens. Every single morning warrior pausing for something as simple as a starchy steamed morsel, or as complex and satisfying as a hearty bowl of porridge. Was this the year 1517, or 2017? It's anyone's guess.

The morning scene and an on-the-go breakfast in China hasn't changed much in millennia. One might ask, "What is it about Chinese morning stalwarts that keeps the millions coming back for more?" Tradition. In a 2015 *Financial Times* opinion article, "In China, breakfast remains a matter of the heart," Shanghai correspondent Patti Waldmeir talked with old and young alike about their breakfast habits. She discovered that, despite undeniable Western influences in cuisine throughout China, the masses still preferred the staples that jump-started their great-grandparents' day.

According to one steamed bun vendor she chatted with, "We've been eating Chinese food for decades and if we suddenly change to foreign food, our stomachs can't get used to it." Though fairly hyperbolic, this sentiment is consistent with folks we've dined with in our years of Chinese breakfasts. Even among the younger set, when presented with the opportunity to lunch at a Western-style burger bar or dine at a chic French bistro, they generally begin their hectic day the same way their ancestors did. Our discussions with the most cosmopolitan among China's young professionals confirm that they, too, are drawn in by sidewalk steamers serving up Steamed Pork Dumplings (page 53) and Steamed Eggplant or Pork Buns (page 49) on the way to their tech startup's garage.

We have a good friend named Dave Fan. He was born and raised in Chengdu, Sichuan, and was the face (and name) behind one of Chengdu's original expat bars, *Dave's Oasis*. Tony Bourdain once Sharpied his signature across one of the walls at the *Oasis*. Dave recently moved to Beijing to live the "Chinese Dream" of hitting it big in the capital city. As an entrepreneur who spends many of his days connecting foreigners with Chinese companies, Dave frequently eats at steakhouses, pizza joints, brew pubs, and sushi counters. "But breakfast," confirms Dave, "is all about eating the familiar and comforting, the food from our childhood."

On a recent feeding frenzy, by which we mean *a visit to Beijing*, we shared a morning walk with Dave through a shiny new neighborhood that markets itself to a younger, affluent crowd. China's now notorious nouveaux-riches. He suggested that we start the stroll by stopping into one of his favorite breakfast spots, Yinji Noodle House. "I've eaten steamed buns all over China. I don't know Mr. Qin's secret, but this dude's out of baozi by 9 o'clock and switches to noodles. They're amazing," promised Dave. According to him, what new neighborhoods like this one offer his hungry contemporaries is tradition done right. The vendors aren't necessarily breaking old models or changing many recipes, but they are trying to outdo one another by perfecting the breakfast experience. "In this part of town," argues Dave, "if you're not perfect, you're going to close down." We agreed that Mr. Qin was producing the perfect baozi. He's safe.

As we thoroughly enjoyed our freshly steamed Zhejiang Province-style buns, we were at ease in an elegant climate-controlled environment with a sparkly dark-tiled floor, deep redwood furniture, and an immaculate, open, modern kitchen in which delicate, perfect little bundles of joy were being stuffed and steamed. These days, we find that, especially in larger cities like Beijing and Shanghai, many vendors are taking their street food operations indoors. In some scenarios, it's the government restricting open-air vendors. Still, some sellers are heading inside to maintain a consistent, appetizing atmosphere, away from the elements, and once inside, in the case of Yinji, to also craft your street snack journey amidst modern luxury. That day, it was quite obviously 2017.

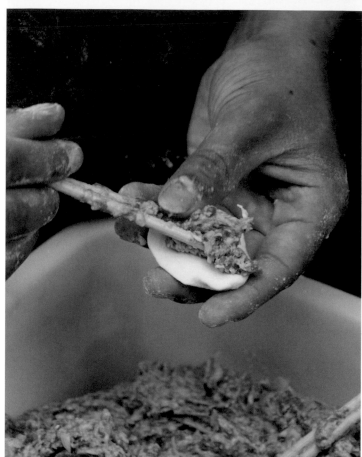

Qiezi Baozi / Zhurou Baozi
茄子包子 / 猪肉包子
(Steamed Eggplant Buns) or (Steamed Pork Buns)

Barbarians once again rear their ugly heads! If you remember all the way back to Chapter 1, you'll recall the story of *mantou*, or "barbarian heads," and the gruesome way in which they got their name. At some unfortunate point in history, the original "barbarian heads" which had stuffing in the middle (you know, the *brains*) took on their modern incarnation as plain steamed white buns. The stuffed version morphed to become known as *baozi*, or simply "filled packages." Perhaps the Chinese food naming gods got the notion that baozi would become incredibly popular and couldn't risk having a gross backstory. There are some small pockets of purists who, in the shadows, still use *mantou* when referring to baozi. *Shh.*

Baozi are, hands-down, our go-to breakfast while traipsing around the Middle Kingdom, and are some serious memory food. On one particularly harrowing adventure through rural Yunnan Province, we were waiting for a hired van to drive us back to relative civilization, and bought some freshly steamed wild mushroom baozi for the road. Long story short, China + cliffs + one-lane roads + 80 mph + hairpin turns = white-knuckled Howie, holding on for dear life, and a sleeping, occasionally laughing Greg. At least this hungry duo could agree on the awesomeness of wild mushroom baozi.

What's waiting for us inside the package may change according to where we travel, but the journey, for us, is all about the adventure. Whether we're relishing the savory pleasures of soupy Zhejiang-style buns, being surprised by spicy and sour eggplant brilliance outside the city walls of Xi'an, or satisfying our sweet tooth with a creamy bean paste-filled pillow, baozi span the gastronomic spectrum of China. Steamed buns are a book unto themselves, but you can join our baozi fan club by choosing between our favorites below.

WRAPPERS:

1 uncooked dough recipe from
 Mantou (Steamed "Barbarian
 Head" Buns) on page 11

EGGPLANT FILLING:

1 large globe eggplant, or 3 Japanese
 eggplants
2 cloves garlic, peeled, minced
2 scallions, minced
1 Tbsp cilantro leaves, roughly
 chopped
1 Serrano chile or green bell pepper,
 minced
½ tsp salt
½ tsp granulated sugar
2 tsp cornstarch
1 Tbsp Lajiao You (Chile Oil) with
 sediment from page 132
1 tsp soy sauce
2 tsp Chinese black vinegar

PORK FILLING:

1 lb ground pork
½ cup pickled cabbage or mild kimchi,
 drained, minced
2 scallions, minced
1 inch ginger, peeled, minced
2 cloves garlic, peeled, minced
1 Tbsp soy sauce
1 Tbsp chicken broth *or* broth from
 Jirou Tang (Chicken Soup) on page
 189
2 tsp Chinese rice wine or dry sherry
1 tsp cornstarch
½ tsp salt
½ tsp granulated sugar
1 tsp five-spice powder

OPTIONAL DIPPING SAUCE:

1 recipe Dipping Sauce from Zhurou
 Jiaozi (Steamed Pork Dumplings) on
 page 53

TO FILL BAOZI WITH THE EGGPLANT FILLING:

Prepare the Mantou dough from page 11 up to the first rising of the dough. While the dough is rising, preheat the oven to 375°F. Pierce the eggplant skin with 4–6 slits using the tip of a sharp knife. Place the eggplants directly onto an oven rack. We place a sheet pan on the rack below in case the eggplant drips fluid while roasting. Roast the eggplant for one hour, flipping halfway through. Remove the eggplant from the oven and place on a plate to cool while you prepare the rest of the filling.

In a large mixing bowl, combine the remaining Eggplant Filling ingredients. When the eggplant is cool enough to handle, cut in half and remove the flesh from the skin and roughly chop. Add the eggplant flesh to the mixing bowl of filling ingredients. Stir to combine evenly. Set the mixture aside.

TO FILL BAOZI WITH PORK FILLING:

In a large mixing bowl, combine all of the Pork Filling ingredients. Stir to combine evenly. Set the mixture aside.

Uncover the dough, dust the work surface with flour, transfer the dough atop the flour and evenly hand-roll it onto a 2-inch-thick log. Cut the dough into 1-inch pieces. Knead and roll the dough pieces into balls. Flatten each dough ball by hand, then use a rolling pin to create a 4-inch round. Try to leave the center of the round a bit thicker than the outer inch.

Place 1–2 tablespoons of filling onto the center of one dough round. Stretch and pinch the edges into pleats, surrounding the filling until you come full-circle. If you have a small gap at the end, pinch the edges together to form a seal.

Prepare steamer baskets by lining them with cheesecloth or parchment paper. (We prefer to cut individual 3-inch x 3-inch squares of parchment paper for individual buns.) Place the filled dough parcels atop the lining, about 2 inches apart. Cover the steamer basket(s) with their matching lid(s). Let the parcels rest for 20 minutes.

Place a skillet or pot over medium heat, fill with 2 inches of water, and bring to a boil. Carefully place the steamer baskets atop the pot of boiling water, cover, and steam the buns for 20 minutes.

Serve baozi hot, on their own as a snack on the go, or with a dipping sauce.

Zhurou Jiaozi / Baicai Jiaozi
猪肉饺子 / 白菜饺子
(Steamed Pork Dumplings) or (Steamed Cabbage Dumplings)

Most culinary cultures on the globe have a few characteristic dumplings. To the Chinese, on the other hand, dumplings account for an entire school of cooking. In the South, cavernous dim sum halls teem with metal carts rolling around to tables, offering little morsels that are steamed, fried, boiled, baked, and griddled. All manner of filling stand to be the surprise in the center. Of course, regional differences abound, lamb in the Muslim-influenced Northwest, wild mushrooms in the deep Southwest, seafood along the southeast coast. In the Northeast, however, though you may find some dumpling diversity, the pork and cabbage jiaozi rule breakfast. The dumplings of Heilongjiang, Jilin, and Liaoning Provinces are also the simplest and oldest on record. The first mention of these particular *jiaozi* in literature dates back to 256 BCE.

In the late 1990s, Howie taught English in rural Liaoning Province. When he first arrived, site and language unseen and unstudied, one of the Chinese teachers, Mr. Zhu, felt it his duty to give Howie an intensive lesson on street food, and notably, dumplings. It was love at first bite. Mr. Zhu reminisced fondly about jiaozi, its relation to family bonds and fortune. "The jiaozi is the shape of an old Chinese gold ingot. That means for every dumpling you eat, you are increasingly lucky, and may get rich!" Throughout millennia, during Chinese Spring Festival celebrations, families get together and as tradition maintains, fill dumplings as a team, in hopes of bringing new fortune in the coming year. Whether it's the big holiday or a quick snack on the morning commute, jiaozi means much more than a filling breakfast.

Total Time: 45 minutes | Serves: 6–8

PORK FILLING:
1 lb ground pork
1 inch ginger, peeled, minced
2 cloves garlic, peeled, minced
3 scallions, minced
1 Tbsp soy sauce
1 tsp toasted sesame oil

2 tsp Chinese rice wine or dry sherry
½ tsp salt
½ tsp ground white pepper
2 Tbsp chicken broth *or* broth from Jirou Tang (Chicken Soup) on page 189
1 egg, beaten

CABBAGE AND EGG FILLING:
6 eggs, beaten
1½ tsp salt, divided
1 head green cabbage (about 1 lb),
   rinsed, finely chopped
4 scallions, thinly sliced
2 cloves garlic, peeled, minced
1 tsp vegetable or canola oil

1 16-oz package wonton or gyoza
   skins, round preferred
Water for sealing the dumplings, plus
   more for steaming

DIPPING SAUCE:
½ cup soy sauce
2 Tbsp Chinese black vinegar
1 Tbsp toasted sesame oil
2 cloves garlic, mashed into paste
1 Tbsp Lajiao You (Chile Oil) with
   sediment from page 132 (optional)

TO FILL THE JIAOZI WITH PORK FILLING:

In a large mixing bowl, thoroughly combine all of the Pork Filling ingredients.

TO FILL THE JIAOZI WITH CABBAGE AND EGG FILLING:

In a mixing bowl, whisk the eggs with ½ teaspoon of salt, scramble them in a skillet over medium heat, and set aside to cool. In a separate large mixing bowl, combine cabbage with 1 teaspoon of salt, and set aside for ten minutes.

Squeeze handfuls of cabbage to get rid of any liquid and place in a separate large mixing bowl. Add the remaining Cabbage Filling ingredients. Finely chop the scrambled eggs and add to the bowl, mix thoroughly.

In the middle of one wrapper, place 2 teaspoons of filling. With a wet finger, moisten the edges of the wrapper. Fold the wrapper in half around the filling and seal by pinching the edges completely. Optionally, you may fold pleats where the edges meet, thereby creating a little purse, rather than a half-moon. Repeat with the remaining filling and wrappers.

Prepare steamer baskets by lining them with cheesecloth or parchment paper. Place the filled dough parcels atop the lining in a single layer. If you have stackable steamer baskets, continue to fill baskets. Otherwise, steam dumplings in batches. Cover the steamer basket(s) with their matching lid.

Place a skillet or pot over medium heat, fill with 2 inches of water, and bring to a boil. Carefully place the steamer baskets atop the pot of boiling water, cover, and steam the dumplings for 10 minutes.

In a mixing bowl, whisk together the dipping sauce ingredients. Serve jiaozi along with a bit of dipping sauce.

Hongtang Sanjiao
红糖三角
(Steamed Brown Sugar–Filled Triangle Buns)

Maybe it's us, but the Chinese seem to go out of their way to avoid calling dark things black. Black tea is dubbed "red tea," black bean sauce is simply called "fermented beans," and (our favorite) black licorice is translated as "sweet grass"! Black is the color of corruption, catastrophe, death, and basically all things evil. Avoiding it whenever possible makes sense. Every once in awhile you'll run into a translated Chinese recipe that calls for "black sugar." Uh oh. By this, they generally mean something close to Western brown sugar . . . that they, of course, call "red sugar." Seeing as how red is the color of happiness, fortune, luck, and basically all things good, using it whenever possible makes sense, too.

Speaking of *all good things*, according to Chinese medicine, red sugar or *hongtang* is said to be an elixir for many ailments from simple annoyances like headaches to deadly blood abnormalities. This superfood characterization is similar to what we've become accustomed to believing about dark chocolate and red wine. Brown sugar buns are therefore an antioxidant, anti-inflammatory, pain reliever, and cholesterol killer all in one! Even though it's a dessert, or a mid-afternoon guilty pleasure, you're completely doing positive things for the old body! So, when you make these sweet treats at home, just remember that it's more like taking a vitamin and less like a trip to the donut shop. Totally.

Total Time: 3 hours | Serves: 4–6

WRAPPERS:
1 uncooked dough recipe from Mantou (Steamed "Barbarian Head" Buns) on page 11

FILLING:
2 cups dark brown sugar, packed
2 Tbsp molasses
½ tsp salt
Water for steaming

Prepare the Steamed "Barbarian Head" Buns from page 11 up to the first rising of the dough.

In a mixing bowl, thoroughly combine brown sugar, molasses, and salt. Set the mixture aside.

continued on page 57

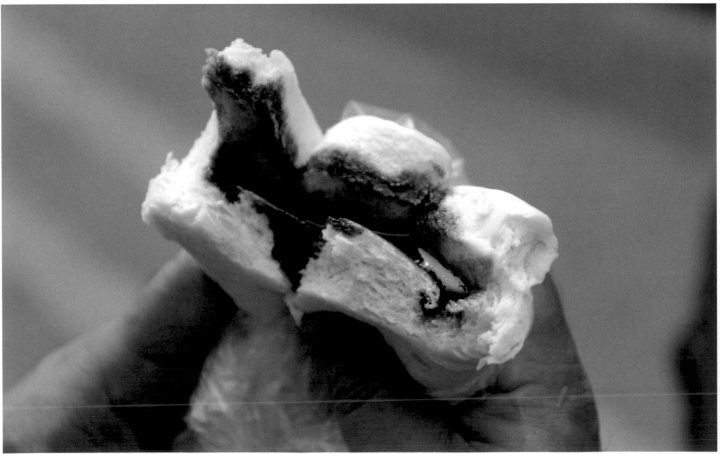

Uncover the dough, dust the work surface with flour, transfer the dough atop the flour and evenly hand-roll it onto a 2-inch thick log. Cut the dough into 2-inch pieces. Knead and roll the dough pieces into 2-inch balls. Flatten each dough ball by hand, then use a rolling pin to create a 3½-inch round. Try to leave the center of the round a bit thicker than the outer inch.

Place two tablespoons of filling onto the center of one dough round. Gather together and pinch together three points equally spaced around the edge of the dough. Continue to seal each open gap, outward to the edge of the dough. Repeat until you use all of the dough rounds.

Prepare steamer baskets by lining them with cheesecloth or parchment paper. (We prefer to cut individual 3-inch x 3-inch squares of parchment paper for individual buns.) Place the filled dough parcels atop the lining, about 2 inches apart. Cover the steamer basket(s) with their matching lid. Let the parcels rest for 20 minutes.

Place a skillet or pot over medium heat, fill with 2 inches of water, and bring to a boil. Carefully place the steamer baskets atop the pot of boiling water, cover, and steam the buns for 20 minutes.

Serve sanjiao baozi immediately on their own and enjoy the oozy, gooey results.

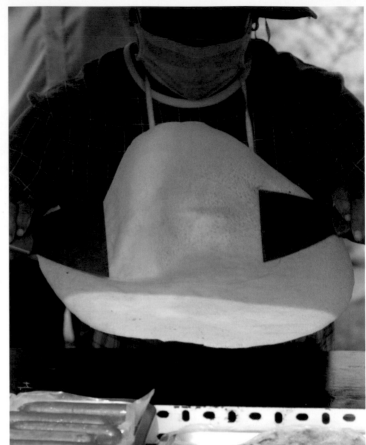

Tianjin Jianbing
天津煎饼
(Tianjin-Style Pancake Wraps)

We once asked our archaeologist friend, Qu Feng, about the origin of the wok. He related it, as he did with most of his food history tales, to the ingenious way the ancient military used its limited resources. Of course. "After battles, soldiers would first feed their horses out of their big shields. Then, they would wipe it out, put it over the fire and cook up a rabbit they caught in the field," he said. We asked, "How could there possibly be rabbits around with all of that war mayhem going on?" Qu Feng's response was expected, "Rabbits are pretty unaware and that's why we eat them." Well, when the soldiers awoke from their bunny-fueled slumber, those same handy shields were used for relative good: pancakes!

Gone are the days of feeding horses out of fairly talented shields, and stir-fries and pancakes took divergent paths. Where woks generally took refuge in restaurant kitchens, jianbing are sold out of small street carts, equipped with a big round griddle, not unlike what you may see at a Parisian crêpe stand. In fact, though jianbing are solidly more complex than a crêpe, we'll still call them cousins. As the title of this recipe indicates, there are many styles of jianbing. The most popular across China hails from Tianjin, a coastal city near Beijing. Texturally, it falls somewhere between an omelette and a burrito. Its cousin, the Shandong-Style Pancake Wrap on page 61 is a crispier affair.

We often seek out jianbing based on the length of the queue. The longer the line, the better the reason to wait, right? On a visit to Chengdu, we waited in a lengthy line with a food-obsessed student at Sichuan University named Yao Dan (English name "Alice"), who was excited to show us her latest jianbing crush. The cart was chock-full of more filling choices than we've experienced: little sausages, deep-fried chicken thighs, shredded barbecued pork, Bibb lettuce, fried dough sticks, red miso paste, creamy peanut sauce, and all the normal accoutrement. Alice chimes in upon ordering, "I usually choose the normal kind, and I add shredded pork. Since the youtiao are fried, I think the pork is healthier!" Ah, but when have we ever turned away from fried goodness? Below is an ode to the classic vegetarian, dough stick and all.

WRAPPERS:

1 cup flour
1¼ cup water
½ tsp salt
6 tsp vegetable or canola oil
6 eggs
2 Tbsp white or black sesame seeds

FILLING:

6 Tbsp black bean sauce, sweet bean sauce (tianmianjiang), *or* hoisin sauce
6 Tbsp chile paste *or* Lajiao You (Chile Oil) with sediment on page 132 (optional)
1 bunch cilantro, roughly chopped
5 scallions, thinly sliced
12 Youtiao (Fried Dough Sticks) on page 67 *or* 8 crispy wonton wrappers from Shandong Jianbing on page 61

In a mixing bowl, whisk together flour, water, and salt. Using a paper towel, smear 1 teaspoon of oil across a skillet over medium-high heat. After 1 minute, pour ¼ cup of batter into the skillet and swirl it around so that it evenly reaches the edges. Add a bit of batter to fill in any gaps. Alternatively, if you have a crêpe squeegee, use it to create an even layer.

When the bottom of the pancake has cooked, after about 1½ minutes, crack one egg on top of the pancake, break it up and evenly spread it using the back of a spoon. Sprinkle with some sesame seeds. Allow the pancake to cook for another 60 seconds, then carefully flip it over.

Brush 1 tablespoon of black bean, sweet bean, or hoisin, and chile paste (if using) across the top. Sprinkle with some cilantro and some scallions to taste. Then place some youtiao *or* crispy wonton wrappers on top. After 60 more seconds of cooking, fold the pancake from both edges, over the fried dough, use spatula to push a crease in the center, then fold the jianbing lengthwise. Set aside and repeat the process using the remaining batter, eggs, and fillings. Enjoy.

Shandong Jianbing
山东煎饼
(Shandong-Style Pancake Wraps)

Many years ago, we decided to take a culturally mandated hike up Taishan Mountain. Taishan, in Shandong Province, is one of the five great mountains of China, and it is mythologically connected to the origin of humanity and/or Chinese civilization. Depends on who you ask. Anyhow, it's super important, and we wanted to be a part of civilization. We've been up many Chinese mountains, and so we knew what to expect: thousands of stone stairs, and eventually, a peak with a terrific view. We'd been told it's best to head up Taishan in the early AM, so we choked down a baozi or three outside of our hotel, laced up our boots, and got to walking, perhaps in that order.

We were about halfway up this scenic, temple-dotted hunk of granite and decided that a well-deserved sitting break was in order. Maybe there would be a pot of tea waiting for us at that next landing? Lo and behold, as it was breakfast time, naturally there was a jianbing vendor. About 2400 feet up? That's one heck of a commute! The food gods were with us that day, friends. One big difference between Tianjin style jianbing and that of Shandong is the equipment. Where Tianjin-style is made on a stationary sizzle plate, Shandong-style uses a much larger, about 3-foot-wide spinning griddle.

We were transfixed as the cook deftly spun and spun the griddle, poured some batter, laid a squeegee down to spread it into a perfect, gigantic disc; he cracked two eggs, and squeegeed them to cover the now-cooked batter. The eggs essentially scrambled as they whirled about. Then, he took what can only be described as a putty knife, stuck the corner of the blade under the edge of the crispy pancake, and pushed inward, scraping toward the center of the griddle, as it continued to spin at high velocity. The pancake flew up in the air and onto a workbench, awaiting some fillings and a good rolling. It's like he'd done this thousands of times before. And he had. We finally made it to the peak at 3:00 p.m. We were quite full. You won't have nearly as much fun making these at home, but they're delicious.

CRISPY WONTONS WRAPPERS:
1–2 cups vegetable or canola oil
8 wonton wrappers

FILLING:
6 Tbsp sweet bean sauce
    (tianmianjiang) *or* hoisin sauce
6 Tbsp chile paste *or* Lajiao You (Chile
    Oil) with sediment on page 132
    (optional)
4 scallions, thinly sliced

1 bunch cilantro, roughly chopped
8 crispy wontons wrappers
6 big leaves Bibb lettuce

WRAPPERS:
1 cup flour
1¼ cup water
½ tsp salt
6 tsp vegetable or canola oil, divided
6 eggs, beaten

In a pot over medium heat, add oil to a depth of at least ½ inch, and heat to 360°F. No thermometer? Use the **Handy Trick** within the Doufunao recipe on page 31.

Fry the wonton wrappers in batches until golden brown. Remove to a paper towel-lined plate.

In a mixing bowl, whisk together flour, water, and salt. Using a paper towel, smear 1 teaspoon of oil across a skillet over medium-high heat. After 1 minute, pour ¼ cup of batter into the skillet to coat the bottom and swirl it around so that it evenly reaches the edges. Add a bit of additional batter to fill in any gaps. Alternatively, if you have a crêpe squeegee, use it to create an even layer.

When the bottom of the pancake has cooked, after about 1 minute, pour a few tablespoons of the beaten egg across the top of the pancake, and evenly spread it using the back of a spoon. Increase the heat to medium-high and allow the thin layer of egg to fully cook, about 2–2½ minutes. Slide the pancake from the skillet and fold in two edges so that they meet in the middle. Set aside while you continue to make pancakes using the remaining batter and eggs.

Upon each pancake, brush 1 tablespoon of sweet bean or hoisin and chile paste (if using) across the top. Sprinkle scallions and cilantro to taste, lay down some crispy wontons, then a leaf of lettuce. Tightly roll the pancake around the fillings. Serve immediately.

Xianggu Zhou

香菇粥

(Mushroom Rice Porridge)

We like visiting second-tier cities throughout China. You know, not the capital of a province but the next city, the one that travelers hear about but hardly consider worthy of a visit. Qujing, in southwestern Yunnan Province, is one such place. It's in these obscure locations that we find hidden culinary gems. We met our friend Tang Hao for a stroll around the one centuries-old street in Qujing that hasn't been razed and replaced with skyscrapers. It's a really interesting site, and not uncommon throughout China. Strings of ornate, one-story wooden shops with archetypal wide, flared, tiled roofs in the foreground and gleaming modernity, reaching for the sky in the background. At least gazing upward, it's pretty easy to remember what year it is.

Tang Hao takes us to one of his favorite breakfast haunts on the aptly named "Old Street." In the glass showcase up front are a series of pancakes. Some made of wheat, most made of corn, even tasty-looking little gems that are spiked with dill (in China?). But, as Tang Hao put it, "You can ignore the stuff up front. Everyone comes here for the rice porridge with mushrooms." In fact, the dozen or so other eaters in the joint had a steaming bowl of *zhou*, and nary a table with a corn pancake in sight. We immediately got excited, as the variety of wild mushrooms in Yunnan number in the hundreds! Tang Hao orders up a bowl of magic with a Fried Dough Stick (page 67), and we follow suit. Happiness ensued. We love second-tier cities.

Total Time: 2 hours, 15 minutes | Serves: 4–6

9 cups water, boiling
3 oz Chinese black wood ear or other dried mushrooms
2 tsp vegetable or canola oil
10 oz shiitake mushrooms, thinly sliced
1 inch ginger, peeled, minced
2 tsp salt
2 Tbsp soy sauce
2 cloves garlic, minced
1 cup jasmine or other long-grain white rice

GARNISH:
4–6 tsp sesame oil
4–6 Tbsp mushroom or other dark soy sauce
3 scallions, thinly sliced
2 Tbsp white or black sesame seeds

In a heatproof bowl, pour boiling water over dried mushrooms, cover, and allow them to rehydrate for 30 minutes. You may need to weigh the mushrooms down with a plate. Once they are rehydrated and cool enough to handle, slice them into thin strips. Reserve the steeping liquid.

Add oil to a large pot over medium heat. When the oil begins to shimmer, add shiitake mushrooms, the rehydrated black mushroom strips, ginger, and salt, and sauté until the mushrooms have softened and begun to brown, 8–10 minutes. Add soy sauce and garlic and continue to sauté for 2 minutes.

Add rice and the mushroom steeping liquid and bring to a boil over medium-high heat. Reduce the heat to medium-low and continue to cook for 1 hour, stirring occasionally to ensure the rice doesn't stick to the bottom of the pot. Reduce the heat to low, continue to stir and simmer for an additional 30 minutes. If the porridge gets too thick during cooking, feel free to add water 1 cup at a time.

Offer steaming bowls of zhou to guests with the listed garnish options. Serve hot with Chadan (Tea-Poached Eggs) on page 167 and/or Youtiao (Fried Dough Sticks) on page 67.

Youtiao
油条
(Fried Dough Sticks)

Just like calling *roujia mo* the "Chinese hamburger" (ugh, more rant on page 248), folks tend to take the uniqueness away from Chinese culinaria by using bad adaptive names in English. *Youtiao* have been called "Chinese churros," "Chinese donuts," and "Chinese crullers." They're not. They're youtiao, or rather plainly, "fried dough sticks"! We get it, it's natural to want to assign some relation, some excitement and something of an allure to an unfamiliar food. But, youtiao are *boring* as a stand-alone snack, and are *always* served alongside a delicious companion. Sweetened, warm soy milk is a good friend to youtiao, as is the snuggly inside of a Tianjin-Style Jianbing (page 59). But, our hands-down favorite use is tearing apart a stick or two and mixing it in with rice porridge (page 65).

Around the world, fried dough is as old as the acknowledgment that raw flour tastes horrible. As such, there's no way to pinpoint the first fried dough made in China. But, the unique shape and symbolism around youtiao is pretty disturbing. According to a certain ex-vice-minister of culture (a good buddy of ours who likes to call Greg "The Mexican," for unknown reasons), youtiao's structure, two strips of dough, sealed together down the center recalls a scheming Song Dynasty minister and his wife, who were found guilty of treason and summarily boiled in oil. Yep, youtiao is also known as "fried devils." Ain't Chinese food fun? Now, go and enjoy a Chinese churro, er, you know what we mean!

Total Time: 3 hours, 35 minutes, or overnight, plus 1 hour, 35 minutes | Serves: 4–6

2 cups all-purpose flour, plus more for dusting
½ tsp salt
½ tsp baking soda
1 tsp baking powder

1 egg
½ cup soy or cow's milk
1 Tbsp vegetable or canola oil, plus more for deep-frying

In a large mixing bowl or the bowl of stand mixer, whisk together flour, salt, baking soda, and baking powder. In a separate mixing bowl, whisk together egg, milk, and 1 tablespoon of oil. Using clean hands or the dough hook of the stand mixer, incorporate the wet ingredients into the dry ingredients until a smooth dough forms.

continued on page 69

dough to ‗‗‗‗
wrap and let it rest at ‗‗‗‗

If you've refrigerated the dough, remove it ‗‗‗‗ are
temperature for one hour.

In a pot over medium heat, add oil to a depth of at least 2 inches, and heat to 360°F. No thermometer? Use the **Handy Trick** within the Doufunao recipe on page 31.

Prepare a wire rack over a baking sheet and place next to the stove. When the oil is heated, reduce the heat to medium-low to maintain the desired heat.

While the oil is heating, dust the work surface with flour. Unwrap the dough, and cut it into 5 x 1-inch wide strips.

Place one strip of dough on top of another strip. Place a chopstick lengthwise down the middle of the top strip and gently press the dough strips to bind them down the middle. Grab the ends of the double dough strip, lightly twist, and stretch the connected strip to about 7-inches in length.

Gently place the dough strip into the hot oil and gently roll it over as it fries, until golden and puffed, about 1½-2 minutes. Remove youtiao from the pot and place on the wire rack. Repeat this process for the remainder of the dough. Work in very small batches if you choose to fry more than one at a time.

Serve when all of the dough has been fried, along with warm soy milk, Danhua Tang (Egg-Drop Soup) on page 278, or Xianggu Zhou (Mushroom Rice Porridge) on page 65. Or, use them inside of Tianjin Jianbing (Tianjin-Style Pancake Wraps) on page 59.

Dust the countertop or work surface with additional flour and transfer the dough on top. Dust the top of the dough, knead, and form the dough into a smooth ball and let it rest for ten minutes. Dust the work surface once again with flour. Using a rolling pin, flatten the dough to a ¼-inch thick rectangle, roughly 5 inches wide. Wrap the sheet of dough in plastic wrap and let it rest at room temperature for 3 hours or in the refrigerator overnight.

If you've refrigerated the dough, remove it from the refrigerator, and allow it to rest at room temperature for one hour.

In a pot over medium heat, add oil to a depth of at least 2 inches, and heat to 360°F. No thermometer? Use the **Handy Trick** within the Doufunao recipe on page 31.

Prepare a wire rack over a baking sheet and place next to the stove. When the oil is heated, reduce the heat to medium-low to maintain the desired heat.

While the oil is heating, dust the work surface with flour. Unwrap the dough, and cut it into 5 x 1-inch wide strips.

Place one strip of dough on top of another strip. Place a chopstick lengthwise down the middle of the top strip and gently press the dough strips to bind them down the middle. Grab the ends of the double dough strip, lightly twist, and stretch the connected strip to about 7-inches in length.

Gently place the dough strip into the hot oil and gently roll it over as it fries, until golden and puffed, about 1½-2 minutes. Remove youtiao from the pot and place on the wire rack. Repeat this process for the remainder of the dough. Work in very small batches if you choose to fry more than one at a time.

Serve when all of the dough has been fried, along with warm soy milk, Danhua Tang (Egg-Drop Soup) on page 278, or Xianggu Zhou (Mushroom Rice Porridge) on page 65. Or, use them inside of Tianjin Jianbing (Tianjin-Style Pancake Wraps) on page 59.

Tang Youbing
糖油饼
(Fried Brown Sugar Dough)

If youtiao, or "fried dough sticks," are boring on their own, and you're looking for a stand-alone pastry to tuck into over some coffee, *tang youbing* are the Chinese donuts you've been looking for. Big, crispy, chewy, satisfying, and fairly reminiscent of an elephant ear, if for only the shape. What's unique, however, is its construction. With one side salty and the other side sweet, it offers something that an elephant ear just can't, a conversation between the two in your mouth. Imagine a salted caramel slathered atop fried bread. Tang youbing is yet another example of Chinese cookery finding balance within a single bite.

Tang youbing eluded us for years, as we would pass by fry stalls and eschew relatively boring youtiao in favor of the bamboo steamers down the block. Ah, baozi. At times we would bow to the youtiao if only to grab some as a foil for a steamy bowl of rice porridge (page 65) or egg flower soup (page 278). But, we never loitered to see what else was coming out of the fryer. On one visit to Beijing, we were hanging out with social entrepreneur Dave Fan. Dave loves greasy breakfasts and so we timidly followed him into what turned out to be an extended deep-fried love fest. Less important was how much we ate, and we ate a lot. Much more important was that we spent about two hours at one stand just watching entire processes.

All sorts of fried goodies went into the burbling oil. But, when it came to the dude making tang youbing, we were entranced. A deep tan slab of dough got rolled out, then paired with a typical white dough. When he merged the two together, cut some slits in the middle, and swept them into the wok, we were mesmerized. *What is this gruesomely beautiful thing?* We never look back, and seek out tang youbing whenever we can. Thanks for ruining us forever, Dave!

Total Time: 1 hour, 30 minutes | Serves: 4–6

SALTY DOUGH:
3 cups flour
½ tsp salt
½ tsp baking powder
¼ tsp baking soda
1 cup water

SWEET DOUGH:
1 cup flour
½ cup brown sugar, packed
¼ cup water, cold

2–3 cups vegetable or canola oil for frying

To make the salty dough, in a mixing bowl or the bowl of stand mixer, whisk together flour, salt, baking powder, and baking soda. Using clean hands or the dough hook of the stand mixer, incorporate water until a smooth dough forms. Knead the dough into a ball, dust the top with flour, cover with plastic wrap, and set aside.

To make the sweet dough, in a mixing bowl or the bowl of stand mixer, whisk together flour and brown sugar. Be sure that the sugar is thoroughly mixed into the flour. It may be necessary to use clean hands to break down clumps of brown sugar. Add the water and continue to knead until a tacky dough forms. Dust a work surface and transfer the sweet dough on top. With floured hands, form the dough into a ball, wrap in plastic, and place in the refrigerator for one hour.

After the hour, uncover the salty dough, divide it into quarters, and roll each segment into a ball.

Dust the work surface. Roll one dough ball into a ¼-inch thick disc. Remove the sweet dough from the refrigerator, unwrap, and divide into quarters. With floured hands, roll one quarter into a ball and place in top of the salty dough disc. Dust with flour and gently spread the sweet dough across the top of the salty dough with a rolling pin. Roll the paired doughs to a thickness of ¼-inch. Repeat with the remaining dough segments.

In a pot over medium heat, add oil to a depth of at least 1 inch, and heat to 360°F. No thermometer? Use the **Handy Trick** within the Doufunao recipe on page 31.

Prepare a wire rack over a baking sheet and place next to the stove. When the oil is heated, reduce the heat to medium-low to maintain the desired heat.

Slash two 1-inch slits near the middle of the rolled dough. Gently place one dough pairing into the hot oil and fry on one side until golden and puffed, 2–2½ minutes. Flip the youbing and fry the other side until the sweet dough has darkened a bit and puffed, about 1½ minutes. Remove youbing from the oil and place on the cooling rack. Fry the remaining dough pairings.

Serve hot alongside Xianggu Zhou (Mushroom Rice Porridge) on page 65, or Danhua Tang (Egg-Drop Soup) on page 278. Alternatively, serve these with a steaming hot cup of coffee.

Xiangchang Juanbing
香肠卷饼
(Hand-Rolled Sausage Pancake)

Awhile back, we were bouncing off of Beijing en route to Hunan Province to eat spicy things. Since we had most of a morning to kill before the train, we naturally set out to a farmers' market to scope out delicious snacks to eat onboard. As our history should have warned us, we were sidelined by a simple pancake stand. We're suckers for jianbing and can't resist the artistry and sheer skill of most purveyors. Oddly, we rolled up to perhaps the only jianbing stand in Beijing owned and operated by a Tibetan gentleman, the affable Mr. Sonam. Nice fella. Great pancakes.

In addition to the classic Tianjin-style jianbing, Mr. Sonam was also cooking *juanbing*, hand-rolled pancakes. It's quite an undertaking to do both, and to do both well, at that. Most stands offer one or the other. Nonetheless, Mr. Sonam and his lovely wife, Dema, were deftly taking orders for both types of pancakes, and somehow, miraculously whipping them up, perfectly, three, four at a time on a 3' × 2' griddle! So here's this Tibetan couple, preparing traditional Han Chinese snacks, better than most we've eaten. We asked Mr. Sonam how he picked up this skillset. He said, "Back in Tibet, my parents read about these and thought they looked great. Once they taught me, I opened a stand in Lhasa, one of a kind! Then, we moved to see what Beijing was like. Now, we're also one of a kind here, also much busier!"

Jianbing and juanbing share similar ingredients, but the techniques differ. Watching Dema simultaneously create both atop the griddle was a sight to behold. Left hand spreading egg on top of the jianbing and right hand, as if by some Tibetan mojo, pouring egg beneath the juanbing so it puffs up slightly. Needless to say, the pancakes never made it to the train.

WRAPPERS:
1 cup flour
1¼ cup water
½ tsp salt
6 tsp vegetable or canola oil
3 eggs, lightly beaten

FILLING:
6 Tbsp sweet bean sauce
　　(tianmianjiang) *or* hoisin sauce
6 Tbsp chile paste *or* Lajiao You (Chile
　　Oil) with sediment on page 132
　　(optional)
1 small red onion, finely diced
½ bunch cilantro, roughly chopped
6 big leaves Bibb lettuce
6 Chinese ham sausages or premium
　　hot dogs, grilled or griddled

In a mixing bowl, whisk together flour, water, and salt. Add 1 teaspoon of oil to a nonstick skillet over medium-high heat. When the oil begins to shimmer, pour ⅓ cup of batter into the skillet and swirl it around so the batter evenly reaches the edges. Add a bit of additional batter to fill in any gaps. Alternatively, if you have a crêpe squeegee, use it to create an even layer.

When the bottom of the pancake has cooked, after about 1½ minutes, lift up one edge of the pancake and pour 2 tablespoons of beaten egg underneath. Gently shake the pan so that the egg travels evenly across the skillet. Allow the egg to fully cook, about 1–1½ minutes before flipping the pancake over.

Continue to cook the pancake until the bottom is golden brown, about 2 minutes. Slide the pancake out of the skillet. Set aside as you continue to make pancakes using the remaining batter and eggs.

Upon each pancake, brush 1 tablespoon of sweet bean or hoisin and chile paste (if using) across the top. Sprinkle red onion and cilantro, lay down a leaf of lettuce, and then place the sausage or hot dog. Tightly roll the pancake around the fillings.

Either serve one pancake to each guest, or cut the pancakes into pieces and serve with toothpicks.

Yumi Bing
玉米饼
(Oven "Fried" Cornbread)

One of the popular morning markets in Chengdu is in the Yulin neighborhood. Throngs of early birds queue up for the freshest meats, produce, and handmade noodles in the city. The most popular stand by far is the one hawking halal beef and offal. Like, a line-up of 150 people by the 9:00 a.m. opening bell! Since fresh lung slices weren't our cup of tea, we opted for the second longest line in front of the decidedly more breakfast-y cornbread stand! According to E.N. Anderson in his brilliant book, *The Food of China*, corn has been around China since at least 1555. They've been innovating around corn for over 400 years. Yet, a humble cornbread brought us to our knees.

We were waiting in line behind an English-speaking woman who was looking to get her language on, this early Saturday morning. We had spotted her before in the halal offal queue, where she sheepishly shouted, "Good morning!" Now, here she was and a longer conversation ensued. We asked her, "What is so famous about that halal stand, and was it worth the wait?" She giddily replied, "I am happy to have gotten some lung slices for my friends back in Shanghai!" Shanghai? Turns out that she wasn't from Chengdu, but any responsible gastronome traveling through Chengdu would be remiss to forget these nationally celebrated bits of viscera for her buddies back home.

We wished her well without an ounce of envy and enjoyed the hottest, sweetest cornbread we'd ever experienced. Slightly crispy on the outside, light as a feather on the inside. In talking with the vendor, we were surprised to hear that since their corn was so naturally sweet, there wasn't any sugar in the batter. That was hard to believe, but we trusted it, and swore we needed to add sugar to our recipe to recreate the taste. Not for nothing, but our little cornbread stand was also boiling fresh corn, blending, straining, and serving hot corn juice. It's one of the most pleasurable, simple surprises. You should try it.

Total Time: 45 minutes | Serves: 4–6

2 cups cooked or canned corn kernels
½ cup, plus 2 Tbsp vegetable or canola oil, divided
2 cups cornmeal
¾ cup all-purpose flour
1 tsp baking powder
2 eggs
⅓ cup sugar
1 tsp salt
1½ cups soy or cow's milk

In a food processor, pureé corn kernels and strain over a bowl using a fine-meshed sieve. Reserve the corn juice. Add ½ teaspoon of oil to each cup of a muffin tin, place it into the oven and preheat to 400°F. In a large mixing bowl, whisk ½ cup oil and all remaining ingredients together. Whisk in ½ cup of the reserved corn juice.

Carefully remove the muffin tin from the oven. Ladle ⅓ cup of batter into each cup. Transfer the muffin tin back into the oven and bake for 15–20 minutes, or until the tops of the muffins are golden brown.

Remove the muffins from the oven, and allow them to cool for at least 5 minutes before consuming the whole lot.

Paocai Kaomantou
泡菜烤馒头
(Pickled Vegetables on Grilled Buns)

You may be familiar with the tale of John Montagu, the Earl of Sandwich, making his famous order of meat between bread so he wouldn't get his poker cards greasy. It doesn't take much smarts to figure out that folks have been *sandwiching* stuff between two dry things for long before the Earl. As our luck would have it, the Chinese have been *sandwiching* things for millennia. The most famous (and most enraging, see our rant on page 248) is Roujia Mo, the Chinese version of a pulled pork delight. But, we contend that a very close runner up is this brilliant breakfast offering: *paocai kaomantou*.

Sometimes, you just have a hankering for the familiar, even in the case of two deeply dedicated Chinese food snobs. There's just *something* about eating a very Chinese version of a typical snack from the States. Ah, a little bit of West in the Far East. The setup is always the same: Gas grill and a small round griddle set alongside a wooden table covered with tins of quick-pickled vegetables, farm eggs, a sauce or three, and freshly steamed *mantou* buns to grill. We come running whenever we're within earshot of a vendor boasting "kaomantou!" Our usual order involved nearly every tin on the table, a smear of sweet hoisin sauce, and of course, that oozy goodness of a fried egg. The breakfast of champions, with not an *earl* in sight.

Total Time: Overnight, plus 15 minutes | *Serves: 6–8*

TYPICAL FILLING:

8 cups water

6 cups of julienned vegetables, including:

    russet or gold potatoes

    carrots

    daikon radishes

    green cabbage

    smoked or baked tofu

¼ cup rice vinegar

⅓ cup soy sauce

1 Tbsp vegetable or canola oil

2 Tbsp toasted sesame oil

2 Tbsp red chile oil *or* Lajiao You (Chile Oil) page 132

½ tsp salt

½ tsp white pepper

1 tsp sugar

ADD-ONS:

¼ cup sweet bean sauce (tianmianjiang) *or* hoisin sauce

4–6 fried eggs, salted

¼ cup red chile oil *or* Lajiao You (Chile Oil) with sediment on page 132

4 scallions, thinly sliced

1 bunch cilantro, roughly chopped

ROLLS:

1 recipe cooked Mantou (Steamed "Barbarian Head" Buns) on page 11

Add water to a large pot and bring to a boil over high heat. Add julienned vegetables to the boiling water and cook for 2 minutes. Remove and drain the vegetables. In a large mixing bowl, whisk together vinegar, soy sauce, oils, salt, pepper, and sugar. Be sure that the salt and sugar dissolve. Fold in the blanched vegetables. Cover and refrigerate overnight. At least once while the vegetables are chilling, give them a toss to re-distribute the dressing.

Light and lightly oil a grill, griddle, or skillet. Brown the steamed buns on both sides and cut in half to fill as a sandwich. Add-ons are optional, but to get and give the full Xi'an experience, dress the bottom of a roll with sweet bean or hoisin sauce, drop on a freshly fried egg, top with drained vegetables, add some excitement with red chile oil, and finally garnish with cilantro and scallions. Put on the top of the roll, and travel to Xi'an.

Youtiao
油条
(Fried Dough Sticks)

Just like calling *roujia mo* the "Chinese hamburger" (ugh, more rant on page 248), folks tend to take the uniqueness away from Chinese culinaria by using bad adaptive names in English. *Youtiao* have been called "Chinese churros," "Chinese donuts," and "Chinese crullers." They're not. They're youtiao, or rather plainly, "fried dough sticks"! We get it, it's natural to want to assign some relation, some excitement and something of an allure to an unfamiliar food. But, youtiao are *boring* as a stand-alone snack, and are *always* served alongside a delicious companion. Sweetened, warm soy milk is a good friend to youtiao, as is the snuggly inside of a Tianjin-Style Jianbing (page 59). But, our hands-down favorite use is tearing apart a stick or two and mixing it in with rice porridge (page 65).

Around the world, fried dough is as old as the acknowledgment that raw flour tastes horrible. As such, there's no way to pinpoint the first fried dough made in China. But, the unique shape and symbolism around youtiao is pretty disturbing. According to a certain ex-vice-minister of culture (a good buddy of ours who likes to call Greg "The Mexican," for unknown reasons), youtiao's structure, two strips of dough, sealed together down the center recalls a scheming Song Dynasty minister and his wife, who were found guilty of treason and summarily boiled in oil. Yep, youtiao is also known as "fried devils." Ain't Chinese food fun? Now, go and enjoy a Chinese churro, er, you know what we mean!

Total Time: 3 hours, 35 minutes, or overnight, plus 1 hour, 35 minutes | Serves: 4–6

**2 cups all-purpose flour, plus more
  for dusting**
½ tsp salt
½ tsp baking soda
1 tsp baking powder

1 egg
½ cup soy or cow's milk
**1 Tbsp vegetable or canola oil, plus
  more for deep-frying**

In a large mixing bowl or the bowl of stand mixer, whisk together flour, salt, baking soda, and baking powder. In a separate mixing bowl, whisk together egg, milk, and 1 tablespoon of oil. Using clean hands or the dough hook of the stand mixer, incorporate the wet ingredients into the dry ingredients until a smooth dough forms.

continued on page 69

Jiucai Hezi
韭菜盒子
(Garlic Chive Pancakes)

Americans love a good egg. Scrambled, poached, fried, hard-boiled, omelets! Sadly, that's just about where the list ends. When we first started to eat our way through China, the enormous diversity with which they use the simple chicken egg astounded us. Sure, Americans enjoy the ubiquitous chopped up scramble in their fried rice at Hunan Dynasty down the block, but that barely scratches the surface of Chinese ingenuity. Stir-fried egg and tomato, dumplings with a thin film of whisked egg as the wrapper, and tea eggs (page 167) are among our favorites. But, where that list offers some complex Chinese culinary magic, its basic use in garlic chive pancakes makes us smile.

Throughout China, you will find hundreds of dishes that make use of a chopped-up scramble, mixed into stuffing of all stripes. But, within this dish, though it doesn't even get top billing, the egg shines. Jiucai, or garlic chives with egg, is simply a dream team. In this recipe, we suggest that you *can* use a blend of typical chives and baby spinach if you can't find garlic chives, but try really hard to source them. If it's spring and you live near a Chinese grocer, go. They'll be there. If you have a green thumb, you can buy seeds online and make many new neighborhood friends (they're prolific plants). You will like the flavor profile of garlic chives with egg so much that you'll even start to put them in your omelet . . . or make this recipe, a farmers' market stalwart.

Total Time: 1 hour | Serves: 6–8

WRAPPERS:
3 cups all-purpose flour
½ tsp salt
1 cup water, hot from the tap

4 tsp vegetable or canola oil for frying
½ cup water for steaming

FILLING:
4 eggs, beaten
½ tsp salt
8 oz garlic chives (or chives plus baby spinach), stems removed, roughly chopped
1 clove garlic, minced
1 Tbsp soy sauce
1 tsp sesame oil
1 tsp five-spice powder

In a large mixing bowl or the bowl of stand mixer, whisk together flour and salt. Using clean hands or the dough hook of the stand mixer, incorporate water until a smooth dough forms.

Dust the countertop or work surface with additional flour and transfer the dough onto the flour. Dust the top of the dough, knead, and form the dough into a ball. Transfer the dough to a large, clean, lightly oiled bowl and cover with plastic wrap. Allow the dough to rest for 30 minutes.

In a mixing bowl, whisk the eggs and salt, scramble them in a skillet over medium heat, and set aside to cool. In a separate mixing bowl, combine garlic chives (or chives and spinach), garlic, soy sauce, sesame oil, and five-spice powder. Finely chop the scrambled eggs and add to the bowl, mix thoroughly.

Uncover the dough, dust the work surface with flour, transfer the dough atop the flour and evenly hand-roll it onto a 2-inch-thick log. Cut the dough into 2-inch pieces. Knead and roll each of the dough pieces into a ball. Using a rolling pin, flatten the ball into a ¼-inch thick oval. Place 1–2 tablespoons of filling into the center of the oval. Pinch to seal the two long edges together over the filling. Use the rolling pin to gently flatten the parcel. Set aside and continue to make similar packages with the remaining dough and filling.

In a wide-bottomed skillet with a matching lid, heat 2 teaspoons of oil over medium heat. When the oil begins to shimmer, place dough parcels, sealed-side down, along the bottom of the skillet. It is okay if they touch, but do not overcrowd the skillet. Work in batches if necessary.

Fry the bottom of the parcels until they are golden brown, about 2–3 minutes. Flip the parcels, and cook for an additional 2 minutes. Then, carefully pour ¼ cup of water into the skillet, cover with a lid, and continue to cook for 4 minutes. Transfer the jiucai hezi to a paper towel-lined plate for serving, hot. These treats may not need a dipping sauce at all, but a simple soy sauce or Chinese black vinegar would match them well.

Zhurou Xianbing
猪肉馅饼
(Pan-Fried Pork Pockets)

An inordinate number of street food legends begin with Emperor Such-and-Such sneaking away from the palace for a forbidden snack. Xianbing is no exception. We've suspected that many of these *forbidden snack* stories are one and the same. But, in this specific case, our skepticism may be misplaced. The tale of xianbing must be true, since it's the only filled pancake in the Chinese universe of filled pancakes to earn the literal name xianbing, or "filled pancake." It may also be true since it came from a pretty reliable source, our archaeologist buddy, Qu Feng. We also find his retellings to be elaborately entertaining.

According to Qu Feng, in the early 700s, the Xuanzhong Emperor of the Tang Dynasty was trying hard to avoid his first wife, Yang Guifei. "She was always threatening to get him kicked off the throne, or kill him. She wasn't a very good wife," he says. So, as the story goes, he went as far as ducking out of the Imperial compound dressed as a commoner. She must have been really annoying. Qu Feng continued, "One time, curiosity got the better of him, as the smell of something frying led him to a long queue awaiting some street snack. When he finally got up to the front, the aroma was so intoxicating that he bought up all of the xianbing." So much for his *commoner* disguise! From that day forward, *this* filled pancake was *the* filled pancake of the empire.

Total Time: 1 hour, 30 minutes | Serves: 6–8

WRAPPERS:
3½ cups all-purpose flour, plus more
   for dusting
½ tsp salt
1½ cup water, hot from the tap

FILLING:
1 lb ground pork
1 inch ginger, peeled, minced
2 cloves garlic, peeled, minced
3 scallions, minced

1 Tbsp soy sauce
1 tsp toasted sesame oil
2 tsp Chinese rice wine *or* dry sherry
½ tsp salt
½ tsp ground white pepper
2 Tbsp chicken broth *or* broth from
   Jirou Tang (Chicken Soup) on
   page 189

¼ cup vegetable or canola oil for frying

Place flour and salt in a large mixing bowl or the bowl of stand mixer fitted with a dough hook. Slowly stir in the hot water until a single mass of dough forms. You may not need all of the water.

Dust the work surface with flour and transfer the dough on top. Knead and form the dough into a smooth ball. Dust the top of the ball with flour and cover with a clean dish towel or plastic wrap. Allow the dough to rest for 30 minutes.

In a large mixing bowl, combine all of the Filling ingredients. Stir to combine evenly. Set the mixture aside.

Dust the work surface with flour. Uncover the dough, transfer the dough atop the flour and evenly hand-roll it into a 1½-inch-thick log. Cut the dough into 1½-inch pieces. Knead and roll the dough pieces into balls. Use a rolling pin to create a 4-inch round.

Place 2–3 tablespoons of filling onto the center of one dough round. Stretch and pinch the edges into pleats, surrounding the filling until you come full-circle. If you have a small gap at the end, pinch the edges together to seal the pouch. Place the pleated side of the pouch down. Use a rolling pin to evenly flatten the pouch to a 4–5-inch disc. Set aside while you fill the remaining dough.

Add 1 tablespoon of oil into a skillet and heat over medium. When the oil begins to shimmer, place a few filled dough discs into the skillet. Don't crowd the pan. Fry for 3–4 minutes or until the bottom is golden brown. Flip the pancakes, cover with a lid, and fry for another 2 minutes. Remove the lid and continue to fry for 2 minutes. Remove the pancake to a paper towel–lined plate and repeat for the remaining dough discs.

Serve hot as a quick snack.

Baicai Bing
白菜饼
(Cabbage Pancakes)

Apart from the well-known Japanese dishes with a Chinese origin story, like ramen and gyoza, we had never run into a dish that *screamed* of a Japanese favorite without ever being thought of as having a cross-border relationship. That is, until one early morning in 2016. A cold snap had hit central Shanxi Province with abandon. We were on a potentially misguided winter mission to hike to the top of a frigid Mianshan mountain to find some mummies. That's right, mummies of Buddhist monks who were preserved in the lotus position after having gained enlightenment, by which we mean they died. We woke up in Pingyao at 4:30 in the morning and for some reason, we thought there would be street vendors to sell us breakfast. Instead, we walked out into pitch black but for one light coming from our hired car for the day. *V'room*, off we went, into the darkness.

About 14 miles into the drive, our tummies rumbling, we spotted billows of glowing steam coming from a covered stall just off the highway. We've been around the Chinese block a few times, so we assumed we would recognize whatever they were selling. We didn't, but it looked and smelled delicious. We began to ID some ingredients on the skillet, definitely a flour and egg pancake, absolutely cabbage, obvious highlights of scallion peeking out. Still, it was the first bite that blew us away. *It's okonomiyaki!* We had to ask, "Do you have any friends from Japan? This is a Japanese recipe, no?" She laughed and responded, "Are you kidding? I'm not that well-travelled. My family has been preparing these from the same little stone house, right over there, for a couple of hundred years. I doubt my great-great-grandmother had been to Japan." Heck, okonomiyaki may actually be *Chinese*!

It makes sense, right? Napa cabbage (no, not named for the valley) was cultivated in central China from a wild variety around the 1400s and gained wide popularity after the Ming court designated it as a medicinal plant. Pancakes in dozens of shapes and sizes are found throughout China, but aside from okonomiyaki, very few are found across Japan. We're claiming it, right here and now. Baicai bing is the original okonomiyaki, and it all started with Mrs. Zhao's ancestors right there in Lianfu village, Shanxi Province. Friends, have we discovered something? Has history been altered forever? Should we begin to alert the okonomiyaki halls of Tokyo? Will we be ultimately held responsible for bringing the two nations together in the most meaningful way since their shared love for karaoke? If you need us, we'll be in the limo.

Okay, we realize that this is all tongue-in-cheek, but it really felt like running into a streetside goulash in Oaxaca.

1 cup flour
½ tsp salt
½ cup soy or cow's milk
3 eggs
1 Tbsp canola or vegetable oil, plus
    more for frying

1 Tbsp soy sauce, plus more for dipping
3 scallions, thinly sliced
2 cups cabbage, shredded

In a large mixing bowl, vigorously whisk together flour, salt, milk, eggs, 1 tablespoon of oil, and 1 tablespoon of soy sauce. Stir in scallions and cabbage and set aside for 10 minutes. Stir once again.

Add 1 teaspoon of oil to a skillet over medium heat. Once the oil is shimmering, place just enough batter into the skillet to reach the edges and flatten with the back of a spatula. Cover the skillet and cook for 4–5 minutes. Gently lift the edge of the pancake to see if the bottom is beginning to brown. Flip the pancake. Leave skillet uncovered and cook for an additional 4–5 minutes, or until the underside is beginning to brown. Remove the pancake to a paper towel-lined plate and repeat with remaining batter.

Serve with soy sauce for dipping.

Fanqie Chaodan Tangmian
番茄炒蛋汤面
(Tomato and Egg Noodle Soup)

One of the first restaurant dishes in China that flattened us to the ground was *fanqie chaodan*, or simply, "'tomato and scrambled egg." *Scrambled egg with stewed tomato? You can do that?* This was a constant refrain the first several times we ordered it. Just amazing. Talk about two great tastes that taste great together, well, this was it. There was just something about the juxtaposition between the rapidly fired egg, slightly crispy around the very edge yet still creamy in the middle, and the acidic and oddly sweet punch of a gently softened tomato. Wow. Whenever we got home from any China trip, we'd pester whoever would listen. *Dear family and friends, have you tried this? Let me make this for you? Could you have ever imagined this combination?* We've consistently left our kin hungry for more.

Flash forward to 2001, our first trip to Chengdu together. This is when we tripped upon the next natural revelation. Take that flash fried egg, throw in those wonderfully weakened tomatoes . . . toss them in the best chicken broth we'd ever experienced and make it a noodle soup! For breakfast! The innkeepers where we had lodged the night before told us about this joint down the block but never conceived that we would run back to them immediately after our first bowl and thank them like no foreigner had thanked them before. Sure, they thought we were nuts. Like that's news. Then, we waltzed right back to the street stand that left our knees weak for yet another bowl. Keep your bagels and lox. We'll take some more of this, please.

Total Time: 25 minutes | Serves: 8–10

BROTH:
12 cups chicken broth *or* broth from Jirou Tang (Chicken Soup) on page 189
6 tomatoes, thin strips

NOODLES:
1 gallon water
1 Tbsp salt

1 lb Chinese thin wheat noodles *or* thin spaghetti

GARNISH:
1 dozen eggs
1 tsp salt
½ tsp ground white pepper
12 tsp vegetable or canola oil, divided
5 scallions, thinly sliced (optional)

Add broth and tomatoes to a pot and bring to a boil over medium–high heat. Reduce the heat to medium and maintain a rolling simmer while you cook the pasta and eggs. In a separate pot, cook the noodles according to package directions. Drain, rinse, and set aside. Then, reduce the heat under the broth to low and maintain a simmer.

In a mixing bowl, whisk together eggs, salt, and pepper. Add 1 teaspoon of oil to a skillet over high heat. When the oil begins to slightly smoke, quickly scramble the equivalent of 1 egg. Remove from the skillet and set aside. Repeat the scrambling 11 times with the remaining oil and eggs.

Evenly distribute drained noodles and broth into bowls. Then, top with one scrambled egg and optionally, some scallions.

CHAPTER 3: MUSLIM STREET

ONE OF OUR AMBITIONS AS we've journeyed throughout China is to venture well beyond the modern comforts of huge cities like Beijing and Shanghai. Traveling deeper into China, we often feel as if we've gone through a time warp. Visiting cities like Xi'an in Shaanxi Province is one such pleasure, and a culinary delight.

In addition to being China's capital for several dynasties, Xi'an was the eastern terminus for the ancient Silk Road. Traders from as far away as Western Europe toted their wares toward the Middle Kingdom for hundreds of years and had a lasting impression upon China's cuisine. Though cookery methods and ingredients flowed back toward the West as well, the impact of culinary trade is still felt, seen, smelled, and tasted in Xi'an today.

The Silk Road enjoyed its golden age during the Tang Dynasty in the 600s. This is when Islam found its way well past the Chinese border, and into the heart of the country. The oldest and largest mosques in China are highlights of any visit to Xi'an. As with many a migration story, along with religion came cuisine. Surrounding the Great Mosque in the Muslim Quarter is a unique, highly diverse, and round-the-clock street food Nirvana.

Originally staged to provide nourishment for road-weary traders, this centuries-old marketplace is the singular reminder of a hallmark of the Silk Road: rather than clashing, cultures came together. They shared tales of rugged adventure, sips of unfamiliar elixir, and of course, food. Where each cobbled-together street stand was once manned by people from different corners of the globe, today, the Muslim-Chinese, or the *Uyghur* and the *Hui* minorities, have become the purveyors of cookery that represents the accumulated culinary knowledge of 4300 miles of Silk Road.

Dozens of narrow alleys, packed with busy vendors, cooks, diners, and fortunate local residents, teem with clouds of perfumed smoke and the unmistakable aroma of cumin and piquant chiles. Ubiquitous are hardwood charcoal grills blanketed with sizzling grilled lamb skewers (page 111). Earthen ovens, reminiscent of an Indian tandoor, dot the sidewalks, producing hundreds of baked flatbreads by the hour (page 113). Giant woks cooking not a flashy stir-fry, but rather enormous piles of aromatic rice and lamb pilaf (page 118). In Xi'an beef and lamb are queen and king. The Chinese penchant for pork is but a sideshow. These sights inspire one to consider whether this is China or the Middle East.

On one sweltering Xi'an summer morning a while back, while cycling through a dizzying maze of fruit stalls, honking cars, throngs of hungry shoppers, and the occasional lucky dog, we are drawn from our saddles by the aroma of what appears to be a simple cauldron of beef soup. Though her sidewalk eatery is jammed to the gills with slurping commuters, a grandmotherly Mrs. Liu grabs us by the arms, foists us into the two remaining seats just behind the soup pot. She asks, "Where are you from and what do you think of our food?" Greg says, "This is why we come to China. We travel to eat, and Xi'an is quite famous!" Our new friend replies, "We have been making this same food for a hundred years, you're in the right place." Right place, indeed.

As we awaited our next helping of Mrs. Liu's morning fortification, we used the opportunity to stretch and talk with her husband, Mr. Ma, about the bone broth recipe. It seems the secret was in the beef: the meat was cured for days before being stewed as a base of the soup. Not unlike a cured brisket that is then boiled for a St. Patty's day corned beef and cabbage, this beef is a labor of love. Though it is not uncommon throughout Shaanxi Province to see cured, steamed beef sold on the streets like an alfresco deli, Mr. Ma's technique of long simmering is rather unique. Despite our inquiry into his exact recipe being met with a chuckle and unsurprising vagueness, we think we finally nailed it (Niurou Gutou Tang on page 101).

Hospitality being what it is in China, Mrs. Liu fed us bowl after bowl of her family's deliciously famous beef bone soup, but she refused our money repeatedly. "You're our foreign guests," was her refrain after repeated attempts to fill her till with cash. We snuck it under bowl #4 (or #5?) upon our satisfied, lumbering exit.

La Niurou
腊牛肉
(Cured Beef)

Chinese cuisine is much more pork-centric than most. Beef is historically considered to be pretty posh, as beef cattle are fewer in volume than hogs, even today. Traditionally, steer was considered crucial for agricultural field-work, and therefore off-limits to the inventive local chef. What spare beef was available, therefore, was generally cured to last through the winter, mostly to flavor soups, stews, and stir-fried dishes in need of a savory, salty punch. As Islam found its way to China and became more popular, primarily in the central and northwestern provinces, so did beef. Accordingly, an industry built around it, family-run Muslim butchers set up shop, beef cattle grew in numbers, and today, it's common to see as much fresh beef as cured.

On yet another eating adventure through Shaanxi Province, we met and spent a lunch hour with Mr. An. He is a 5th generation cured beef seller from Xi'an. His brand of la niurou has been gaining in popularity in its 100-year tenure. They've built a small chain throughout the city, and still today, lines form around the block in the early morning hours. They're out of beef by noon. Rather than the typical salt-only cure, Mr. An's forefathers developed a wet cure that produces unique, delicious results. Katz's Delicatessen in New York has nothing on this joint.

Total Time: 4 days, (plus 4 hours and 30 minutes, if cooking immediately)

CURE:
¼ cup sugar
¼ cup salt
¼ cup soy sauce
2 Tbsp dark soy sauce
¼ cup Chinese rice wine or
  dry sherry
3 lb beef brisket

BOIL:
1 gallon water
4 scallions
2 inches ginger, washed, halved
  lengthwise
2 star anise
1 stick cinnamon

In a mixing bowl, whisk together all Cure ingredients, except for the beef. It's not important that the salt and sugar dissolve at this point. Place the beef in a large ziplock plastic bag or in a storage container that fits the beef snugly at the bottom. Pour the mixture over the beef. Turn the beef so that it is initially painted with curing liquid, seal, and refrigerate.

continued on page 100

Each day, turn the beef once more to ensure even exposure to the curing paste. After four days, remove the beef from the refrigerator and rinse under cold water. At this point, you can wrap the beef tightly in plastic wrap, seal tightly in a ziplock bag and/or use the uncooked beef for recipes such as "Lurou" Huoshao on page 163, Niurou Gutou Tang on page 101, Mala Zhangfei Niurou on page 141, or Xiangcao Rou on page 126.

To cook the beef for general use: sandwiches, stir-fries, or just to munch on, bring water, scallions, ginger, anise, and cinnamon to a boil over high heat. Reduce the heat to low to maintain a simmer. Add beef to the pot and simmer, uncovered, for 3 hours. Turn the heat off, place a lid on the pot and allow the beef to cool for one hour in the liquid.

Remove the beef from the pot to a rimmed plate. Allow it to cool for an additional 30 minutes before slicing and eating.

(Beef Bone So

Though soups abound in Chinese cuisine, and the more simple renditions as street food, this specimen is unique. Making use of bones, cured and seasoned beef, and sundry aromatics, the broth develops an unmistakable savory quality, with a richness not found in most other soups. It's deep. Where the broth is the star of the bowl, a supporting cast of bean thread noodles, slices of beef, bright herbs, and bits of chewy bread to soak up the goodness make this soup a well-rounded show. In fact, Mr. Ma is indeed putting on a show, right there on the sidewalk. How can passersby resist the alluring aroma of the beefy steam and the freshness of the ingredients being ornately, expertly piled into a breakfast bowl of the gods?

By the way, suggest that your guests tear the bread to bits themselves. According to Chinese tradition, the smaller the pieces, the smarter the eater.

Total Time: 5 hours, 45 minutes | Serves: 8–10

BEEF AND BROTH:
1½ gallons water, divided
3 lb beef soup bones, butcher-cut into 2-inch segments
1 recipe uncooked La Niurou (Cured Beef) on page 99
2 inches ginger, peeled, halved lengthwise
2 heads garlic, unpeeled, halved lengthwise
1 bunch scallions
2 cinnamon sticks
4 star anise
1 Tbsp Sichuan peppercorns
2 Tbsp salt
3 Tbsp Shaoxing, other Chinese rice wine, or dry sherry

TO FINISH:
2 cups water, boiling
½ lb bean thread or vermicelli noodles
½ recipe Baiji Mo (Baked Sandwich Buns) on page 105
4 scallions, thinly sliced
1 bunch cilantro, roughly chopped

La Niurou
腊牛肉
(Cured Beef)

Chinese cuisine is much more pork-centric than most. Beef is historically considered to be pretty posh, as beef cattle are fewer in volume than hogs, even today. Traditionally, steer was considered crucial for agricultural field-work, and therefore off-limits to the inventive local chef. What spare beef was available, therefore, was generally cured to last through the winter, mostly to flavor soups, stews, and stir-fried dishes in need of a savory, salty punch. As Islam found its way to China and became more popular, primarily in the central and northwestern provinces, so did beef. Accordingly, an industry built around it, family-run Muslim butchers set up shop, beef cattle grew in numbers, and today, it's common to see as much fresh beef as cured.

On yet another eating adventure through Shaanxi Province, we met and spent a lunch hour with Mr. An. He is a 5th generation cured beef seller from Xi'an. His brand of la niurou has been gaining in popularity in its 100-year tenure. They've built a small chain throughout the city, and still today, lines form around the block in the early morning hours. They're out of beef by noon. Rather than the typical salt-only cure, Mr. An's forefathers developed a wet cure that produces unique, delicious results. Katz's Delicatessen in New York has nothing on this joint.

Total Time: 4 days, (plus 4 hours and 30 minutes, if cooking immediately)

CURE:
- ¼ cup sugar
- ¼ cup salt
- ¼ cup soy sauce
- 2 Tbsp dark soy sauce
- ¼ cup Chinese rice wine or dry sherry
- 3 lb beef brisket

BOIL:
- 1 gallon water
- 4 scallions
- 2 inches ginger, washed, halved lengthwise
- 2 star anise
- 1 stick cinnamon

In a mixing bowl, whisk together all Cure ingredients, except for the beef. It's not important that the salt and sugar dissolve at this point. Place the beef in a large ziplock plastic bag or in a storage container that fits the beef snugly at the bottom. Pour the mixture over the beef. Turn the beef so that it is initially painted with curing liquid, seal, and refrigerate.

continued on page 100

Each day, turn the beef once more to ensure even exposure to the curing paste. After four days, remove the beef from the refrigerator and rinse under cold water. At this point, you can wrap the beef tightly in plastic wrap, seal tightly in a ziplock bag and/or use the uncooked beef for recipes such as "Lurou" Huoshao on page 163, Niurou Gutou Tang on page 101, Mala Zhangfei Niurou on page 141, or Xiangcao Rou on page 126.

To cook the beef for general use: sandwiches, stir-fries, or just to munch on, bring water, scallions, ginger, anise, and cinnamon to a boil over high heat. Reduce the heat to low to maintain a simmer. Add beef to the pot and simmer, uncovered, for 3 hours. Turn the heat off, place a lid on the pot and allow the beef to cool for one hour in the liquid.

Remove the beef from the pot to a rimmed plate. Allow it to cool for an additional 30 minutes before slicing and eating.

Niurou Gutou Tang
牛肉骨头汤
(Beef Bone Soup)

Though soups abound in Chinese cuisine, and the more simple renditions as street food, this specimen is unique. Making use of bones, cured and seasoned beef, and sundry aromatics, the broth develops an unmistakable savory quality, with a richness not found in most other soups. It's deep. Where the broth is the star of the bowl, a supporting cast of bean thread noodles, slices of beef, bright herbs, and bits of chewy bread to soak up the goodness make this soup a well-rounded show. In fact, Mr. Ma is indeed putting on a show, right there on the sidewalk. How can passersby resist the alluring aroma of the beefy steam and the freshness of the ingredients being ornately, expertly piled into a breakfast bowl of the gods?

By the way, suggest that your guests tear the bread to bits themselves. According to Chinese tradition, the smaller the pieces, the smarter the eater.

Total Time: 5 hours, 45 minutes | Serves: 8–10

BEEF AND BROTH:

1½ gallons water, divided

3 lb beef soup bones, butcher-cut into 2-inch segments

1 recipe uncooked La Niurou (Cured Beef) on page 99

2 inches ginger, peeled, halved lengthwise

2 heads garlic, unpeeled, halved lengthwise

1 bunch scallions

2 cinnamon sticks

4 star anise

1 Tbsp Sichuan peppercorns

2 Tbsp salt

3 Tbsp Shaoxing, other Chinese rice wine, or dry sherry

TO FINISH:

2 cups water, boiling

½ lb bean thread or vermicelli noodles

½ recipe Baiji Mo (Baked Sandwich Buns) on page 105

4 scallions, thinly sliced

1 bunch cilantro, roughly chopped

In a large stock pot, bring ½ gallon of water to a boil and add soup bones. Boil the bones for 3 minutes, then remove, set aside, and discard the water. Rinse out the pot.

In the pot, combine boiled bones, cured beef, ginger, garlic, scallions, cinnamon, star anise, peppercorns, salt, rice wine, and the remaining 1 gallon of water. Bring to a light simmer over medium heat. Simmer, covered, for 4 hours. Turn off the heat and allow the contents to rest in the covered pot for one hour.

Use a large slotted spoon to transfer the cured beef from the pot to a rimmed plate. Strain the broth into a large pot through cheesecloth or a fine-meshed sieve. Keep the pot of strained broth warm on the stove over low heat. Transfer the cured beef to a chopping board and cut into ½-inch thick slices. Set aside.

In a mixing bowl, pour boiling water over bean thread noodles or vermicelli and soak for 10 minutes. Drain the noodles and set aside. While the noodles are soaking, tear Baiji Mo buns into small bits, about the size of peas, and set aside.

Evenly distribute drained bean thread noodles or vermicelli and beef slices into bowls. Then ladle in simmering broth before topping with scallions and cilantro. Serve immediately with bread pieces for folks to add at will.

Baiji Mo
白吉馍
(Baked Sandwich Buns)

When we first started traveling in northeast China more than twenty years ago, steamed or fried breads were traditional and expected. Baked breads were *not the rage*. Every once in a while, you would run into a street vendor from some far-off province, admire their oven, and enjoy what were decidedly foreign snacks. As we ventured toward the West, however, we began to see these breads with more frequency. Thanks to food hopping the borders of central Asia and the Indian subcontinent, notably along the Silk Road, flatbreads and the occasional leavened bread became *all the rage*. Today, as bread recipes easily jump aboard cheap planes and trains, baked breads are increasingly common throughout the country. Baiji Mo bread, popular in Xi'an, is traditionally served as a chewy sandwich bun or torn into bits and stirred into soups.

Despite the rise of baked breads in China, it's always astounding to see that the equipment used is still very much old style, particularly with small vendors on the street. It's always a *treat* to be around bakers when the central China summer is in full swing. Stone and sometimes wood ovens, blazing at 600°F, clear discomfort for passersby and curious travelers such as ourselves, and yet, the bakers keep a smile, and hand over hot, fresh buns. Worth every drop of sweat!

Total time: 2 hours, 45 minutes | Serves: 6–8

**3½ cups all-purpose flour, plus
   more for dusting**
2 tsp rapid-rise yeast

1 tsp salt
1 cup of warm water

In a large mixing bowl or the bowl of stand mixer, whisk together flour, yeast, and salt. Using clean hands or the dough hook of the stand mixer, incorporate water until a smooth dough forms.

Dust the countertop or work surface with additional flour and transfer the dough onto the flour. Dust the top of the dough, knead, and form the dough into a ball. Transfer the dough to a large, clean, lightly oiled bowl and cover with plastic wrap. Allow the dough to double in size, about one hour to 90 minutes.

continued on page 106

Uncover the dough, dust the work surface with flour, transfer the dough atop the flour, and evenly hand-roll it onto a 2-inch-thick log. Cut the dough into 2-inch pieces. Knead and roll each of the dough pieces into a ball. Dust the top of the dough balls and cover with towel or plastic wrap. Allow the dough balls to rest for 30 minutes. Preheat the oven to 375°F.

After the dough balls have rested, remove one from the plastic wrap and hand-roll it into a 1-inch log. Using a rolling pin, roll the dough into a long oval, about ¼-inch thick. Starting from one narrow end, roll it up as you would a poster. Stand the roll on its end and gently flatten and roll it into a 4-inch disc. If an outer edge sticks out, fold it under the bottom of the disc as you flatten it. Set aside and continue to make discs with the remaining dough balls.

Heat a lightly greased skillet or griddle over medium-low heat for 4 minutes. Pick up one of the dough discs and using two hands, with thumbs atop the dough, gently push the center to slightly stretch out the middle, forming a bowl shape before placing it flat into the skillet. This step assures that the middle will not overly rise. Cook the dough on one side for 1-2 minutes, or until the bottom is beginning to brown. Flip the dough over and continue cooking for one minute. Remove the partially cooked disc from the skillet and place on a sheet pan. Finish browning the remaining dough discs.

Transfer the sheet pan(s) to the oven and bake the dough until the buns are cooked through, about another 15–20 minutes. They should be puffed up and golden brown. Once the buns are done, set aside for Roujia Mo (Stewed Pork Sandwiches) on page 248, Niurou Gutou Tang (Beef Bone Soup) on page 101, or Yangrou Paomo (Lamb and Bread Soup) on page 107.

Yangrou Paomo
羊肉泡馍
(Lamb and Bread Soup)

According to legend, awesome warrior Zhao Kuangyin invented this dish. It seems he was tired, poor, and toting a couple of loaves of stale bread along an arduous journey back to his hometown after some bloody battle or another. Anyhow, he stopped into a small inn and asked for a delicious handout. Thinking he was out of luck, he ripped up his bread into tiny bits and put them in a bowl. Just then, a waiter came and took the bowl and gave Mr. Zhao a coat check ticket. "Why'd you take my bread, dude?" he asked in a huff. The waiter came back several minutes later with his bread bits soaked in lovely, nourishing lamb soup. With all those proteins and carbs coursing through his body, Mr. Zhao went and started a mutiny against the Zhou emperor and founded the Song Dynasty.

Okay, it may not have gone down exactly this way, but today in Xi'an, they do give you a numbered medallion that identifies your bowl of bread so they don't mix up the impending steamy bowl of mushy bread and lamb soup.

Total time: 5 hours | Serves: 8–10

LAMB AND BROTH:
16 cups water, divided
3-lb lamb shoulder on the bone
2 inches ginger, peeled, halved
    lengthwise
1 large onion, halved
10 cloves garlic, peeled
1 large carrot, 2-inch pieces
2 tsp five-spice powder
2 tsp cumin powder
1 Tbsp Sichuan peppercorns

FINISHING:
2 cups water, boiling
½ lb bean thread or vermicelli noodles
½ recipe Baiji Mo (Baked Sandwich
    Buns) from page 105
2 Tbsp Shaoxing, other Chinese rice
    wine, or dry sherry
2 Tbsp soy sauce
1 tsp salt
3–4 tsp Chinese black vinegar
6–8 tsp sesame oil
4 scallions, thinly sliced
Chile paste (optional for serving)

In a stock pot or Dutch oven over high heat, bring 8 cups of water to a boil. Add the lamb and cook for 1 minute, rolling it over so that each side is in contact with boiling water for at least 30 seconds. Carefully transfer the lamb from the water, rinse with cold water, and set on a plate.

Wipe out the pot and add lamb, remaining 8 cups of water, ginger, onion, garlic, carrot, five-spice, cumin, and Sichuan pepper. Bring the mixture to a light simmer over medium heat. Reduce the heat to low, cover, and continue to simmer for 3½ hours.

Turn off the heat and allow the lamb to rest in the covered pot for one hour. Use a large slotted spoon to transfer the lamb from the pot to a rimmed plate. Strain the broth into a mixing bowl or another pot through cheesecloth or a fine-meshed sieve. Transfer the lamb to a chopping board, remove the bone, and thinly slice the meat. Set aside.

In a mixing bowl, pour 2 cups of boiling water over bean thread noodles or vermicelli and soak for 10 minutes. Drain the noodles and set aside. While the noodles are soaking, tear Baiji Mo buns into small bits, about the size of peas, and set aside.

To build the soup, in a separate pot over medium-high heat, combine the strained broth, rice wine or sherry, soy sauce, and salt, and bring it to a boil. Reduce the heat to low, add the bread pieces, stir, and allow the mixture to simmer for 5 minutes.

Evenly distribute drained bean thread noodles or vermicelli and lamb slices into bowls. Add ½ teaspoon of vinegar and 1 tsp of sesame oil into each bowl. Then ladle in simmering bread soup before topping with scallions. Serve immediately with chile paste for folks to add at will.

Yangrou Chuan
羊肉串
(Grilled Lamb Skewers)

Kebabs were the brainchild of hungry ancient soldiers who threaded the flesh of recently hunted field game onto their swords and cooked over an open fire. Thought to be originally conceived of in Turkey, meat kebabs have taken on the honor of being one of China's most beloved and ubiquitous street snacks. Though you can find pork, beef, seafood, and sundry vegetables on *shaokao* skewers across China (page 229), lamb kebabs, or *yangrou chuan*, are the clear favorite. Through all of our China eating adventures, watching the yangrou chuan process in lesser-known cities never ceases to amaze. Shop-owners' kids, some as young as eight years old, propped up on a ladder, expertly butchering a hanging lamb carcass, shaving meat from the ribs, the legs, and the shoulders, depositing the cuts into a marinade, or directly onto skewers, ready for the grill. Thanks, kids!

Speaking of kids, our most memorable yangrou chuan experience involved students, fresh out of class in Chengdu. As we're waiting for our skewers to grill to perfection, down the street from an elementary school, the bell rings and a couple dozen 5th graders bound down the block, straight for the string of kebab stands. Out came whatever pocket change they had; each skewer was about 12 cents. In China, queues are hard to come by, and the kids amassed, almost on top of the grill. This was a hungry mob, vying to get their money to the vendor first! Then, they began to compete with how much spice they could handle. School letting out is different and yummy in China.

Total Time: 2 hours, 20 minutes | Serves: 4–6

20 wooden skewers
2½ lb lamb shoulder, boneless, cut into 1-inch chunks
2 Tbsp soy sauce
1 Tbsp vegetable or canola oil
1 Tbsp sesame oil

1 Tbsp Shaoxing rice wine or dry sherry
3 cloves garlic, minced to paste
1 Tbsp ground cumin
1 Tbsp Ancho or other chile powder
2 tsp ground white pepper

In a baking dish filled halfway with water, soak the wooden skewers for 2 hours. In a large mixing bowl, combine lamb, soy sauce, vegetable oil, sesame oil, rice wine, and garlic. Cover with plastic wrap, and refrigerate for 2 hours.

In a small mixing bowl, mix together cumin, chile powder, and white pepper and set aside.

Light a grill and make sure you have an area of the grill that is high heat and an area that is medium-low. Thread a few chunks of marinated lamb onto drained skewers and place on the medium-low side of the grill. After 5 minutes, flip the skewers and grill for an additional 5 minutes. Repeat this process for all of the skewers until all the meat has been cooked.

As the meat is cooked for 10 minutes, dust each skewer with the spice mixture and sear on the high heat side of the grill for one minute on each side. Serve the kebabs hot off the grill with Nang (Baked Flatbread) on page 113, or keep them warm under aluminum foil until all of the meat has been cooked.

Nang
馕
(Baked Flatbread)

It's not hard to see the progression of flatbreads across the Middle East, into the Indian subcontinent and finally into China. In fact, the word *nang* is likely the Chinese transliteration of the word *naan* from Hindi (though the bread's format is closer to a Persian style flatbread). In fact, they're even made in a tandoor oven. Spiced with cumin and various seeds, *nang* is a Chinese Muslim staple that could be eaten alone as a snack, but is frequently paired with skewered meat or dipped into soup. The texture is somewhere between a pizza crust and a bagel. What's not to love?

A lot of street food in China is not obvious from down the street. Most of the time, you won't know what folks are cooking up until you're right in front of the stand. Nang, on the other hand, can probably be spotted on satellite imagery. Bakers start the day by making stacks upon stacks of golden brown loaves to put on large, picturesque display tables next to the tandoor. Many are ornate, with a flowery design, speckled with sunflower or sesame seeds. Along with their unique food aesthetic, nang vendors are also mainly Uyghurs from Xinjiang Province, in China's far Northwest, and offer some ethnic diversity to the street food scene.

Total Time: 2 hours | Serves: 6–8

4 cups flour, plus more for dusting
1 Tbsp rapid-rise yeast
1 cup water, warm from the tap, plus
   more for brushing
1 Tbsp salt
1 tsp sugar

3 Tbsp yogurt
1 large egg, beaten
1 Tbsp ground cumin
2 Tbsp black or white sesame seeds, or
   sunflower seeds

In a large mixing bowl or the bowl of a stand mixer, whisk together flour and yeast. In a separate mixing bowl, whisk together water, salt, sugar, and yogurt. Then, whisk in the egg. With the dough hook attached to the stand mixer or with clean hands in the mixing bowl, slowly incorporate the liquid mixture into the flour mixture. When there is no longer visible flour, knead the dough for 3 minutes.

continued on page 115

Dust the countertop or work surface with additional flour, and pour the dough from the mixing bowl atop the flour. Briefly knead the dough to form a smooth ball. Dust the top of the dough ball with additional flour, cover with plastic wrap, and allow to ferment on the counter for 1 hour. The dough will become bubbly and much larger in size.

Generously dust the countertop or work surface with flour and transfer the now very loose dough on top of the flour. Using a knife or a bench scraper, divide the dough into equal quarters. Form each quarter into a ball, dust with flour, cover with plastic wrap, and let it rest for 25 additional minutes.

Preheat the oven to 450°F.

Remove the plastic wrap. Using your fingertips, avoiding the edges, flatten and stretch each ball to an even 8–10 inch circle. It should end up looking like you're making a pizza. Use a fork to pierce the dough, avoiding the edges, 20–25 times, evenly across the surface.

Transfer the dough circles to flour-dusted sheet pans, brush the top of the dough with water, and sprinkle with cumin and sesame or sunflower seeds. Transfer the dough to the oven and bake it for 10–12 minutes, or until it is golden brown and the edges have puffed up. Remove the nang from the oven and serve hot with Yangrou Chuan (Grilled Lamb Skewers) on page 111, or as the bread for any meal.

Fenzheng Rou
粉蒸肉
(Flour-Steamed Beef)

The Chinese are big into texture, the more unexpected the better. On their face, flour coated hunks of steamed meat don't seem that appealing. Add a bit of Chinese ingenuity and voilà, a dish that presents meat that is silky, delicate, and meltingly tender. This dish is found in many different contexts. There's a restaurant version that tends toward rice flour and piquant pork, steamed in single serving vessels, atop potatoes that soak up the drippings and spice. Then there's the street version, wheat flour and beef steamed in huge baskets, nothing underneath to soak up anything left behind by the meat. And, in a very central Chinese fashion, it may be served up on a less-than-expected scallop shell.

We very much enjoy the street version. It's simple, delicious, completely filling, and, c'mon, who doesn't love food served in a scallop shell? But, the restaurant rendition is complex and really very appealing. There is a middle ground. We found it. Back in the early 2000s, we met a street vendor in Yibin, Sichuan, who used the highly seasoned restaurant ethic and applied it to the traditional Muslim beef version. It's truly a surprise that more cooks haven't happened upon this hybrid before. You are lucky recipients of fusion Chinese cuisine.

Total Time: 2 hours, 45 minutes | Serves: 4–6

1½ lb beef flank steak, boneless short rib, *or* chuck roast, boneless, diced
1 inch ginger, peeled, minced
2 scallions, minced
1 Tbsp soy sauce
1 tsp toasted sesame oil
2 tsp red chile oil *or* Lajiao You (Chile Oil) on page 132
1 tsp sweet bean sauce (tianmianjiang) or hoisin sauce

1 tsp Chinese rice wine or dry sherry
½ tsp salt
½ tsp ground white pepper
1½ lb russet or gold potato, ½ inch thick half-moons
5 Tbsp all-purpose flour
Water for steaming

In a large mixing bowl, thoroughly mix beef, ginger, scallions, soy sauce, sesame oil, chile oil, sweet bean or hoisin, rice wine, salt, and pepper. Set aside to marinate for 30 minutes.

Place 2 pie pans or other rimmed plates into stackable steamer baskets and lay potato pieces at the bottom of the plate. Add flour to the marinated beef and evenly coat it by hand. Transfer the beef mixture atop the potatoes.

Place a deep skillet or pot over medium heat, fill with 3 inches of water, and bring to a boil. Reduce the heat to medium. Carefully place the steamer basket atop the pot of boiling water, cover, and steam the dish for 2 hours.

Serve hot.

Shouzhua Fan
手抓饭
("Grasping" Rice and Lamb Pilaf)

The name is a fun one. Originally called *shouzhua fan*, or "hand-grabbed rice," it was a dish to be enjoyed communally with the fingers as dining implements. Where the Chinese traditionally consider this method to be barbaric and opt for a spoon or chopsticks to consume rice, the name may be shortened to *zhua fan*, or simply "grabbed rice" and has all but lost its literal meaning. To boot, Chinese do not traditionally make pilaf-style rice. The concept of cooking raw rice alongside aromatic spices, fatty meat, and vegetables is definitively alien. However, when you get to the middle of China, and farther west, you begin to see the cuisine of northwestern Uyghurs, who of course get their concepts of rice from their Middle Eastern and Turkic ancestors. Alien food, done right.

The Uyghurs are an interesting part of the Chinese landscape. They tend to view themselves as foreigners living among the Han. Additionally, not unlike the bread vendors we mentioned previously, their signs are often in Arabic and internal communications are often in a Uyghur tongue. We've even had a number of experiences of a language block when chatting them up about their food. In the case of our preferred pilaf peddlers in Xi'an, Greg's passing knowledge of Arabic script helped in our recipe research more than any Chinese we could muster.

Total time: 2 hours, 20 minutes | Serves: 4–6

1 cup jasmine or other long grain white rice
4 cups water, divided
¼ cup vegetable oil
1 lb lamb shoulder, diced
1 ½ tsp salt, divided

1 onion, thinly sliced half-moons
½ lb carrots, ¼-inch x 2-inch sticks
8 cloves garlic, lightly crushed
1 Tbsp cumin
1 tsp ground black pepper

Preheat the oven to 350°F. In a mixing bowl, combine rice with 2 cups of water and set aside.

Heat a skillet over medium heat and add the oil. When the oil begins to shimmer, add the lamb and 1 teaspoon of salt to the skillet and sauté, stirring often until all of the meat has browned, about 6–8 minutes. Using a slotted spoon, remove the lamb to a plate and set aside.

continued on page 119

Add onions to the skillet and sauté until the onions have softened and begin to brown, about 8–10 minutes. Add carrot, garlic, cumin, and black pepper, and continue to sauté for an additional 6–8 minutes, or until the carrots have softened but not broken. Add the remaining 2 cups of water to the skillet and bring to a boil. Reduce the heat to low, add the browned lamb, cover, and simmer for 1 hour.

Turn off the heat and uncover the skillet. Drain the soaking rice and evenly distribute it across the top of the contents of the skillet. Sprinkle the remaining ½ teaspoon of salt across the top. Using the back of a spoon, make sure the rice is submerged in liquid, but do not mix it with the lamb mixture. Cover and transfer the skillet to the oven for 45 minutes.

Remove the skillet from the oven. Allow the zhua fan to rest, covered, out of the oven for 15 minutes. Remove the lid, stir everything together, and serve directly to bowls.

Suantang Shuijiao
酸汤水饺
(Boiled Dumplings in Sour Sauce)

We never gave the term *suantang shuijiao* much thought, and before we could distinguish the character for garlic from the character for sour, we just presumed this snack was dumplings in garlic soup. So, a while back we were in Xi'an for... what else? Food. On a rather crowded afternoon in the alleyways of the Muslim Quarter, we found relief on two little plastic stools and ordered up a bowl of what we assumed was our first garlicky treat of the day. Our first bite seemed to confirm it: beef dumplings with big shards of raw garlic mixed into the filling. The beef seemed a supporting player. This was garlic to the nth degree. Then, we stirred it up with the sauce. Wham! Powerfully sour soup! Long story short, we learned to tell the characters apart.

It's a very common ethic to simply dip Chinese dumplings into a soy sauce concoction, maybe some vinegar. It's basic and flavorful. But, the Chinese actually enjoy the occasional "mix-in!" There are several in the street food pantheon, but Red Oil Boiled Dumplings (page 135) and this recipe are among the finest. Why dip when you can surround the dumplings with a coating of savory, sweet, and/or spicy elixir? What are you missing? It's here.

Total Time: 45 minutes | Serves: 6–8

FILLING:
1 lb ground beef
2 leeks, stemmed, washed, diced
1 inch ginger, peeled, minced
2 cloves garlic, peeled, minced
1 Tbsp soy sauce
1 tsp toasted sesame oil
2 tsp Chinese rice wine or dry sherry
2 Tbsp beef stock
½ tsp salt
½ tsp ground black pepper
½ tsp baking soda
2 tsp cornstarch

SAUCE:
½ cup beef stock
¼ cup soy sauce
½ cup Chinese black vinegar
⅓ cup Lajiao You (Chile Oil) with sediment on page 132
½ tsp salt
½ tsp sugar
2 cloves garlic, mashed into paste
1 16-oz package wonton or gyoza skins, round preferred
1 gallon plus 1 cup water for boiling, plus more for sealing the dumplings

GARNISH:
1 bunch cilantro, roughly chopped
4 scallions, thinly sliced

In a large mixing bowl, thoroughly combine all of the filling ingredients. In a separate mixing bowl, whisk together the sauce ingredients. Be sure that the salt and sugar dissolve.

In the middle of one wrapper, place 2 teaspoons of filling. With a wet finger, moisten the edges of the wrapper. Fold the wrapper in half around the filling and seal by pinching the edges completely. Optionally, you may fold pleats where the edges meet, thereby creating a little purse, rather than a half-moon. Repeat with the remaining filling and wrappers.

Bring water to a boil over high heat. Stir the pot to create a current such that as you drop the individual wontons into the water, they are not likely to stick together. When the water comes to a boil again, add 1 cup of cold water and continue to cook for an additional 6–8 minutes. Remove dumplings from the water to a plate using a slotted spoon or sieve.

Evenly distribute sauce into bowls. Then top with cooked dumplings and garnish with cilantro and scallions. Serve hot, and suggest that guests mix it all together before enjoying.

Guantang Baozi
灌汤包子
(Steamed Soup Dumplings)

In the US, at least in larger cities, Shanghai-style *xiaolongbao* are a big deal. Soup dumplings. In fact, most Americans just assume that xiaolongbao means "soup dumplings." It doesn't. It means "little steamer" dumplings. *Guantang baozi* literally means "soup-inside-buns." Yeah, it may still be confusing since baozi are typically thought of as steamed buns rather than steamed dumplings, but let's forgive the Chinese this linguistic snafu. That being said, connoisseurs of soup dumplings know the trick to eating them. Bite the very edge, suck out some of the soup inside, dip the rest of the dumplings into something dumpling-worthy and consume the remainder. During our first go at soup dumplings in China, Greg was unaware; popped the whole thing into his soon-to-be-sorry mouth. Scalding soup explosion! Be careful.

On one particularly hot night in Xi'an, we happened upon a shop serving guantang baozi that was unique. The purveyors didn't employ a fancy sealing technique or an aesthetic beyond the simple. Half-moons instead of finicky, perfect little purses. Their flavor was their currency. Where xiaolongbao in Shanghai is ornate with some exact number of pleats, these were just as good if not a bit better without all the fuss—luscious packages of hot broth and luscious filling. The spirit of soup dumplings was strong that day.

Total Time: 1 hour, 30 minutes | Serves: 6–8

FILLING:
2 cups beef broth *or* broth from Jirou Tang (Chicken Soup) on page 189
2 tsp gelatin powder
1 lb ground beef
1 inch ginger, peeled, minced
2 cloves garlic, peeled, minced
3 scallions, minced
1 Tbsp soy sauce
1 tsp toasted sesame oil
2 tsp Chinese rice wine or dry sherry
½ tsp salt
½ tsp ground white pepper

WRAPPERS:
1 16-oz package wonton or gyoza skins, round preferred
Water for sealing the dumplings, plus more for steaming

OPTIONAL DIPPING SAUCE:
1 recipe Dipping Sauce from Zhurou Jiaozi (Steamed Pork Dumplings) on page 53

Add broth to a pot over medium-high heat. Once the broth boils, turn off the heat, sprinkle gelatin over the broth and stir it in until it dissolves. Pour the broth into a baking dish and refrigerate uncovered for at least 45 minutes or until the broth is gelatinized and completely cool. Remove the gel from the baking dish in one sheet and dice into very small blocks.

In a large mixing bowl, thoroughly combine the remaining filling ingredients. Then, evenly stir in the gel blocks.

In the middle of one wrapper, place 1 tablespoon of filling. With a wet finger, moisten the edges of the wrapper. Fold the wrapper into a half-moon around the filling and seal by pinching the edges completely. Repeat with the remaining filling and wrappers.

Prepare steamer baskets by lining them with cheesecloth or parchment paper. Place the filled dough parcels atop the lining in a single layer, with the sealed edges facing up. If you have stackable steamer baskets, continue to fill baskets. Otherwise, steam dumplings in batches. Cover the steamer basket(s) with their matching lid(s).

Place a skillet or pot over medium heat, fill with 2 inches of water, and bring to a boil. Carefully place the steamer baskets atop the pot of boiling water, cover, and steam the dumplings for 10 minutes.

Serve guantang baozi very hot, optionally with a bit of dipping sauce.

Xiangcao Rou
香草肉
(Steamed Corned Beef Rolls)

Pingyao is a small city in Shanxi Province. It's one of the only remaining towns with its old city wall intact. It's a pretty neat place to visit. Despite the ancient-coolness factor, it's not a town with a whole lot of street food going on, but for one of our favorite morsels ever, *xiangcao rou*. The name itself translates to "fragrant straw meat," as it's traditionally steamed in neat little straw capsules that are said to impart a unique aroma to the beef. We disagree, and feel that the flavor of this dish is directly in line with the curing process, and perhaps the earthy tones of rice wine. It's also said that Pingyao-style cured beef is unique, different from all others around China. We love you, Shanxi Province, but your cured beef is pretty much the same as your next door neighbor, Shaanxi Province.

So, you can breathe a sigh of relief that 1) you don't have to make any other cured beef than our Cured Beef from page 99, and 2) you don't have to fly to Pingyao to buy your own collection of fragrant straw baskets! Also comforting is that this dish will remind you of something . . . It's basically a corned beef wrap which had us pining for some deli mustard and rye bread the first time we tried it. One would think that this delicious little package would make its way around China. Boggles the mind that it hasn't. We will have to settle for the home kitchen, and frequent visits to Pingyao.

Total Time: 45 minutes | Serves: 4–6

1 lb (½ recipe) uncooked La Niurou (Cured Beef), ground or minced
1 egg white
1 tsp sesame oil
2 tsp Chinese rice wine or dry sherry
1 Tbsp cornstarch
1 tsp salt

1 scallion, minced
4 Tbsp cold water, divided, plus more for steaming
2 Tbsp all-purpose flour
12 sheets tofu skins, trimmed to 5 × 6-inch squares

In a large mixing bowl, combine beef, egg white, sesame oil, rice wine, cornstarch, salt, scallion, and 1 tablespoon of water. Mix thoroughly with clean hands or a wooden spoon, briskly and in one direction. The mixture will lighten in color as air gets incorporated, which ensures a light-textured beef roll. In a small mixing bowl, whisk together flour with 3 tablespoons of water.

Brush one tofu skin with flour paste. Place ¼ cup of meat mixture in the middle, and wrap as you would a spring roll or burrito with closed ends. Place seam-side down on a plate and repeat with remaining meat mixture and tofu skins.

Prepare steamer baskets by lining them with cheesecloth or parchment paper. Place the tofu parcels atop the lining. Cover the steamer basket(s) with their matching lid(s). Place a skillet or pot over medium heat, fill with 2 inches of water, and bring to a boil. Carefully place the steamer baskets atop the pot of boiling water, cover, and steam the rolls for 35 minutes.

Serve the Xiangcao Rou hot.

Xigua Shiliu Zhi
西瓜石榴汁
(Watermelon Pomegranate Juice)

Far be it for us to tell you that finding a juice recipe in a book about Chinese street food is normal. But, if you've ever been to Xi'an, you know that watermelon and pomegranates are plentiful. There's a juice stand on most corners in most seasons. We have the Silk Road to thank, once again. Pomegranates are native to central Asia and watermelon hails from southern Africa. One thing led to another and once traditional Chinese doctors got a hold of both fruits, it was love at first bite. Alone, either fruit is healthy, refreshing, and a good foil for hot climates, but together, let's just say, Chinese medical practitioners consider the combination, um, potent for potency.

Total Time: 1 hour | Serves: 4–6

**1 large watermelon, seedless, flesh
   scooped away from the rinds**
3 cups pomegranate seeds

Working in batches, place watermelon flesh and pomegranate seeds in a blender and puree. Transfer the puree to a fine-meshed strainer or sieve over a large bowl. Using a spatula or a spoon, coax the juice out of the pulp by stirring and gently pushing. The less pulp that gets pushed through the strainer, the better.

Chill resulting juice in the refrigerator for at least 30 minutes and serve ice-cold.

CHAPTER 4: WHEN MA MET LA

SICHUAN PROVINCE IS FAMOUS, WORLDWIDE, for its distinctive and fiery cuisine. In fact, when one merely mentions Sichuanese cuisine to most Americans, and dare we say, to most global citizens with access to a Sichuan restaurant, smoke alarms go off and visions of three-alarm meals are top of mind. These days, whether at a Chinese joint or any other restaurant with spicy offerings, the ubiquitous menu symbol for spicy is the red chile pepper, but you may be surprised to know that the Sichuanese were fans of palate-altering spices well before they met the red chile.

Sichuan pepper, related to neither the chile pepper nor the peppercorn, is actually the berry of a prickly ash bush. Since the days when Confucius wrote odes to the magical orb more than two millennia ago, cooks in southwestern China have been toasting the berries, crushing them, and adding them to dishes for a unique gastronomic kick: as Chinese cuisine is a carnival of more than just flavor, this additive numbs any membrane with which it comes into contact. The Chinese call this sensation *ma*. As you may have guessed, Sichuan pepper also found its way into the medical arena with great success.

So, you have a population that is already a huge fan of things that make you go *whoa*. Sometime around the turn of the 15th century, along came Portuguese traders via Mexico. They introduced the Chinese to the chile pepper, fresh from South America. Agriculturally curious Chinese plant the bush, and, long story short, it thrives throughout hot, sweaty Sichuan Province. Upon chewing on the chiles, the Sichuanese simultaneously sweat, feel relief from the heat, and get that oh-so-famous mouth burn, which they call *la*.

We can only imagine the conversation that led to the meeting of *ma* and *la*, but it probably went something like this: *Hey, you got chile peppers on my prickly ash berries. Hey, you got prickly ash berries on my chile peppers. What? Delicious!* Well, perhaps we're just two 40-somethings who watched too many TV ads in the 80s. But, the joining of spicy and numbing was such a hit that to this day, when one talks of Sichuan cuisine, it goes hand in hand with *mala*. It's so intertwined that we don't think we've ever had a conversation in China about Sichuan cuisine that didn't feature the phrase *mala* within the first 12 seconds.

Given the characteristic cuisine that makes one's mouth pop, tongue melt, and ears steam, you may think that the people of Sichuan are of equally fiery spirit. On the contrary, Sichuan is also famous for its laid-back lifestyle. Perhaps it is this culture, as much as our love for the piquant food, that keeps us coming back to this province. The hot summer days, playing mahjong and sipping tea by the lake. The long nights, drinking beer and trying to learn the arcane rules of Chinese poker without losing too much money in the process. The relaxed crowds, idling away in the parks, awaiting a cheap chair massage or a cringe-worthy ear cleaning. This is the much-more-than-food feeling that *mala* evokes for us.

Lajiao You
辣椒油
(Chile Oil)

One of the great joys of traveling around China is tasting the many and varied *lajiao you*, or "chile oils." From the simple red chile flake variety found throughout the world and the blackened chile specimen laced with sesame oil and star anise, popular in southwestern China; to a surprising sugar-infused ground yellow lantern pepper example from the only tropical island in China, sampling lajiao is essentially a Napa Valley wine tasting of spicy goodness. On one of our many "wine tasting" trips to Sichuan, a friend told us about a city called Zigong. It was only a couple hours away from Chengdu and was known for its dinosaur museum and its gingko trees. We went there for the dinosaurs and, as it turned out, spice.

There are lots of great stories to share about Zigong. For example, ever see a guy attempt to light a cigarette at a bus stop that also happens to be a natural gas station? Or, ever been to a town where every vehicle on the road seems to feel it necessary to honk at least once every four seconds, whether moving or not? But, relevant to chile oil, we'll tell you that, back in 2002, if you walked about three blocks south of the dinosaur museum, you'd find an open-air spice market. Nestled between a vegetable stand and a tea vendor there was a guy selling sixteen varieties of local chile oil. For those of us who enjoy such things, it was like walking into a Zinfandel tasting, only without the spit barrels. Whether, sixteen years later, he's still there, we'll just have to go back to Zigong to check. But that memory, and the resultant scars on our tongues, will remain for a lifetime.

Total Time: 45 minutes

2 cups vegetable or canola oil
1 cinnamon stick
5 star anise

3 Tbsp Sichuan peppercorns, whole
1 cup crushed red chile flakes

In a pot over medium-low heat, combine oil, cinnamon, anise, and Sichuan pepper. Bring the mixture to a light simmer and reduce the temperature to low. Maintain a light simmer for 30 minutes.

Place the crushed chile flakes in a heat-proof mixing bowl. Using a sieve over the mixing bowl, carefully strain and pour the aromatic-flavored oil over the chile flakes and stir. Discard the aromatics in the sieve. Allow the chile oil to cool, covered, for 2 hours before pouring both oil and chile flakes into a jar. The chile oil can be stored in a cool, dry cabinet for up to 6 months.

The resulting chile oil is used for a great many recipes in this book.

Hongyou Chaoshou
红油抄手
(Red Oil Boiled Dumplings)

The first time we were in Chengdu, it wasn't even to be in Chengdu. We hadn't yet fallen in love with the numbing heat and aroma of Sichuan peppercorn, or spent our days idling with Li Yan, along the riverfront, hearing firsthand stories about World War II, the triumph of Mao, and the tragedy of the Cultural Revolution. It was even before we spent our nights drinking beer at *Dave's Oasis*, enjoying his latest version of kung pao chicken pizza. Before all that, Sichuan was just someplace we *had* to stop to get our transit pass to our ultimate destination—Tibet.

Well, Tibet was marvelous, but since that first stopover, we keep returning to Chengdu with no further destination. Our love affair with Spice City started with a bowl of *hongyou chaoshou*, literally, "red oil crossed hands." A 30-hour train ride from Beijing, with nothing to eat but instant noodles and tubes of Spam, can make you hungry. Real hungry. So, once off the train, when we happened upon a dumpling guy with a stack of steamers, we figured we'd hit gold. Turns out, we'd hit red. He took those dumplings—those pillows of pork, scallions, and flour—and placed them in a bowl. As we were reaching for the bowl, he proceeded to douse them with more chile oil than either of us had ever seen. And then he added even more.

We were tempted to pay, smile, and walk away. But he was so nice, and so obviously proud of his food, we dared to take a bite. Unbelievably, it was spicier than it looked. But it was also amazing. The harshness of the spice juxtaposed with the cloudlike dumpling was a revelation. Halfway through the bowl, our impulse to leave was even stronger—our faces were sweating, our noses dripping. But we couldn't stop. Quite frankly, this book would have never been written if we had.

Total Time: 45 minutes | Serves: 6–8

FILLING:
½ recipe Pork Filling from Zhurou Jiaozi (Steamed Pork Dumplings) on page 53

SAUCE:
2 Tbsp soy sauce
½ tsp sugar

⅓ cup Lajiao You (Chile Oil) with sediment on page 132
3 cloves garlic, mashed into paste
1 16-oz package wonton or gyoza wrappers, square preferred
1 gallon plus 1 cup water for boiling, plus more for sealing the dumplings
4 scallions, thinly sliced

In a large mixing bowl, thoroughly combine all of the Filling ingredients. In a separate mixing bowl, whisk together the Sauce ingredients. Be sure that the sugar dissolves.

In the middle of one wrapper, place 1–2 teaspoons of filling. With a wet finger, moisten the edges of the wrapper. Fold the wrapper in half into a triangle around the filling and seal by pinching the edges completely. Then, wet the two tips from the long side of the triangle and pinch them together in front of the filled center. Repeat with the remaining filling and wrappers.

Bring water to a boil over high heat. Stir the pot to create a current such that as you drop the individual dumplings into the water, they are not likely to stick together. When the water comes to a boil again, add 1 cup of cold water and continue to cook for an additional 6–8 minutes. Remove dumplings from the water to a plate using a slotted spoon or sieve.

Evenly distribute sauce into bowls. Then top with cooked chaoshou and garnish with scallions. Serve hot, and suggest that guests mix it all together before devouring.

Mala Xiao Longxia
麻辣
(Boiled Spicy Crayfish)

We've seen them grown in vast aquaculture developments adjoining railroad tracks and wheat fields. And we've seen children fishing for them in the Panlong River that runs through Yunnan Province. Throughout China, crayfish are treasured for their rich color, for their sweet taste, and for the ease and speed at which they can be raised. But nowhere in China are crayfish more popular than on Ghost Street in Beijing, where several dozen restaurants specializing in this traditional street food line the boulevard. As with many formerly-street-foods in Beijing, things have been cleaned up a bit. Yes, as in the street-food days, they still let you order by the pound. Yes, as in the street-food days, they still serve the crawfish from a boiling cauldron of chile-infused broth. Yes, as in the street-food days, they still serve them whole, expecting you to rip them to pieces with your bare hands. But now—in the age of the civilized restaurant—they give you thin plastic gloves. Progress!

Our favorite story of Ghost Street involves our good friend, Ray. You see, this was Ray's first trip to China, and, like all reasonable people, he was mad about the food. (Wait, we have to complain about Ray for a moment. It used to be that *we* were the exotic foreigners walking around the Forbidden City asking to have our photo taken with dozens of families. This time, it was all about Ray! *What gives*? It was exhausting, but must have been a real hoot for our good buddy. We digress.) On our last night, fatigued from watching Ray be a rockstar, we were sitting around the oil-soaked plates and piles of fish bones that indicate a proper Chinese feast, when our friend Zhang Ping mentioned the Crayfish of Ghost Street. Though clearly filled to the brim, Ray began drooling. It took a couple hours of walking and beer-drinking to build up another appetite, but we spent the midnight hour digging our plastic-clad hands through a trough of sweet, fiery crayfish.

¼ cup red chile oil with sediment *or* Lajiao You (Chile Oil) on page 132

4 cloves garlic, peeled, smashed

3 inches ginger, peeled, smashed

5 scallions, 2-inch segments

¼ cup Chinese broad bean paste (optional)

½ cup Chinese rice wine or dry sherry

2 star anise, whole

2 Tbsp Sichuan peppercorns, whole

1 Tbsp white peppercorns, whole

1 Tbsp salt

2 tsp granulated sugar

1 gallon water or chicken stock

3 lb crayfish, whole, live

Add chile oil to a large pot over medium heat. Open some windows. When the oil begins to shimmer, add garlic, ginger, and scallions and sauté for 4–5 minutes, until the scallion whites are translucent. Add broad bean paste (if using) and sauté for an additional 2 minutes. Add rice wine, raise the heat to medium-high, and continue to cook until the wine has almost evaporated, about 3 minutes.

To the pot, add star anise, peppercorns, salt, sugar, and water or stock. Bring to a boil, reduce heat to medium, and maintain a high simmer for 20 minutes.

Carefully wash the crayfish under cold running water and use an old toothbrush to ensure there's no dirt on the shells. Add live crayfish to the pot and continue to simmer for 5–8 minutes, until all of the crayfish are bright red and fully cooked. Turn off the heat, cover, and allow the crayfish to soak up flavor for 30 minutes.

Carefully remove just the crayfish from the pot and serve hot, with plastic gloves like they do in China. Get crackin'!

Mala Zhangfei Niurou
小龙虾
(Spicy Cured Beef Salad)

With 4,000 years of written history, you can forgive the Chinese people if they don't remember every emperor, general, poet, and artist who has come and gone. Do you even remember who was elected President in 1836? Okay, smarty, good guess. How about Vice President? So, what's a society to do? How do you remember and honor the old greats, if there are too many to possibly remember? The Chinese have hit upon the perfect solution. Naming food after them.

What's the best way to lay tribute at the feet of the great Zhang Fei, the General who led thousands of horsemen for future Han emperor, Lui Bei, in the early 200s? The man who valiantly covered his troops' retreat by turning his horse around, facing the enemy across a short bridge, face red with anger, screaming, "I'm Zhang Fei, but you may know me by my other name, Yide! You wanna fight? Fight me!" How to remember him when there are hundreds of other notable generals from that era? It's simple; mimic his angry red face and spicy character in a delicious beef salad. He'll be remembered forever.

Think of it, if we called that famous fried chicken with 11 herbs and spices "Dick Johnson Chicken," you just might have a better shot of remembering that Dick Johnson was our 9th Vice President. Genius!

Total Time: 3 hours, 15 minutes | Serves: 8–10

1 recipe uncooked La Niurou (Cured Beef) on page 99
1 cup water
1 cup red chile oil with sediment *or* Lajiao You (Chile Oil) on page 132
⅓ cup Chinese black vinegar
1 Tbsp Sichuan peppercorn, ground

½ tsp salt
8 stalks Chinese celery, *or* 4 stalks Western celery, with leaves, julienned
3 jalapeño, serrano, or Thai bird chiles, stemmed, thinly sliced
½ cup white sesame seeds

Preheat the oven to 325°F.

Place the cured beef on a roasting rack in a roasting pan. Pour enough water in the bottom of the roasting pan until it is at least ½-inch deep. Carefully transfer the pan, rack, and beef into the oven and roast for 2 hours.

In a large mixing bowl, whisk together oil, vinegar, Sichuan pepper, and salt. Stir in the celery, chiles, and sesame seeds.

Remove the beef from the oven, set aside on a rimmed plate, and allow it to rest for 15 minutes. Transfer to a cutting board and cut the beef, across the grain, into ¼-inch thick slices. Add beef slices to the mixing bowl with the oil mixture. Stir thoroughly.

Cover and transfer the bowl to the refrigerator for at least 45 minutes. Remove the salad from the refrigerator, stir to redistribute the dressing, and serve as a cold appetizer.

La Qiaomai Mian
辣荞麦面
(Spicy Buckwheat Noodles)

Save for one famous landmark, and what other travelers will tell you, Datong is not a destination city. It is surrounded by coal mines and the power plants that burn it. Twenty years ago, when we tried to get to the big tourist attraction, the historic and (we're told) beautiful Yungang Grottoes, filled with thousands of stone Buddhas carved into cliff sides and caves, we failed, epically. When the bus that we were assured went all the way to the grottoes came to what seemed like a screeching halt at the end of a paved road, we began to scratch our heads.

What does a Buddha-loving duo do now? Upon exiting the bus we were met by what felt like a hundred, but was more likely a dozen, motorcyclists who were willing to take us the rest of the way to Yungang along a gravel road for a hefty fee. After negotiating a bit, it was clear that they *all* wanted in on our action, and thus a fight broke out. We were able to slink away. Our collective skin crawls whenever someone barely mentions caves. For the record, Chinese tourism has come a long way in the last twenty years. It's all fine, now . . .

All this being said, even after the place itself leaves a bad taste in our mouths, food swooped in to save the day. We quickly retreated from our near catastrophe at the end of the bus ride and perhaps in a comedic twist, sought *another* bus to get us out of town on the double. The next departure for Beijing was leaving in two hours and with no interest whatsoever in being the guys about town, lest more disaster strike, we opted to grab some street grub and eat on the bus. Right there in front of the station was a dude hawking spicy buckwheat noodles!

Just our luck! It turns out that, despite Greg's Eastern European grandparents' love of kasha varnishkes, buckwheat does not come from Poland or Romania. It was, in fact, first cultivated in central China, right around Datong, and brought to Europe about a thousand years ago via the Silk Road. How about that for a poetic end to a terrible day? A local specialty, at that! Who needs grottoes, anyway?

NOODLES:
1 lb thin buckwheat or Japanese soba
   noodles
1 gallon water
2 Tbsp salt

SAUCE:
1 cup red chile oil or Lajiao You (Chile
   Oil) with sediment on page 132
⅓ cup Chinese black vinegar
⅓ cup soy sauce
1 Tbsp sesame paste
1 Tbsp toasted sesame oil
½ tsp granulated sugar

GARNISH:
¾ cup peanuts, roughly chopped
½ cup white sesame seeds
5 scallions, thinly sliced

Cook the noodles with water and salt according to package directions. Drain, rinse the noodles, and set aside. In a mixing bowl, whisk together all sauce ingredients.

Evenly distribute sauce, then noodles into bowls. Then top with the garnishes. Suggest that guests mix it all together before enjoying.

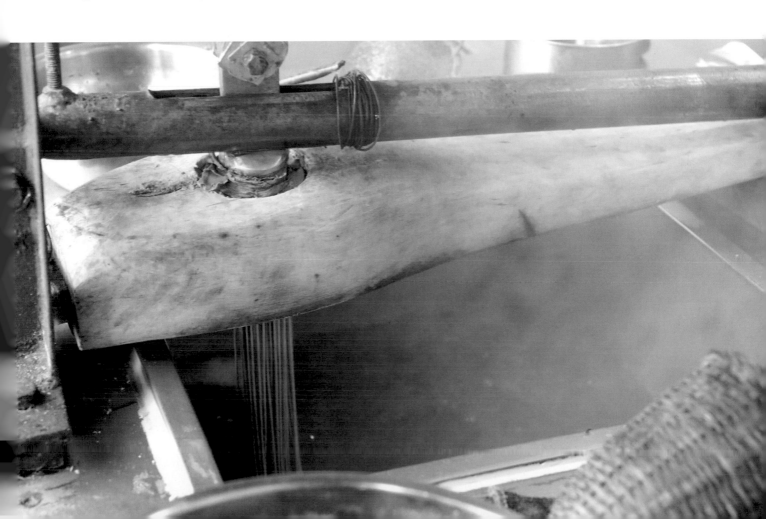

CHAPTER 5: YOU'LL LOVE THIS, WE PROMISE

WE WERE IN A RESTAURANT in Shenyang, in northeastern Liaoning Province, in 1999. It was a friend's birthday dinner and it was, by all measures, a lavish affair. When we say lavish, we're not talking about red carpets, limousines, or champagne. For us, lavish almost always means dozens of exquisite dishes on a single table. For ten people, that's lavish. It was one of our first single meals in China that offered a real panoply of flavors, textures, aromas, mouthfeel, and unique specimens. Chinese culinaria never disappoints when challenged to present true diversity in one sitting. That being said, when the chicken feet came out, we finally reached our limit. The appeal of chicken feet is, of course, the crunch of cartilage. Not what we call appetizing.

A university administrator we became friendly with named Fu Qiang (English name "Steven"), put our sudden displeasure this way: "Americans always expect that flavor is the only reason that you eat something. You also think that if something is unappealing to look at or smell, it will be bad to eat. Chill out." That last bit was a new phrase to Steven, and he employed it frequently. In this case, he made the right suggestion. We do stop at the mere idea, sight, or odor of something and decide against it. Think of the first time you were presented with a super-ripe Camembert or a tiny fork with which to pull escargot from its shell. "Keep that away from me," was your first response, but after a little coaxing, nose-pinching, and perhaps a double-dog-dare, admit it, you totally loved it.

The Chinese excel at hitting every mark when offering up things to eat. They consider not only taste, but the way something feels on the lips, cheeks, teeth, the way a dish makes you think, the way something wafts through the air, reaching the nose, the way something catches the eye, and, of course, the way something finally meets the palate. To eat in China is to experience totality. Within the street food universe, this philosophy still applies. If you watch enough travel TV, you may believe that eating street food in Asia is full of intellectual and/or gastronomical challenge, but the truth is that there are very few examples that may have you initially think, "Um, I'll pass."

This chapter is dedicated to that very challenge and a promise. You'll love this stuff. Our names are staked upon it. From the rather viscous, dare-we-say offensive texture of *hula tang*, the olfactory-alarming *chou doufu*, and the downright creepy looking *chadan*, you will come to adore what you never believed you would adore in a million years. Even donkey! Okay, perhaps we're over-promising there. These dishes also offer you the opportunity to surprise dinner party guests and give them stories to walk away with. Who needs more than that? Just be appreciative that we don't go to the level of chicken feet. We're proud to say, there is no cartilage crunching here.

Miancha
面茶
(Sesame Millet Porridge)

This dish could easily fit into the "What's in a Name" chapter as well as here. *Miancha*, or "flour tea," contains no tea and would seem terribly unappealing if it did. It's essentially *gruel*, an entire genre of food that sounds less than appetizing from the outset. So, untold centuries ago, in the heart of Beijing's labyrinth of alleyways, Chinese Goldilocks had to decide whether her mush was too thick, too soupy, or *just goopy enough*, and everyone else just went with it. In fact, Goldilocks went a step further and said to herself, "You know what this gruel needs? Another layer, perhaps something gooey," and proceeded to drop some sesame paste on top. Fabulous addition, and the combined viscosity was indeed reminiscent of hot glue. Sure, we're laying it on pretty thick, but once you get the past the concept, the name, and the appearance, it's filling, nutritious, and truly delicious. Surprise!

One winter's day four years ago, we were in Beijing to eat. Go figure. It being morning, we wandered into the old narrow hutongs for something traditional, warming, and cheap. The school day was just about to begin, and throngs of young children, mostly with a grandparent, were grabbing a quick bite before the drop-off. We can't resist a long queue-up for street food, as it typically results in us eating something delicious. On this particular day, we had no idea what was about to be slopped into our bowls. Once up at the front, we pay our cash, we take our mush, and naturally begin to play with it. Just then, an unexpected, stern reprimand came from an otherwise kindly looking older woman seated next to us. "Stop looking at it. Stop swirling it around with that spoon. Just eat it, already," she insisted! We of course complied. We'd rather face gloopy than disappoint grandma. That one difficult step led to an odd sense of pleasure. Trust us.

2 cups millet, wheat, or rice flour
⅔ cup white sesame seeds, plus more
    for garnish
2½ tsp salt, divided
7–9 cups water

1 Tbsp ground ginger powder
1 cup fine cornmeal
1 cup light or dark sesame paste
2 Tbsp toasted sesame oil

Add flour to a dry skillet over medium heat. Constantly whisk for up to 10 minutes. Your goal is to toast the flour and your aim is a light brown color. Remove toasted flour from the skillet and set aside.

Add sesame seeds and ½ teaspoon of salt to a separate skillet over medium-low heat. Toast the sesame seeds, constantly stirring for 5 minutes, or until the seeds are toasted.

In a large pot over medium heat, thoroughly whisk together 7 cups water, ginger powder, cornmeal, 2 teaspoons of salt, and toasted flour. Continually stir the contents in one direction as it heats up to a low simmer. You should see small bubbles come to the surface within 7–10 minutes. Continue to stir and cook as the mixture thickens. The ideal texture will be that of a thick paste, after about 25–30 minutes. If the mixture becomes too thick before this time, add water ½ cup at a time.

In a small bowl, whisk together sesame paste, sesame oil, and the remaining ½ teaspoon of salt. Evenly distribute porridge into bowls, top with some sesame sauce and toasted sesame seeds. Enjoy a taste of old Beijing.

Hula Tang
胡辣汤
(Black Pepper Beef Soup)

Just before this recipe, we waxed sarcastic about the texture of (delicious) miancha being goopy, gluey, and just plain gooey. Sometimes, there are no appetizing words to describe a dish that is so stark in its traits. But, since miancha already took goopy, gluey, and gooey, we're going to have to go with *slippery, sticky,* and *slimy* to describe hula tang. Sounds delectable, no? Well, wait until you pull a spoonful from the bowl and watch the trail stretch from the surface and finally break somewhere close to your mouth. Tasty! Texturally, there is no way around the initial challenge of hula tang. But, once you've enjoyed a hot, thick serving of this viciously viscous stew, you'll wonder why you've never thought of adding a ton of potato starch to all of your soups. *Stick to your ribs* never meant so much.

The name *hula tang* literally means "black peppercorn spicy soup." Though black peppercorns are used in many Chinese dishes, we find it interesting when one very specific recipe gets to keep the name of an ingredient. During the 400s, somewhere between the Eastern and Western Jin Dynasties, the royal court became enamored of this little black ball of bitterness when it first arrived over the southern borders. *Hujiao,* or "barbarian pepper," was used to add exotic flair, particularly to long-cooked brews, as a deep complexity develops from the pepper over time. One enigmatic stew escaped the royal kitchens of Chang'an (modern day Xi'an) and settled into street food fame. *Dear China, you've hit the nail on the head with this storied, filling, tasty, very black peppery stew. But, why the texture? Why?*

A few months back, we were in Xi'an to see the Terracotta Warriors. Just kidding, we were there to eat. We effortlessly decided to begin our first day of consuming a city we love by visiting the strong hands of Mrs. Liu, our morning soup friend. We were curious about her long-term memory of two foreign friends, and of course, her soup was easily the taste of Xi'an to us. From about twenty yards, through hundreds of other faces on a thoroughly crowded street, she yelled out, "Hey, my foreign boys! I have soup for you!" Maybe we stick out, just a little? We had fawned over her Beef Bone Soup (page 101) a few years earlier, but we had hula tang on the brain. We had to insist and re-insist that she go easy on us that morning. "Fine," she said, "you'll be back for lunch, then?" Of course, Mrs. Liu. Of course. Since she went easy on us that morning, we are paying it forward by going easy on you below: our version is much less of a textural challenge.

Total Time: 2 hours, 45 minutes | Serves: 8–10

BROTH:
1½ gallons water, divided
2 lb beef soup bones, butcher-cut into
   2-inch segments
2 inches ginger, peeled, halved
   lengthwise
1 bunch scallions, halved
1 Tbsp Sichuan peppercorns, whole
2 Tbsp black peppercorns, whole

MEATBALLS:
2 scallions, minced
1 inch ginger, peeled, minced
½ cup water
1 lb ground beef
1 tsp salt
1 tsp ground black pepper
1 tsp white pepper
1 Tbsp potato starch or tapioca starch,
   plus more for dusting

VEGETABLES:
1 Tbsp salt
1 lb potatoes, peeled, 1-inch chunks
1 lb carrots, peeled, 1-inch chunks
½ head green cabbage, diced

STARCH:
½ cup potato starch or tapioca starch
⅔ cup water

GARNISH:
Red chile oil with sediment *or* Lajiao
   You (Chile Oil) on page 132

In a large stock pot, bring ½ gallon of water to a boil and add soup bones. Boil the bones for 3 minutes, then remove, set aside, and discard the water. Rinse out the pot. In the pot, combine boiled bones, ginger, scallions, peppercorns, and the remaining 1 gallon of water. Bring to a high simmer over medium-low heat. Simmer, covered, for 2 hours. Using a slotted spoon or sieve, remove and discard the bones, ginger, and scallions. Maintain a high simmer.

While the broth is simmering, in a small mixing bowl, stir together scallions, ginger, and water. Set aside for at least 30 minutes. In a separate mixing bowl, thoroughly combine beef, salt, black pepper, white pepper, and cornstarch. Add just the scallion-ginger steeped water to the meat mixture and discard the scallions and ginger. Again, mix thoroughly. Dust the counter or work surface with cornstarch. Form 1-inch meatballs by hand, and roll them in the cornstarch.

To the pot of simmering broth, add salt, potatoes, and carrots, and simmer for 12 minutes. Add cabbage and meatballs and simmer for an additional 8 minutes. In a small mixing bowl, whisk together starch and water. Stir the soup and drizzle in the starch mixture, increase the heat to medium-high, and bring to a boil while stirring. Turn off the heat.

Ladle simmering soup evenly into bowls before topping with some red chile oil. Serve immediately.

Rejiao Tuan
热搅团
(Cornmeal Porridge in Sour Soup)

Last summer, we were a few blocks outside of the city walls of Old Town Xi'an. Yes, they let you do that as a tourist, and we highly recommend it. Things are just different and refreshing after a couple of days of lamb skewers and bread soup. Don't get us wrong, we absolutely *love* the Muslim Quarter, but sometimes it's nice to get away from the neon and lean toward lesser street lights. It's hard to put in words, but it's sort of like going back to China for a while. As it was morning, we were naturally after steamed buns, perhaps some spring rolls, maybe a bowl of noodles. As many of our stories go, we stuffed ourselves silly, then we saw tortilla man.

We discovered his name was Mr. Mao, no relation. He was happily standing outside of his tiny shop, peeling and munching on the crispy remnants of whatever was cooking in a big pot on the sidewalk just minutes earlier. "What are you eating?" we ask. He laughs and quickly responds, "It's kind of like a tortilla chip from America! We just cooked a batch of corn porridge for the sour soup." We were immediately intrigued. What's a sour soup? Mind you, he didn't say *sweet* and sour soup, and he didn't say *hot* and sour soup, and he would have if it were the case. He said *sour* soup.

We politely turned and walked to chat with his wife, Ms. Qu, who was doing the actual cooking. We had to get to the bottom of this. "Mr. Mao says you're making a sour soup, can we have a taste?" She didn't hesitate before warning us, "This is not for everyone; it's pretty strong. But, it's supposed to be eaten with this pretty boring cornmeal mush." Out of morbid curiosity, of course we took a sip. Whoa! Then, we asked for the full treatment of cornmeal mush, essentially a really smooth and soft polenta, topped with this astoundingly strong, lip-puckering broth. Complex and pleasing. Now, that's the stuff.

Total Time: 55 minutes | Serves: 8–10

SOUP:
2 Tbsp vegetable or canola oil
3 cloves garlic, peeled, minced
8 ribs celery with leaves, finely diced
4 scallions, thinly sliced
2 large tomatoes, diced
2 lb baby spinach

2 tsp salt
1 Tbsp five-spice powder
10 cups water
¼ cup rice vinegar

continued on page 156

PORRIDGE:
2 cups fine cornmeal
2 tsp salt

6–8 cups water
Lajiao You (Chile Oil) with sediment on
page 132 for garnish

In a pot over medium heat, add oil. When the oil begins to shimmer, add garlic, celery, and scallions. Sauté for 3–4 minutes, or until the whites of the scallions are translucent. Add tomatoes and spinach, and continue to sauté for 4–5 minutes, or until the tomatoes have begun to break down. Add salt, five-spice powder, water, and vinegar, and bring the mixture to a boil. Reduce the heat to low and maintain a simmer for 30 minutes, while you cook the porridge.

In a large pot over medium heat, thoroughly whisk together cornmeal, salt, and 6 cups of water. Continually stir the contents in one direction as it heats up to a low simmer. You should see small bubbles come to the surface within 7–10 minutes. Continue to stir and cook as the mixture thickens. The ideal texture will be that of a thick paste, after about 25–30 minutes. If the mixture becomes too thick before this time, add water ½ cup at a time.

Distribute porridge into bowls, top with the soup, and garnish with lajiao. Enjoy!

Chou Doufu
臭豆腐
(Stinky Tofu)

Throughout China, *chou doufu*, or "stinky tofu," is popular at night markets. It's typically grilled or fried and served with a sweet or savory sauce, perhaps some herbs. Not unlike cheese that is aged, chou doufu is fermented and treated differently, depending on where you travel. In the Northeast, you may find a saltier variety, in the Southwest, a spicier concoction, and in central China, it may have a sweeter punch. But, wherever you may roam, there is one distinction that every permutation can promise, as the name assures: the aroma is alarming! It is no joke. Like those vapor trails emanating from Pigpen in Charlie Brown, you can just about see them. One does not have to seek out chou doufu vendors, their mere presence will find you, and hopefully draw you in. Since, also like aged cheeses, the odor can overwhelm where the taste can be divine.

Still, chou doufu is not for everyone. It can be divisive, like cilantro or yellow mustard. One either loves it or hates it, with very few on the fence opinions. Even in China, it can cause upheavals in relationships. Your two otherwise *brothers from different mothers* authors even disagree on it. Greg refuses to try it. Howie adores it. It can cause great consternation on any of our journeys, and will often cause geographic separation on a nighttime snack walk. Chou doufu is one of those topics that always lights a fire under either a big fan or a vehement hater. "Let me know when you're done eating old smelly socks," Greg may say. Howie may respond, "Fine, go over there and enjoy that plain bowl of rice." Please enjoy the embodiment of one of our great lifelong feuds below.

2 lb firm tofu, sliced into roughly
   1-inch cubes
1 cup water, boiling
2 Tbsp salt

1 Tbsp granulated sugar
1 cup Chinese rice wine or dry sherry
1 tsp dried red chile flakes
1 tsp Sichuan peppercorns, ground

Line a plate with paper towel and place tofu in a single layer across the bottom. Top with another layer of paper towel, then seal the plate with plastic wrap. Place the baking dish in a bright room or next to a window and allow the tofu to ferment for 3–4 days. The tofu will become off-white to yellow in color.

In a mixing bowl, whisk together water, salt, and sugar. Be sure that the salt and sugar dissolve. Then, whisk in rice wine, chile flakes, and peppercorns. Set aside and allow the mixture to cool completely.

Transfer the fermented tofu to a container that will fit the pieces snugly across the bottom. Pour the liquid mixture over the tofu, cover, and place in the refrigerator for at least two weeks. Every once in awhile, give the container a gentle shake to redistribute the liquid and seasoning.

Drain the chou doufu, dry it, and use as a pungent seasoning. If the pieces are dry enough, you can also skewer and grill them, or even deep fry them. This is not a dish to be eaten by itself, but rather as a highly-seasoned addition to an otherwise balanced meal.

Lu Yuwan Tang
绿鱼丸汤
(Green Fish Ball Soup)

When was the last time you heard a meatball referred to as springy enough? Bouncy enough? Chewy enough? In China, *yuwan*, or "fish balls," are judged by these three measures. Once again, in China, texture is of the utmost importance. Sure, according to Chinese gastronomica, even if the fish is delicious and the broth is wonderful, if the yuwan doesn't have just the right toothiness, you may as well order the chicken. We've had plenty of less-than-perky yuwan in our China wanderings. We find that the balls that lack in springiness are often aided by distractingly entertaining features, like color. We've enjoyed orange fish balls infused with carrot and purple fish balls tinted with sweet potato, but oddly, perhaps the most appetizing were green, which used pureed peas in the mix. We've gotten close to perfect texture *and* fun color with this recipe.

We've heard tall tales of yuwan that were constructed of *only fish*, no other ingredients. Can this be true? We know a chef in southwestern Yunnan Province, Yang Jiaquan. He never gives up his secrets, but with his fish balls, apparently there is not even a hint of magic dust. According to him, "It's a matter of perfect technique, a series of slapping the fish flesh against the side of a metal bowl in just the right spot at just the right velocity. This way, the fish meat deconstructs, then reconstructs to distribute equal tension across one little ball of meat." We call malarkey! We love Chef Yang, but we're entirely convinced that some non-aquatic starchy goodness was at work. We submit to you, our magic dust . . . and our food processor.

Total Time: 35 minutes | Serves: 4–6

SOUP:
8 cups fish broth or stock
3 Roma tomatoes, thin wedges
3 cloves garlic, smashed
1 Tbsp soy sauce
1 tsp toasted sesame oil
½ tsp salt
½ tsp white pepper

FISH BALLS:
2 Tbsp cornstarch
1 Tbsp water, plus 4 cups for simmering
2 lb mackerel or other flaky white fish
    fillets, skinless, boneless, diced
1 tsp salt
½ tsp ground white pepper
¼ cup peas, cooked or canned

GARNISH
¼ head iceberg lettuce, shredded
3 scallions, thinly sliced
4 Tbsp red chile paste

Add all soup ingredients to a pot over medium-high heat and bring to a boil. Reduce the heat to low and maintain a simmer while you make the fish balls.

In a small bowl, mix cornstarch and 1 tablespoon of water. To a food processor, add fish, salt, pepper, peas and the cornstarch slurry. Pureé until a smooth paste forms.

In a separate pot on the stove, bring 4 cups of water to a simmer over medium heat, and reduce heat to low. With wet hands, break off a ping-pong-sized ball of fish paste and form a smooth ball. Set aside and continue to make balls. Place the balls into the simmering water and cook for 10 minutes. Remove the fish balls from the water and rinse under warm water. Evenly distribute shredded lettuce into bowls, followed by fish balls then soup, topped with scallions and chile paste. Enjoy the briny warmth.

"Lurou" Huoshao
驴肉火烧
("Donkey" Sandwiches)

We've worn many hats during our relationship with China: English teachers, tour guides, ambassadors for American cuisine, television stars, foreign faces for store openings, and of course, art exporters. About fourteen years ago, we decided that beautiful Chinese scrolls needed to be popularized in the US. So, we started a partnership with an art school in the city of Shenyang and began to import gorgeous paintings. To kick off the business deal naturally, we threw a huge banquet with our archaeologist-turned-art-agent friend, Qu Feng. About fourteen dishes in, out came a favorite dish that we'd always thought to be the best beef we'd ever tasted. Lo and behold, Qu Feng felt it his job to correct us. This was donkey. It turned out, with a northeastern accent, the words for steer and donkey meat were very, *very* close. Alas, *donkey* was the best beef we'd ever tasted.

As is his professional duty with the Indiana Jones hat on, Qu Feng regaled us with a history lesson as we enjoyed the stir-fried *lurou* at the banquet. Donkey-as-cuisine actually has quite a storied past in China. Legend has it that during horrifyingly drawn-out military campaigns of the Ming Dynasty, when soldiers ran out of food, they began butchering their horses for survival. Locals in the war-torn regions followed suit, and *horse d'oeuvres* were all the rage. Ha. Long story short, horses retained military importance, so donkey was used as a substitute. Later, when the railways were built, donkeys lost whatever remaining portage value they had and went lumbering back, in larger numbers, to the dinner table.

Years after our banquet with Qu Feng, some art dealers, and Eeyore, we ran into cured donkey sandwiches at a stall in Hebei Province. Perhaps it was the power of suggestion and/or linguistic confusions of our past, but we agreed that this cured donkey could pass for corned beef any day! Much to our surprise, these sandwiches, lovingly constructed of succulent donkey meat, crispy fresh green peppers, and a fragrant touch of cilantro on a flaky bun, provided a solid alternative to going out for a Reuben. Here, we've gone easy on our dear readers and recreated the sandwiches with beef. It's easier to get. But, if you are up to the challenge and locate a purveyor of donkey meat, we will send you a beautiful scroll painting. We have a lot left.

FILLING:

1 recipe La Niurou (Cured Beef) on page 99
1 large green bell pepper or anaheim chile, diced
1 large red bell pepper, diced
½ bunch cilantro, roughly chopped

ROLLS:

3 ½ cups all-purpose flour, plus more for dusting
1 Tbsp rapid rise yeast
2 tsp salt
1 tsp granulated sugar
1 cup warm water
4 tsp vegetable oil, divided

Preheat the oven to 325°F.

Place the cured beef on a roasting rack in a roasting pan. Pour enough water in the bottom of the roasting pan until it is at least ½-inch deep. Carefully transfer the pan, rack, and beef into the oven and roast for 2 hours.

While the meat is roasting, prepare the dough. In a large mixing bowl or the bowl of stand mixer, whisk together flour, yeast, salt, and sugar. Using clean hands or the dough hook of the stand mixer, incorporate water and 1 teaspoon oil until a smooth dough forms.

Dust the countertop or work surface with additional flour and transfer the dough onto the flour. Dust the top of the dough, knead, and form the dough into a ball. Transfer the dough to a large, clean, lightly oiled bowl, and cover with plastic wrap. Allow the dough to double in size, about one hour to 90 minutes.

Uncover the dough, dust the work surface with flour, transfer the dough atop the flour, and evenly hand-roll it onto a 2-inch-thick log. Cut the dough into 2-inch pieces. Form each dough piece into a ball. Roll one ball into a ¼-inch thick oval. Starting from a narrow end, roll up the dough as you would a poster. With the loose end down, roll into a flat ¾-inch thick rectangle. Set aside on a sheet pan and repeat with the remainder of the dough balls.

Dust the top of the dough segments with flour, cover with plastic wrap or a clean towel, and allow them to rest for 45 minutes.

When the beef is done roasting, remove from the oven and transfer to a rimmed plate and allow it to rest until the rolls are baked. Reserve the pan drippings. Increase the oven to 400°F.

Heat 1 teaspoon of oil in a skillet or griddle over medium-low heat for 4 minutes. Place some of the dough segments into the skillet, do not overcrowd the skillet, work in batches. Cook the dough on one side for 2–3 minutes, or until the bottom is beginning to brown. Flip the dough over and continue cooking for 2 minutes. Remove the partially cooked dough segments from the skillet and place on a sheet pan. Finish browning the remaining dough.

Transfer the sheet pan(s) to the oven and bake the dough until the buns are cooked through, about another 15-20 minutes. They should be puffed up and golden brown. Once the rolls are done, set aside while you carve the meat.

Open the rolls with a knife and fill with some roasted meat, peppers, and cilantro. Optionally, dress the inside of the roll with some of the pan drippings.

Chadan
茶蛋
(Tea-Poached Eggs)

We've waxed poetic about diverse Chinese uses of eggs, far beyond the basic Western practices of poaching, frying, boiling, and scrambling. They go multiple steps further, yielding hundreds of permutations of eggy goodness. Instead of just scrambling, they scramble, then chop and mix into dumpling stuffing. Instead of just poaching, they drizzle them into simmering savory soups. Instead of just frying, they quickly fry, then wrap up something delicious in a warm egg-blanket. To top it all off, instead of just boiling, they boil, then steep in deeply flavored broth, resulting in *chadan*, or "tea eggs," a unique taste, a unique texture, and a unique and shocking look.

"Why does my hard-boiled egg remind me of an eyeball?" you may ask. It's all in the technique. They could simply have boiled the egg, peeled it, and soaked it in tea, turning a glossy white facade into tan. But, Chinese culinaria being what it is, they needed to be artful. Crack the shell all over, but leave it on the egg while it takes a scrumptious bath. The fissures in the shell allow color to strategically seep into a vein-like pattern. Peel it, et voila, an eyeball! *This* eyeball is frequently the star of a breakfast show, alongside mushroom rice porridge on page 65 and fried dough sticks on page 67.

If you didn't know what they were, you wouldn't find them terribly appealing on the street. "Look, there's a pile of cracked eggs sitting in a weird, dark pool of . . . something?" Just remember that these may be sitting next to another favorite among the Chinese, the hyperbolically named "thousand-year-old egg," which is, of course, *not* a thousand years old. We feel that it may as well be. It's a stinky and gelatinous egg-gone-to-the-dark-side. Opt for the cracked mystery swimmers. Or, just make them at home for all to find a little weird but delectable.

12 eggs, whole
6 cups water
2 Tbsp black tea leaves, or 4 tea bags
2 cinnamon sticks
5 star anise

3 Tbsp soy sauce
2 Tbsp mushroom or dark soy sauce
1 Tbsp black or white peppercorns
1 Tbsp orange zest or 2 dried tangerine
   peels

Add all ingredients to a pot over medium heat. Bring it to a boil, then turn off the heat. Allow the eggs to steep for 25–35 minutes, or until the poaching liquid cools completely. Using a slotted spoon, carefully remove the eggs from the pot and gently tap them with the back of a spoon to crack the shells over the whole egg. Leave the cracked shells *ON* the eggs.

Transfer the eggs and the poaching liquid to a large, sealed container. Place the container in the refrigerator overnight. The next day, peel and enjoy the marbly, flavor-infused eggs.

Zhurou Zongzi / Dousha Zongzi
煮肉粽子 / 豆沙粽子
(Boiled Sticky Rice and Pork Dumplings)
or (Boiled Sticky Rice and Red Bean Dumplings)

When traveling around China, we tend to surround ourselves with friends of like mind, fellow storytellers. Where this tendency offers us hours upon hours of entertainment and more than our fill of Chinese history and folklore, it can be a bit of a time-suck when it comes to devouring a quick bite. Whenever we see a *zongzi* vendor along the street, our lovely, wordy friends love to retell the millennia-old story of the zongzi, each with her or his own elaborations. It used to be that zongzi were only sold around the time of the Dragon Boat Festival in mid-spring. So, the tale could be spun in all of its glory, maybe once a year. But recently, zongzi have gained in popularity at any given festival, or, like, a Wednesday afternoon. Fittingly, we were in need of a much shorter recounting of the story of Qu Yuan, shamed politico of the Warring States Period.

We were in the city of Harbin, deep in the Northeast of China in January. Essentially, this is Siberia. You can imagine the temperatures. We befriended a history professor named Qi Guangying. As she was touring us around her subzero hometown, we happened upon a zongzi stall, hardly visible through the billows of steam emanating from a huge pot of the leaf-wrapped goodies. As we quickly opted for the sweet version with red bean paste, a rather shivery Guangying succinctly noted, "More than 2000 years ago, this guy Qu Yuan was embarrassed at his government job and threw himself into the raging river. The townspeople loved this guy, and didn't want the fish to eat his body. So, they tricked the fish with sweet rice and meat wrapped up in leaves. This is where the Dragon Boat Festival comes from." Though vague with a lot of awesome detail missing, we appreciated her brevity on this cold day. Do look it up—pretty grim stuff.

Total Time: Overnight, plus 3 hours, 30 minutes | Serves: 10–12

2 cups glutinous rice
4 cups water, plus 1½ gallon water
1 Tbsp soy sauce

PORK FILLING:
1 lb pork shoulder or Boston butt,
    boneless, diced small
1 inch ginger, peeled, minced
2 scallions, minced
1 Tbsp soy sauce
1 tsp toasted sesame oil
1 tsp Chinese rice wine or dry sherry
½ tsp sugar
½ tsp salt
½ tsp ground white pepper

RED BEAN FILLING:
8 oz Chinese sweet red bean paste

24 packaged bamboo leaves

In a mixing bowl, combine rice and 4 cups of water. If filling the zongzi with pork, in a separate mixing bowl, combine all of the pork filling ingredients. Cover both and refrigerate overnight. Remove the rice and pork from the refrigerator. Pour off the water from the rice, and rinse until the water runs clear. In a mixing bowl, mix the drained rice with 1 tablespoon of soy sauce.

In a pot over high heat, bring 1½ gallon of water to a boil. Reduce the heat to medium-low. Put bamboo leaves into the simmering water for 30 minutes to soften them. Remove them from the water, set aside to cool, and reduce the heat to low, maintaining a simmer.

Place two bamboo leaves in the palm of your hand, overlapping, widthwise. Grasp the narrow tops of the leaves and roll inward, toward the bottom tips, to form a closed cone. Secure the cone within your hand. Place enough rice in the leaf to come halfway up the cone. Add 1 tablespoon of filling atop the rice, then atop the filling, add more rice to come within ½ inch of the top of the cone. Fold the hanging flaps of extra leaf over the top of the rice, and tie with butcher's twine. Repeat with the remaining leaves, rice, and filling.

Add the tied, filled bamboo leaves to the simmering water and cook for 2½ hours. You may wish to put a heavy plate on top of the zongzi as they cook, to keep them submerged. Using a slotted spoon or sieve, remove the zongzi from the water. Suggest that your guests have the fun of untying before eating the zongzi directly from the leaves!

16元
一只

CHAPTER 6: SIMPLE POETRY

ONE OF THE THINGS THAT American Chinese food gets wrong is the idea of the stir-fry. Chop up some meat, some celery, some carrots, a bit of bell pepper. Slice some cabbage. Wok it all up with a bit of soy sauce and cornstarch, top it with some green onions and that's how they do it in China, right? Well, not usually. By and large, across the dozens of Chinese cuisine genres, when you order eggplant you get a plate of beautiful eggplant. You order cabbage, you get the most stunning cabbage you've ever seen. You order the ribs, what comes out of the kitchen are incredible, undistracted baby backs. No pile of bean sprouts, no slivers of water chestnuts or mushrooms to cost-efficiently fill up the dish. Just the subject at hand, perhaps with a few supporting players, cooked in a manner that brings out its best texture and flavor, placed in a light sauce or broth to bring out its natural strengths.

The best Chinese cuisine is all about highlighting the taste and the feeling of an ingredient. If it's bitter melon, they put it in a light broth so you can really get all that bitterness. If it's pea greens, they quickly fry them with garlic, to bring out the natural bite and tang of the plant. With centuries of practice, the list goes on. In the deep south of Yunnan Province, in all our countryside adventures, we seldom saw a restaurant menu. When you walk into a restaurant, there's a refrigerator. In that refrigerator is the daily haul from the market—meats, greens, herbs, roots, whatever was freshly available and looked good. You order by walking up to the fridge with the server and saying, *I'll take this, lightly fried with a little onion and spice.* Three minutes later, it shows up on your table, prepared in a way that the cook thought was best. And, generally speaking, the cook was right.

Though different in approach, street food is similar in its lean toward simplicity. When you are on the street, you don't have the time or the equipment to craft overly complex dishes. You don't have the luxury of a huge haul from the wet market. You don't have a kitchen brigade to bring you finely shredded garnish or perfectly poached spinach to finish a composed dish. You are forced to keep it simple. This is one huge reason that street food is such a draw for us, such a different, delicious way of approaching food.

Frankly, most of this book could fit in this chapter. What is a Yangrou Chuan (page 111) but a piece of lamb, salted, seasoned, and charred to make it sing? What is Youtiao (page 67) but simple dough crisped to golden perfection in a fryer? What is Niurou Wanzi (page 235) but some ground beef balled up with some aromatics? Here, however, are a few recipes that bubbled up to the top for us in their ability to define pureness of flavor, texture, and presentation. A few nuts, some potatoes, a couple tofu dishes, and a chicken or two. Each bringing out the best of its ingredients. Each a plate of simple poetry.

Kuihuazi Cui
葵花籽脆
(Sunflower Seed Brittle)

Seeds abound throughout Chinese cuisine. The sesame seed is prominent in both savory as well as sweet dishes. They're toasted and sprinkled atop plated beauties, they're bound within meatballs, they are crushed up for a creamy paste and pungent oil with hundreds of culinary uses. Then there's the pumpkin seed. Big and brightly flavored, a little tough to get into, but well worth your dental effort to breach the shell. Heck, in Chinese medicine, they're even touted as antioxidant parasite killers with the knack for lowering blood pressure.

But pity the poor sunflower seed. She begins life as part of an astounding beauty—her flower treasured among home decorators and the subject of Van Gogh's masterwork. As that flower withers, she emerges as a long, lean zebra of color and strength. But crack open that shell, and what you see is only surprising in its blandness. Like a butterfly in reverse, it transforms to emerge as a subtle, taupe-gray speck of a seed. Like a certain wizard from the land of Oz, there's just not a lot going on behind that curtain.

In the West, we typically drown the seeds in salt or in seasoning, losing, to some extent, the beauty of the faintly sweet, intensely earthy taste. One wonders if there's a way to gather the forces of this little seed en masse so that it may gain its rightful place among other, more popular Chinese seeds. This simple brittle, found at street stands throughout China, uses a bit of sugar and salt to accentuate that flavor, and perhaps more importantly, to bind dozens of them together into a small cookie that builds enough volume to make the seed sing.

Total Time: 30 minutes | Serves: 4–6

2 cups raw sunflower seeds, shelled
1 cup granulated sugar
½ cup water
½ tsp salt

Add sunflower seeds to a skillet over medium-low heat. Stir the seeds continuously for 8 minutes. Remove from the heat and transfer to a bowl.

continued on page 176

Line a rimmed sheet pan with parchment paper. Optionally, place ring molds across the parchment.

Add sugar, water, and salt to the skillet over medium-high heat. Stir and cook until the bubbling begins to subside slightly, about 6–8 minutes. Reduce the heat to low, add the seeds, and quickly stir until they are well coated.

Pour the skillet contents into ring molds on the sheet pan and use a spatula to even out the tops. If you're not using ring molds and poured a large single layer, after a few minutes, while warm, use a knife or a biscuit cutter to shape individual bars of brittle. Remove ring molds, or separate the bars and allow them to cool completely before enjoying the crunch.

Gaoshan Xiaotudou
高山小土豆
(Fried Spicy Potatoes)

One of our friends in Sichuan Province is social media darling Jimmy He. He writes this column called *Picky Eater Jim*, so we tend to trust him whenever he suggests a place to pig out. A few years back, Jimmy invited us out to this joint that serves classic Sichuan dishes in their original, artisanal, and arguably better, format: mapo tofu swimming in incendiary stew with unctuous hunks of short rib, kung pao chicken leg meat with deep-fried soy beans, twice-cooked pork belly with islands of melty fat well outweighing strands of flesh. The meal went on for three hours, one dish better than the last. With all this beauty in front of us, we asked Jimmy about his favorite thing to eat. He replied, "Simple fried potatoes on the street." With the decadent spread on our table, he had to be kidding, right?

Jimmy continued, "I don't know why, I just can't resist it every time I see it. It reminds me of my childhood. People had little money. We'd go into the streets to enjoy some little spark of life. So, for us, it's something that's emotionally attached, rather than the just the palate." It began to make sense. We had heard similar notions about how street food brings people back to a simpler time, to an easier age, evoking memories of family, friends, holidays, bonding on a sidewalk over a skewer of this, or a pancake filled with that. There we sat, in a gorgeous private dining room, filling our bellies with complex delights and our minds with historical culinaria, when we could have been spending a more personal afternoon walking the outdoor stalls filling up in a different way. So, without a second thought, we dutifully completed one of the best Chinese feasts of our lives only to roll out the door in search of "fried potatoes on the street." We got to know the real Jimmy that evening.

Total Time: 45 minutes | Serves: 3–4

POTATOES:
1½ lb new potatoes, peeled, or gold potatoes, peeled, 1-inch chunks
1 Tbsp, plus 2–3 cups vegetable or canola oil for frying
1 Tbsp salt

SEASONING MIXTURE:
2 Tbsp red chile oil with sediment *or* Lajiao You (Chile Oil) on page 132
2 tsp Sichuan peppercorns, ground
1 tsp ground cumin
1 Tbsp toasted white sesame seeds
3 scallions, thinly sliced
½ cup cilantro, roughly chopped

Preheat the oven to 350°F. In a large mixing bowl, toss together potatoes, 1 tablespoon of oil, and salt. Place potatoes on a sheet pan, wrap tightly with aluminum foil, and roast for 30 minutes. Remove potatoes from the oven and uncover.

In a large mixing bowl, whisk together chile oil, peppercorns, cumin, sesame seeds, scallions, and cilantro.

In a pot over medium heat, add oil to a depth of at least 1 inch, and heat to 360°F. No thermometer? Use the **Handy Trick** within the Doufunao recipe on page 31.

Carefully add potatoes to the oil and fry until they begin to brown, about 2 minutes. Roll the potatoes around as they cook, to ensure even frying. Do not overcrowd the pan, fry in batches. As the potatoes are done, remove to a paper towel–lined plate.

Add fried potatoes to the seasoning mixture and stir thoroughly to combine. Serve hot.

Kao Huasheng
烤花生
(Pan-Roasted Peanuts)

It's an odd feeling. Walking through a night market in Sichuan, past the exotic hot pot stands, with skewers of vegetables, meat, all manner of offal and of course, duck tongues waiting to be plunged into their fiery cauldrons. Past the pancake griddle, bamboo steamers, lamb-stacked charcoal grill. Past the roasted rabbit heads, staring into your soul. Past the guy selling polyester socks and underwear, along with kitchen utensils. To go from that to the sudden feeling that you are in Yankee stadium is odd, indeed. *Get your peanuts here!*

Pan-roasted peanuts are a staple at night markets across China, but there's something about the aroma of those in Sichuan that bring about the most ball-parky of feelings. The smell is familiar yet unique. The clouds of smoke and steam from the nut roaster has a hint of, what is that, *Buffalo wings*? Must be the spice. When we've been on the road for weeks and are a bit homesick, nothing quite hits the spot like a bag full of Sichuan roasted peanuts and an icy lager. Now, *didn't we see some wings down the block?*

Total Time: 35 minutes | Serves: 8–10

1 lb peanuts, shelled, skinless	2 tsp salt
1 Tbsp canola or vegetable oil	1 tsp sugar
1 Tbsp sesame oil	1 tsp five-spice powder
1 Tbsp red chile oil *or* Lajiao (Chile Oil) with sediment on page 132	1 tsp Sichuan peppercorn, ground (optional)

Warm a skillet over medium-low heat for 2 minutes. Add all ingredients and stir occasionally for 15 minutes.

Transfer the nuts to a bowl and allow them to cool for 20 minutes before devouring the whole crunchy lot.

Zha Doufu
炸豆腐
(Fried Tofu)

We love hanging out with Jimmy He, our social media restaurant reviewer buddy in Chengdu. He always levels our street food perspective by calling it out as an indulgence and an impulse. According to Jimmy, "Every day, once school lets out, all these kids take whatever spare change they have in their pockets and, behind their parents' backs, go find some street snacks." Parents warn kids off these treats. It's not healthy, they'll say. It's not clean, they'll warn. But, as with your humble authors and the local ice cream truck, when it comes to after-school treats, the kids don't listen.

Though it may seem like an exaggeration, he may be right on the money. In China, the numbers are certainly there. He talks of millions of kids flocking to tens of thousands of deep fryers as soon as the bell rings. These "fry guys" sit in their roadside stalls for hours, oil-filled wok heated by coal or gas, with a sprinkling of customers throughout the daytime. But when school's out, hordes of neatly uniformed locusts descend on them. They marshall up their few yuan, sometimes splitting skewers or borrowing from friends, gobbling up sticks of meatballs, donuts, hot dogs, or tofu. *Tofu? Really?* It was a surprise to us, too.

The preparation is simple. Put it on a stick, maybe dust it with a starch, dunk it in the burbling oil, sprinkle with salt and spicy seasoning, or serve it with a bit of a savory, slick dipping sauce. We've seen the details of the sauces vary with region, but not the popularity of the fried morsel itself. If we're being honest, we'll often grab a donut as a chaser. But then, we get clear out of the way of the oncoming student stampede.

Total Time: 25 minutes | Serves: 4–6

TOFU:
- **3 lb firm tofu, cut into 1½-inch blocks**
- **3 tbsp cornstarch**
- **2–3 cups vegetable or canola oil for deep-frying**

DIPPING SAUCE:
- **3 Tbsp sesame paste or tahini**
- **2 Tbsp soy sauce**
- **½ tsp sugar**

Dry the tofu blocks on paper towels. Roll the tofu blocks in cornstarch until they are well coated.

In a pot over medium heat, add oil to a depth of at least 1 inch, and heat to 360°F. No thermometer? Use the **Handy Trick** within the Doufunao recipe on page 31.

Carefully place a few pieces of tofu into the hot oil at a time, being sure not to overcrowd the pot. Turn the tofu until golden brown, about 3–4 minutes. Remove the tofu to a paper towel–lined plate and continue with the remaining tofu.

In a small bowl, combine the dipping sauce ingredients.

Serve hot with toothpicks for piercing, with the dipping sauce.

Tieban Doufu
铁板豆腐
(Iron Skillet Tofu)

It is a mystery to us why tofu is such a recent addition to the Western diet. So recent, in fact, that it wasn't until the early 1970s that the English name, based on the Japanese *tofu*, which was, in turn, based on the Chinese *doufu*, was standardized.

While everything from tea and noodles to buckwheat and fireworks travelled far westward from China, tofu did not. It migrated north, east, and south, and became a staple of the Korean, Japanese, and Southeast Asian diets, so it can't be that the concept wouldn't travel. It can't be that there wasn't enough to go around. Soybeans have been growing cheaply and plentifully for over 3000 years. Soy products have been the peasants' source of protein where they lacked meat for about as long. Perhaps, in trying to capture all the glistening silk and silver of high Chinese culture, Western travelers just overlooked this gem of an ingredient.

But it wasn't completely overlooked. There's a letter, for example, written in 1771 from Ben Franklin. He was writing from Britain, telling his Philadelphia-based correspondent that he had heard about this crazy bean-milk called "tau-fu," which was eaten all over China. There's no sign that old Ben had tasted it, but he did send a few beans along in the letter. Whether it is directly related or not, it's also noted that the soybean itself had grown successfully in the Georgia colony a few years after Ben's letter was received. What a missed opportunity! Perhaps, if old Ben had been a bit more persistent and had planted a few of those beans himself, *Tofurkey* would be the star of any Thanksgiving table.

Total Time: 30 minutes | Serves: 6–8

3 Tbsp soy sauce	1 tsp salt
3 Tbsp hoisin sauce	3 lb firm tofu, drained, dried,
1 Tbsp ground cumin	½-inch slabs
1 Tbsp red chile powder	2 Tbsp vegetable or canola oil
2 tsp Sichuan peppercorn, ground	4 scallions, thinly sliced

In a small bowl, whisk together soy sauce and hoisin. Set aside. In a separate small bowl, whisk together cumin, chile powder, peppercorn, and salt. Evenly sprinkle both sides of the tofu slabs with spice mix and set aside.

continued on page 187

Add 1 Tbsp of oil to a skillet over medium-high heat. When the oil begins to shimmer, add tofu slabs. Work in batches so you don't crowd the pan. Sauté the tofu for 4–6 minutes, until the bottom is beginning to brown. Flip the tofu over, brush the tops with soy-hoisin mixture and allow the bottom to brown for 4 minutes. Flip the tofu and brush the tops with soy-hoisin mixture. Finally, flip the tofu and allow the bottom to brown further, about an additional 3 minutes. Remove the tofu from the skillet and repeat with the remaining tofu and soy-hoisin mixture.

Sprinkle with scallions and serve hot.

Jirou Tang
鸡肉汤
(Chicken Soup)

When we were filming *Sauced in Translation*, a Web series in which we taught some Chinese friends how to cook American dishes, we happened upon Xishan Island, a Hamptons-style getaway for the wealthy of Shanghai and Suzhou. Picture waterfront villas, summertime food festivals, and posh red wines. But, as we were rather busy that summer, we decided that February was a *good idea*. Imagine the northern reaches of Long Island in the middle of winter. Despite the wet, the cold, and the lack of crowds to enjoy our delicious American recipes, we persisted.

At a morning market, we asked a local resident about the best place to eat that wasn't boarded up for the season. She gave us the name "Little Fish," and vague walking directions through a series of alleyways that led to nothing that looked like a restaurant. No signs, we just kept calling out, *Little Fish, Little Fish, does anyone know Little Fish?* Eventually, and likely as a result of our disrupting the neighborhood, someone led us, by hand, to Little Fish and what still didn't look like a restaurant. The central courtyard looked like the playground of a preschool. Turns out it looked that way because it was. But, through the courtyard there was a kitchen, and beside the kitchen was a 3-table dining room. Talk about *hidden* gems.

We aimed to show Little Fish how to make a BLT, and even prepared some semblance of the sandwich for whatever cold-weather, rain-tolerant visitors she could draw in. To construct a BLT was quite an operation given the paucity of either bacon or mayonnaise in China, but we got creative. Perhaps it was our long faces at the end of a rainy, freezing, not entirely successful day, or the hunger brought on by trying to whip up fresh mayonnaise with only chopsticks for a whisk, but we looked like what the cat dragged in. Little Fish showed us what China was made of that day and sat us down for a meal, by which we mean a single soup.

Out came a huge ceramic bowl filled with what became the way we define chicken soup. It was gorgeous in its simplicity: chicken, water, a bit of ginger, garlic, scallions, and salt. Most impressively, it was the most chicken-y chicken we've tasted. Part of the challenge that we have in recreating this soup at home is that we typically get our chickens from the supermarket, not from the courtyard. Did we forget to mention that there were eight chickens pecking around that preschool playground? Make that seven.

Just a note: We realize that this soup is not, in itself, a street food. But, unless you choose to consume the fresh soup as a meal, and we *do* recommend it, the excellent broth and the meat are used throughout this book.

Total Time: 7 hours | Serves: 8–10

4–5 lb chicken, whole or pieces, bone-in

2 inches ginger, peeled, halved lengthwise

1 head garlic, unpeeled, halved lengthwise

1 bunch scallions

2 Tbsp salt

1 gallon cold water

In large stock pot, combine chicken, ginger, garlic, scallions, salt, and water. Bring to a light simmer over low heat. Simmer uncovered for 6 hours. Turn off the heat, cover, and let the chicken and broth cool for 1 hour.

Using cheesecloth or a fine-meshed sieve, strain broth from the solids into a large bowl or another large pot. From the solids, remove garlic, ginger, scallions. Then pick the chicken meat from the bones and cartilage. Set the chicken aside; store in the refrigerator for up to one week. Use the chicken for recipes such as Jirou Shaobing (Chicken Sandwiches) on page 203. Store broth in the refrigerator for up to one week. Use the broth for recipes such as Huntun Tang ("Swallowing Clouds" Soup) on page 25 or Fanqie Chaodan Tangmian (Tomato and Egg Noodle Soup) on page 91.

Kaoji

烤鸡

(Roasted Chicken)

The Chinese are not squeamish about where their meat comes from. Fish are unceremoniously scooped out of tanks and split open for one's approval before cooking. Pork is purchased by asking the man with the cleaver to hack off a couple kilos of belly from the fresh carcass on the table. Whole lambs hang in alleyways as a butcher deftly shaves leg meat to thread onto a barbecue skewer. And chickens, well, chickens usually keep their heads. For what it's worth, most Chinese chickens are still living the life that their "free-range" counterparts in the US could only dream of. They peck at the insects in the ground, flap their wings to deter predators, and build up quite speedy fast-twitch muscles as they repeatedly cross the road. We're still trying to figure out why. Maybe it's the guy with the cleaver?

Where were we? Oh yeah, you'll see those still-headed chickens hanging from hooks in virtually every street market in China. If you're (un)lucky, you may even see them as they are being defeathered especially for you. To the traveler who is accustomed to seeing supermarket meat, neatly encased in Styrofoam and plastic, this can be a disconcerting sight. It can be tough to order a chicken whose eyes seem to be judging you for your moral decisions.

On to cooking. As most Chinese homes do not have an oven or the ability to properly keep the air cool while slow-cooking a chicken, the only option for roasted bird is to buy it from a street vendor. One can only imagine alfresco cooks across China have been expertly spit-roasting chicken since their newly domesticated fowl friends got freaked and hopped over a fire over 9,000 years ago. At least, this recipe feels like it is that refined. Where roasted chicken is technically a street food, but not the snack you imagine, we've been known to make new Chinese friends, buy a bird, and share, hot off the roaster.

Total Time: 2 days, plus 3 hours, 40 minutes | Serves 4–6

¾ cup soy sauce
¼ cup mushroom or dark soy sauce
2 Tbsp Chinese rice wine or
  dry sherry
3 Tbsp granulated sugar
1 Tbsp salt
2 tsp five-spice powder

6 cloves garlic, peeled, smashed
2 inches ginger, peeled, smashed
5 scallions, 2-inch segments
1 3–4 lb chicken, whole, rinsed and
  patted dry
2 Tbsp black sesame seeds

In a mixing bowl, whisk together soy sauce, dark soy sauce, rice wine, sugar, salt, and five-spice powder. Be sure that the sugar and salt dissolve. In a resealable container or large ziplock bag, add garlic, ginger, scallions, and chicken. Pour over the marinade and seal the bag. Refrigerate for 48 hours. Massage the chicken in the bag every once in a while to ensure even seasoning.

Remove the chicken from the marinade, brush away any solids, set on a roasting rack, breast-up over a roasting pan, sprinkle with sesame seed, and air-dry at room temperature for 2 hours. Preheat the oven to 425°F. Transfer the roasting pan into the oven and roast the chicken for 40 minutes. Reduce the temperature to 225°F and continue to roast for 30 minutes.

Remove the chicken from the oven and allow it to rest for 25 minutes before carving, shredding, and serving as a main dish. You may also choose to use the meat for Bangbang Ji / Guaiwei Ji ("Strange-Flavored" Chicken) on page 16.

CHAPTER 7: WHAT CAME WITH THE CAMELS

ONE TENDS TO VIEW CHINESE cuisine as a monolithic thing. China is a huge country with a long history, but without a whole lot of formal immigration. Therefore, the food of China must be completely Chinese, right? Wrong. Where it is true that there have not been mass periods of immigration in China for quite some time, internal migration from borderlands of the country has shaped all forms of cuisine, most notably, street food. The title of this chapter suggests that foodways came along with camels to inform what would become a Chinese food tapestry. Though fun to say and alliterative, it's only partly true. For 1600 years, the Silk Road carried culture, livestock, and of course, recipes from as far away as the Middle East into the heart of China. Camels were indeed around.

You can read more about the impact of central Asian cuisine on China in our *Muslim Street* chapter. Some of our favorite street foods do not fit into the category of those with Islamic beginnings, so we dedicate this chapter to other foreign-born delicacies. Today, we see a wide range of street foods that have their roots outside of China, but have embedded themselves into the hearts, minds, and bellies of the Chinese so deeply that they may be thought of as native. We're here to celebrate the diversity within Chinese kitchens and the *otherness* of these snacks, from the hearty stalwarts such as "these *must* be Chinese" Baked Sesame Buns (page 197) to the rather outlandish "these *must* be from Mars" Fried Mashed Potato Cheese Balls (page 223). Both, equally foreign.

We recently became friendly with a Beijing food writer and historian named Baiwei. He's the hungry mind behind the very comprehensive *Beijing Restaurant and Food Guide*. He's also the guy you want beside you while you hunt for the latest food fad! According to Baiwei, most street food we see today is in fact non-majority cookery; it's built on dynasties and migration. He notes, "Throughout our history, people came from different parts of China to make money in the big city, especially when the rulers were from a different ethnic background. When the Mongols and the Manchus ruled China, there

was a big upswing in the diversity of street foods. A place like Beijing was, and still is, a big attraction for minorities and unique groups. They came to sell their specialties on the streets. In many cases, these snacks were initially seen as outsider food. Eventually, even the oddest examples may be considered *our* food."

Based on the patterns of migration, the internalization of minority foodways in larger cities makes a lot of sense. What makes even more sense is what you see as you near the borders of other countries. As you near the borders of Southeast Asia, you see tropical fruits and delicious things wrapped in banana leaves. When you get close to Russia, you see sourdough bread and purple beets. The closer you get to Mongolia, every shade of dairy pops up around every corner. Fermented mare's milk, anyone? Over time, and with increased ease of cold storage and shipping, these things drill in toward the heart of China and find a place at the street stall.

Back in 2010, we wanted to be a part of this migratory menu magic, and produced a Web series called *Sauced in Translation*. We would show up in a Chinese town, eat the specialties, and decide on which relatable American dish to cook up for the locals. Then, we'd shop at the farmer's market, locate a place to cook, and effortlessly draw a hungry crowd. They were always curious about what we were making, and most of the time, they enjoyed it. We never had any leftovers. On every trip back to China, we're just waiting to see some stall hawking jambalaya, chowder, macaroni salad, or BLTs! One day, perhaps even *we* will be considered camels. Wait. That doesn't sound right.

Zhima Shaobing
芝麻烧饼
(Baked Sesame Buns)

When in China, one may lose an argument about *shaobing* being a foreign street food. A Chinese friend will insist that they are Chinese immediately after telling you the tale of how shaobing came to China from afar. It boggles the mind. Our food writer buddy Baiwei is one such denier, and he's a historian! We sat with him over a beer after meticulously choosing from among a dozen shaobing shops down the street. "Tell us again, how these things are deeply Chinese despite having been invented somewhere around Babylon?" He recoils at the notion, "Sure, sesame bread came from the Middle East, but we've been baking these buns for a thousand years! I love them! My hometown in Shandong makes the best. Everyone in my family adores them, and they have for hundreds of years. That makes them Chinese, no?"

Chinese, indeed. Originally named *hubing*, or "barbarian cake," the concept of clay-oven baked shaobing is thought to have been brought back from central Asia by a Han Dynasty general in the 200s BCE. Of course they would be called "barbarian cakes," as everyone from outside of China must be a barbarian. In fact, the Chinese word for beard also involves the word for barbarian, since all barbarians fought against happen to have had beards. Howie has been known by the name "the great barbarian" among Chinese friends, given his tendency toward ample facial hair. We digress. Shaobing in their simplest form, with a sesame filling, are known and sold throughout China as a quick bite, or as an accompaniment to a hot bowl of soup. At times they are also sliced in half and filled as a sandwich bun (see Chicken Sandwiches on page 203). There are also stuffed versions you will see on the following pages. They are a light, flaky, and have a lot more in common with a Kaiser roll than barbarism . . . or beards.

Total Time: 2 hours, 40 minutes | Serves: 8–12

DOUGH:

3 cups all-purpose flour, plus more
    for dusting
2 tsp rapid-rise yeast
1 tsp salt
1 Tbsp sugar
1 cup water
1 Tbsp vegetable or canola oil

FILLING:

2 Tbsp roasted sesame paste or tahini
2 Tbsp toasted sesame oil
¼ tsp salt
½ tsp sugar

TOPPING:

1 egg white
1 tsp water
½ tsp sugar
⅔ cup white or black sesame seeds

In a large mixing bowl or the bowl of stand mixer, whisk together flour, yeast, salt, and sugar. Using clean hands or the dough hook of the stand mixer, incorporate water and oil until a smooth dough forms.

Dust the countertop or work surface with additional flour and transfer the dough onto the flour. Dust the top of the dough, knead, and form the dough into a ball. Transfer the dough to a large, clean, lightly oiled bowl and cover with plastic wrap. Allow the dough to double in size, about one hour to 90 minutes.

In a mixing bowl, whisk together the filling ingredients and set aside. In a separate mixing bowl, whisk together egg white, water, and sugar for the topping. Place sesame seeds on a separate plate.

Dust a wide area of flour on the work surface, and transfer the dough on top. Use a rolling pin to form a large ¼-inch thick rectangle. Evenly brush a thin layer of the filling paste across the dough. Starting at the bottom (long edge), roll the dough forward onto itself, forming a tight tube. When you reach the end, pinch to seal the edges, lengthwise along the roll.

Cut the tube into 2-inch segments. Dust your hands with flour, and place one segment in your palm with the cut edges facing out. Gently form the dough into a ball. Flatten the ball with your hand into a 2½-3-inch disc. Brush the top of the disc with the egg white mixture and then dip into the sesame seeds. Set the disc aside, sesame seeds up, and repeat with the remaining dough segments. Cover the dough discs with plastic wrap and allow them to rest for 45 minutes.

Preheat the oven to 375°F. Place the dough discs onto a sheet pan (or a few), sesame seeds down, and bake for 10 minutes. Remove the partially baked buns from the oven, flip them over, and continue to bake for an additional 5–10 minutes, or until the tops are golden and the buns have risen.

Serve hot or at room temperature as a sweet snack.

WHAT CAME WITH THE CAMELS

Mogu Shaobing / Niurou Shaobing
蘑菇烧饼 / 牛肉烧饼
(Baked Mushroom Buns) or (Baked Beef Buns)

It's not that often that one spends more than a few minutes at a street food stand, especially since the entire goal of these convenient stalls is a quick bite along one's route. But, when you're as food-obsessed and inquisitive as us, things change. One night a while back, we were hanging out in Beijing with a social media restaurant reviewer named Jianghao. He's one of those dudes whose word is gospel among the local foodies. Once he says that some dish or street stall is the bee's knees, the grueling wait in the impending queue generally matches the deliciousness of the prize at the end. If you're lucky enough to be with him when such discoveries are made, the lack of a line inspires eating as much as you can possibly tolerate. Friends, we were two of those lucky ones that night.

We had met up with Jianghao to visit a quaint tea house hidden deep in the back alleys. We sipped fine jasmine tea, talked about his local favorite haunts, bought way-too-expensive sweet snacks, and then called it a night . . . That is, until we walked him to the nearest bus stop just south of the Lama Temple. That's when we ran into a guy named Zhangyi who was making Shandong-style shaobing. They're different from the Beijing staple (from the previous recipe), in that they're not intricately rolled into exponential layers. They're simple. Roll dough, place filling, close dough, bake. This fella was baking them in a tandoor oven made from a recycled wooden barrel, the kind in which you may go over Niagara Falls!

What started as curiosity led to a pancake binge-fest. Zhangyi was rolling out a dozen or so fillings. We felt it our solemn duty to try them all, with outstanding results. Pork belly with garlic chives, tenderloin with cilantro and eggs, spicy fermented cabbage reminiscent of kimchi; the list (and our long night) went on. The two featured here were the last we sampled and our hands-down top picks. Though we literally could have *rolled* away from this tiny pancake palace after the previous fourteen shaobing, we just couldn't help ourselves and must have eaten three of these each. Somehow, we survived, and as a bonus, we didn't have to stand on the reported 100-person line the next day, once Jianghao recovered enough to post about it!

Total Time: 2 hours, 40 minutes | Serves: 4–6

WRAPPERS:

**1 uncooked dough recipe from
    Zhima Shaobing on page 197**

MUSHROOM FILLING:

**1 Tbsp vegetable or canola oil
4 scallions, thinly sliced
1½ lb cremini or shiitake
    mushrooms, finely chopped
½ tsp salt
2 Tbsp dark or mushroom soy sauce
1 Tbsp sweet bean sauce
    (tianmianjiang) or hoisin sauce
⅓ cup vegetable stock or water
1 tsp cornstarch
1 tsp sesame oil**

BEEF FILLING:

**½ lb ground beef
2 scallions, minced
½ inch ginger, peeled, minced
1 clove garlic, peeled, minced
2 tsp soy sauce
2 tsp Chinese rice wine or dry sherry
½ tsp cornstarch
¼ tsp salt
¼ tsp granulated sugar
½ tsp five-spice powder**

TOPPING:

**1 egg white
1 tsp water
½ cup white or black sesame seeds**

Prepare the Zhima Shaobing dough from page 197 up to the first rising of the dough.

TO FILL SHAOBING WITH THE MUSHROOM FILLING:

Add oil to a skillet and heat over medium high. When the oil begins to shimmer, add scallions, mushrooms, and salt. Sauté until the mushrooms lose their moisture and begin to brown, 10–12 minutes. Stir in soy sauce and sweet bean or hoisin sauce and continue to sauté for 5 minutes. Mix together water or stock and cornstarch. Pour this mixture into the skillet and bring to a boil. Turn off the heat, stir in sesame oil, and set the mixture aside.

TO FILL SHAOBING WITH BEEF FILLING:

In a large mixing bowl, combine all of the Beef Filling ingredients. Stir to combine evenly. Set the mixture aside.

Uncover the dough, dust the work surface with flour, transfer the dough atop the flour, and evenly hand-roll it onto a 2-inch-thick log. Cut the dough into 2-inch pieces. Knead and roll the dough pieces into 2-inch balls. Flatten each dough ball by hand, then use a rolling pin to create a 4-inch round. Try to leave the center of the round a bit thicker than the outer inch.

Continued on page 202

Place two tablespoon of filling onto the center of one dough round. Stretch and pinch the edges into pleats, surrounding the filling until you come full circle. If you have a small gap at the end, pinch the edges together to seal the pouch. Dust a work surface and place the pleated side of the pouch down. Use a rolling pin to evenly flatten the pouch to a 5-inch inch disc. Set aside on a parchment-lined baking sheet (or a few) while you fill the remaining dough.

Preheat the oven to 500°F. In a mixing bowl, whisk together egg white and water for the topping. Brush the top of the dough discs with egg white mixture, sprinkle with sesame seeds, transfer to the oven, and bake for 10–12 minutes, or until the buns have risen and are golden brown.

Serve hot, on their own, as a quick snack.

Jirou Shaobing
鸡肉烧饼
(Chicken Sandwiches)

By the time we got to China in the late 1990s, the golden arches and the white-bearded Colonel's best were very popular, especially among the kids and the beginnings of the nouveaux riches. We would often joke about going, if only for the kitsch value. *Forget about all that great Chinese food, let's grab a bucket and some biscuits and climb the Great Wall! Guess what we ate in China, everybody!* Of course, we've never given in to some weird desire for American fast food while traipsing around China. But, right around that same time, we found the real reason that it was just a really warped idea. If you travelled a mere couple of blocks from any of these trademarked locations, you'd be confronted with a stunning alternative.

Imagine if the Colonel offered three types of cooked chicken and paired it with a crispy on the outside, fluffy on the inside, sesame-seeded bun, and instead of slopping the bread with limp lettuce, tasteless tomato, ketchup, and mayonnaise, it was just slathered in the drippings from said cooked chicken. How would *that* taste? Amazing, right? Why would you ever think of something that comes with a side of mashed potatoes in lieu of bathing in the luxury that is a sloppy, savory, seductive Chinese chicken sandwich? The very first time we encountered this remedy for your run-of-the-mill junk food, we were hooked.

Total Time: 3 hours | Serves: 8–10

BUNS:
1 uncooked dough recipe from
   Zhima Shaobing on page 197
2 Tbsp toasted sesame oil
1 egg white
1 tsp water
½ cup white or black sesame seeds

FILLING:
Stewed chicken from Jirou Tang
   (Chicken Soup) on page 189 *or*
Roasted chicken from from Kaoji
   (Roasted Chicken) on page 191 *or*
Boneless fried chicken pieces

OPTIONAL TOPPINGS:
Ham, thinly sliced
Lettuce leaves
Cilantro, roughly chopped
Scallions, thinly sliced
Chicken broth

Prepare the Zhima Shaobing dough from page 197 up to the first rising of the dough.

Uncover the dough and evenly hand-roll it onto a 2-inch-thick log. Cut the dough into 2-inch pieces. Knead and roll each of the dough pieces into a ball. Dust the top of the dough balls and cover with towel or plastic wrap. Allow the dough balls to rest for 30 minutes.

Preheat the oven to 375°F. After the dough balls have rested, remove one from the plastic wrap and hand-roll it into a 1-inch log. Using a rolling pin, roll the dough into a long oval, about ¼-inch thick. Brush the top of the dough with a thin layer of sesame oil.

Starting from one narrow end, roll it up as you would a poster. Stand the roll on its end and gently flatten and with a rolling pin, roll it into a 4-inch disc. If an outer edge sticks out, fold it under the bottom of the disc as you flatten it. Set aside on a parchment-lined baking sheet and continue to make discs with the remaining dough balls.

In a mixing bowl, whisk together egg white and water for the topping. Brush the top of the dough discs with egg white mixture, sprinkle with sesame seeds, transfer to the oven, and bake for 20–25 minutes, or until the buns have risen and are golden brown.

Remove the buns from the oven and allow them cool for 30 minutes. Cut the buns in half, sandwich-style. Place a handful of chicken on the bottom bun, optionally top with ham, lettuce, cilantro, and scallions. For additional juice, pour a small amount of broth over the chicken. Close the bun and go to town!

Meigancai Niurou Bing
梅干菜牛肉饼
(Baked Pickled Vegetable Beef Cakes)

One rather elaborate version of the shaobing doesn't even go by the name "shaobing." It's *that* special. Rather, when a seller wants to draw people in, it's not the commonly loved baked treat that he wants to highlight. It's the use of *meigancai*, or "molded dried vegetables." Where that doesn't sound terribly appealing, it's the stuff of which culinary dreams are made. Meigancai is the result of thousands of years of Chinese ingenuity. Sure, one could simply salt some vegetables after the harvest and they will last through the winter months. But, why not add layers of flavor by sun-drying, steaming, salting, fermenting, then sun-drying again, only to be re-salted, re-steamed, and dried one last time?

The humble shaobing may have started as "barbarian" import, but the use of meigancai cements *this* bun as solidly Chinese. We once visited with a friend named Yao Dan (English name "Alice"), in Chengdu for some of her favorite Sichuan street snacks. According to Alice, "Before one really gets into our local specialties, you have to try one of the most important flavors in all of China." Of course, we came to Chengdu to have our palates explode with chiles, but Alice had never steered us wrong, so we approach her favorite beef cake stand, just to be good guests. Friends, it was a revelation. We had been accustomed to meigancai steamed with fatty meat to impart an equally salty and umami counterpunch. So, we thought it would overwhelm inside of a simple pancake. It didn't. Relatively lean, sweet beef and some aromatics combined with this dried, salted, and fermented gold inside of a bland, crispy shell was and is a winner among Chinese buns.

As if the original foreignness of shaobing wasn't enough, the vendor drizzled on Japanese kewpie mayonnaise and ketchup along with chile oil before handing over this hot treat. How's that for some cross-border relations?

Total Time: 1 hour | Serves: 6–8

WRAPPERS:
2½ cups all-purpose flour, plus
    more for dusting
½ tsp salt
1 cup water, hot from the tap

FILLING:
1 lb ground beef
½ cup rehydrated meigancai, mild
    kimchi, or other preserved greens,
    drained, minced
2 scallions, minced
1 Tbsp soy sauce
2 tsp sweet bean sauce
    (tianmianjiang) or hoisin sauce

1 Tbsp Chinese rice wine or dry
    sherry
½ tsp salt
½ tsp granulated sugar
1 tsp five-spice powder
1 egg

OPTIONAL TOPPING:
Lajiao You (Chile Oil) on page 132
Japanese mayonnaise, or American
    mayonnaise mixed with a bit of rice
    vinegar and sugar
Ketchup

Whisk together flour and salt in a large mixing bowl or the bowl of stand mixer fitted with a dough hook. Slowly stir in the water until a single mass of dough forms. You may not need all of the water.

Dust the countertop or work surface with flour and transfer the dough onto the flour. Dust the top of the dough, knead, and form the dough into a smooth ball. Transfer the dough to a clean bowl, dust the top with flour, and cover with a clean dish towel or plastic wrap. Allow the dough to rest for 30 minutes.

In a large mixing bowl, thoroughly combine all filling ingredients. Set aside.

Preheat the oven to 450°F. Uncover the dough and evenly hand-roll it onto a 2-inch-thick log. Cut the dough into 2-inch pieces. Knead and roll the dough pieces into 2-inch balls. Flatten each dough ball by hand, then use a rolling pin to create a 4-inch round. Try to leave the center of the round a bit thicker than the outer inch.

Place two tablespoon of filling onto the center of one dough round. Stretch and pinch the edges into pleats, surrounding the filling until you come full circle. If you have a small gap at the end, pinch the edges together to seal the pouch. Dust a work surface and place the pleated side of the pouch down. Use a rolling pin to evenly flatten the pouch to a thin, 6-inch disc. Set aside on a parchment-lined baking sheet (or a few) while you fill the remaining dough.

Transfer to the oven and bake for 15–20 minutes, or until the pancakes are golden brown. Serve hot, optionally brushed with topping ingredients.

WHAT CAME WITH THE CAMELS

Dabing
大饼
(Sweet or Spicy Bread)

Within the dizzying kaleidoscope that is Chinese street food, *dabing* stands out. It's right there in the name. Where other street snacks, or *xiaochi*, are literally "small eats," dabing means "big pancake!" It's often sold whole to customers to bring home as part of bigger meal, but is also offered in hacked off pieces for eaters on-the-go, similar to pizza by-the-slice. That's not where the similarity to pizza ends. Dabing is essentially a folded and continually rolled pizza, only without the cheese. It can be sweet or savory, mild or spicy, herby or oily, and pairs exquisitely well with a morning Mushroom Rice Porridge on page 65, or a soup like Black Pepper Beef Soup on page 151. Though we've tried a range of dabing lined with the entire pantry, the two found throughout China are timeless: sweet sesame and spicy chile oil.

So far as history, dabing shares its lineage with shaobing. It's essentially a permutation of the same filled dough, only really big. Its size makes it quite a challenge to cook in a tandoor-style oven, like other baked Chinese treats. So, it stands to reason, where the inspiration for baked yeast breads came from abroad, the format of dabing is pretty darned Chinese. On the streets, when you see a huge *pingdi guo*, or "flat-bottomed pan," with a hinged lid, you should stay there and await flatbreads of all stripes. Mostly, the pingdi guo is used for hybrid pan-frying and steaming for the likes of Scallion Pancakes on page 272 and Pan-Fried Pork Pockets on page 85, but when neither oil nor steam are used, the pan turns into what amounts to a flat oven. Welcome to the wonderful world of big bread!

Total Time: 2 hours, 10 minutes | Serves: 8–10

DOUGH:
3 cups flour, plus more for dusting
1 Tbsp rapid-rise yeast
1 cup water, warm from the tap, plus
   more for brushing
1 Tbsp salt
2 tsp sugar

CHILE FILLING:
½ cup chile paste *or* red chile oil with
   sediment *or* Lajiao You (Chile Oil) on
   page 132

SESAME FILLING:	TOPPING:
2 Tbsp roasted sesame paste or tahini	**1 egg white**
2 Tbsp toasted sesame oil	**1 tsp water**
¼ tsp salt	**3 Tbsp white or black**
½ tsp sugar	**sesame seeds**

In a large mixing bowl or the bowl of a stand mixer, whisk together flour and yeast. In a separate mixing bowl, whisk together water, salt, and sugar. With the dough hook attached to the stand mixer or with clean hands in the mixing bowl, slowly incorporate the liquid mixture into the flour mixture. When there is no longer visible flour, knead the dough for 3 minutes.

Dust the countertop or work surface with additional flour, and pour the dough from the mixing bowl atop the flour. Briefly knead the dough to form a smooth ball. Dust the top of the dough ball with additional flour, cover with plastic wrap, and allow to ferment on the counter for 1 hour. The dough will become bubbly and much larger in size.

To make the Sesame Filling, in a small bowl, whisk together sesame paste, sesame oil, salt, and sugar.

Generously dust the countertop or work surface with flour and transfer the now very loose dough on top of the flour. Using a rolling pin, form a large rectangle, about ¼-inch thick. Brush a thin layer of either the Chile filling or Sesame filling across the top of the dough, leaving a ½-inch gap at the edges.

Fold the dough in half lengthwise and pinch to seal the loose edges. Then, fold it in half again widthwise, and seal the edges. Dust with flour and roll the dough to ¼-inch thickness. Repeat the folding technique lengthwise, then widthwise, and finally roll to ½-inch thickness. Transfer the dough to a baking sheet. Dust with flour, cover with plastic wrap, and let it rest for 25 additional minutes.

Preheat the oven to 450°F.

Remove the plastic wrap. In a small bowl, whisk together egg white and water for the topping. Brush the top of the dough with egg wash and sprinkle generously with sesame seeds. Transfer the dough to the oven and bake it for 12–15 minutes, or until it is golden brown and puffed up. Remove the dabing from the oven and serve hot with Xianggu Zhou (Mushroom Rice Porridge) on page 65, Hula Tang (Black Pepper Beef Soup) on page 151, or as an interesting bread for any meal.

Suannai
酸奶
(Beijing-Style Yogurt)

Dairy is not the first thing that comes to mind when one thinks about the foods of China . . . or the second, third, fourth, or 1000th. There's the fabled lactose intolerance among Chinese folks, but that's more of a result than a reason. For millennia, bovines were a source of field work rather than a meal; therefore, neither beef nor cow's milk was commonly consumed. It was simply more valuable to keep cattle closer to a plow than to a grill or a milkmaid. On the northern borders and the coasts, fresh milk came and went with traders, but where refrigerated shipping hadn't been mastered until the last century, most of China didn't see a nice frosty glass of milk until relatively recently. In fact, even today, fresh milk is still not common.

All this being said, the popularity of suannai, literally "sour milk," comes as quite a surprise. We once asked Qu Feng, our archaeologist friend, about why most Chinese folks don't eat cheese. He replied, "Most Chinese don't drink milk. Why do you think we would like old, spoiled milk?" At the time it made sense, and it was funny, but the more we noticed the enjoyment of yogurt all over China, the more perplexing it became. We recently hung out with Qu Feng in Beijing and asked a slightly different question: "You don't like cheese, but you love yogurt; why?" "Ah," he said, as if a lightbulb went on above his head; "yogurt is sour. We love sour things more than we hate cheese." It's all so simple. We treated Qu Feng to a cold ceramic jar of yogurt, popped our straws through the foil top, and enjoyed the irony.

Total Time: 6½ Hours | Serves: 12–16

1 gallon milk (whole, light, or skim)
4 Tbsp natural yogurt
Honey for serving

Preheat the oven to 200°F. Turn it off and let it cool down while you prepare the fermentation mixture.

In a pot over medium heat, warm milk to 200°F, or just before it comes to a boil. Turn off the heat, cover the pot, and let the milk cool to 115°F. If you're not using a thermometer, a clean finger should be able to withstand this temperature for ten seconds. Gently whisk in the yogurt until it is fully incorporated.

Transfer the fermentation mixture into clean glass jars with lids. Four quart-sized mason jars is ideal. Place closed jars into the oven, with the oven light turned on, for four hours.

Remove the jars from the oven and refrigerate for at least 2 hours before mixing in some honey and sipping through a straw—Beijing-style!

Zhuye Niurou
竹叶牛肉
(Steamed Rice and Beef Cups)

We have a college buddy named Ray. Several years back, Ray decided that he wanted to go to China with us, if only to get us to stop asking him to come along. We'd been yammering on and on about how great the food was and he wanted in. Without knowing too much about the deep southwestern Chinese menu, we made the Yunnan borderlands our target. Notably, our aim was the "Water Splashing Festival." (Look it up—Most. Fun. Ever.) What we did not know was that most of the food we'd been bending Ray's ear over for years was fairly hard to find way down there. It was replaced with some of the most interesting dishes we'd come across in China. This was true cross-border magic. We sampled street foods that reminded us more of Bangkok, Saigon, or Vientiane than Beijing, Chengdu, or Shanghai.

Yunnan Province was one of the last holdout regions to Chinese empire during the Ming and Qing Dynasties. When borders were finally solidified, centuries-old clans remained on the Chinese side of the line. To this day, they represent many of the minority groups whose cultural heritage, traditions, and recipes thrive far from Beijing. Dialect is also among the things that survive within these small enclaves in Yunnan. That led to some surprising food finds, as we could mostly point, pay, and hope for the best. We relied on sights and smells and seldom went wrong. We mean, we *did* go wrong, but that's for a different book. These steamed beef and sticky rice bundles of joy, wrapped in bamboo leaves, were a real mystery, then a delight, and one of Ray's favorites. Who knew Ray was getting four countries for the price of one?

Total Time: Overnight, plus 1 hour, 45 minutes | Serves: 10–12

2 cups glutinous rice
4 cups, plus 1 gallon water, divided, plus more for steaming
1 lb ground beef
2 scallions, thinly sliced, white parts and green parts separated
1 Tbsp Chinese black bean sauce
1 tsp Chinese rice wine or dry sherry
½ tsp sugar
½ tsp salt
½ tsp ground white pepper
24 packaged bamboo leaves
½ cup chile paste, red chile oil *or* Lajiao You (Chile Oil) with sediment on page 132 (optional)

In a mixing bowl, combine rice and 4 cups of water. Cover and refrigerate overnight. Remove the rice from the refrigerator. Pour off the water from the rice, and rinse until the water runs clear. In a large mixing bowl, thoroughly combine drained rice, beef, scallions, black bean sauce, rice wine, sugar, salt, and pepper.

In a pot over high heat, bring 1 gallon of water to a boil. Reduce the heat to medium-low and put bamboo leaves into the boiling water for 30 minutes to soften them. Remove them from the water, set aside to cool.

Place two bamboo leaves in the palm of your hand, overlapping, widthwise. Grasp the narrow tops of the leaves and roll inward, toward the bottom tips, to form a closed cone. Secure the cone within your hand. Place enough of the rice filling to come within ½ inch of the top of the cone. Fold the hanging flaps of extra leaf over the top of the rice, and tie with butcher's twine. Repeat with the remaining leaves, rice, and filling.

Prepare steamer baskets by lining them with cheesecloth or parchment paper. Place the filled bamboo leaves atop the lining in a single layer. If you have stackable steamer baskets, continue to fill baskets. Otherwise, steam bamboo leaves in batches. Cover the steamer basket(s) with their matching lid(s).

Place a skillet or pot over medium heat, fill with 2 inches of water, and bring to a boil, then reduce the heat to medium. Carefully place the steamer baskets atop the pot of simmering water, cover, and steam the bamboo leaves for 45–60 minutes, until the rice is cooked fully. Remove the zhuye niurou from the steamer, cut free just the top flap, so that you may serve the bamboo leaves as delicious steamy bowls. For a spicy kick, suggest that guests add chile paste or oil before enjoying the dish!

Boluo Fan
菠萝饭
(Pineapple Rice)

We can all admit to thinking pineapple *must* be a part of Chinese cookery based on the Friday night take-out menu of our collective youth. Remember that sweet and sour pork with goopy, day-glow orange sauce coating chewy chunks of pork belly, highlighted with what was otherwise a tropical fruit? So do we, though, needless to say, we much prefer the version made in China, where the sweet is sugar and the sour is vinegar. Sometimes, American Chinese food can be confusing. Pineapple? Really? That said, pineapple is authentically used in southwestern Chinese cooking, but not in such a silly way. The Spanish brought pineapple from its original home in South America to the Hawaiian Islands, then on to southern Asia where it thrived within striking distance of China.

This dish was another example of street snacks we encountered in Yunnan Province more than a decade ago. Pineapple was everywhere, baked into buns, grilled on a stick, and steamed along with some glutinous rice, as we present here. Though you can now find *boluo fan* in many a night market across China, when it's made with freshly picked fruit, the sweetness cannot be beat. Fruit and rice together is not top-of-mind when it comes to creating a dessert, but it should be. Sticky rice is a natural friend to differing levels of sweet. That and the textural combination of chewy rice and unctuous pineapple may never replace a slice of chocolate cake, but it is a great option for surprising your dinner guests. We've also given you an entire two paragraphs of dinner table conversation. You're welcome, and we'll give you more if you promise never to put pineapple in sweet and sour pork again.

Total Time: Overnight, plus 1 hour, 15 minutes | Serves: 3–4

1 cup white or black glutinous rice
2 cups water, plus more for steaming
1 (2–3 lb) pineapple, peeled, top and bottom removed, cut into 3–4 (1½-inch) discs

1½ Tbsp sugar
¼ tsp salt
½ cup carrot, peeled, shredded

In a mixing bowl, combine rice and 2 cups of water. Cover and refrigerate overnight. Remove the rice from the refrigerator. Pour off the water from the rice, and rinse until the water runs clear.

Create pineapple "bowls" by cutting out a cone from each disc. Starting ¾ inch from the edge of one disc, insert a small knife at an angle and cut down toward the center of the bottom without breaking through. Run the knife around the disc, complete a circle and remove the cone. Repeat with the other pineapple discs.

Discarding the core, dice up the scooped out pineapple. In a mixing bowl, combine drained rice with pineapple chunks, their juices, sugar, salt, and carrot. Fill the pineapple cups with about ⅓ cup of filling.

Place the filled pineapple bowls on plates on steamer racks in a single layer. Cover the baskets with their matching lids.

Place a skillet or pot over medium heat, fill with 2 inches of water and bring to a boil, then reduce the heat to low. Carefully place the steamer baskets atop the pot of simmering water, cover, and steam the pineapple rice for 45–60 minutes, until the rice is cooked fully. Serve warm or at room temperature as a sweet treat.

Yindu Xiangjiao Feibing
印度香蕉飞饼
(Flying Indian Banana Pancakes)

We love Chengdu in Sichuan Province. It's a foodie paradise by all measures. Whenever we ask our friends in China what their favorite regional cuisine is, nine times out of ten, the answer is Sichuan food. What they're usually referring to is Sichuan's tendency to offer up spice! We feel the same way about Sichuan cooking, but sometimes when we visit China's spice capital, we need to give our tummies a break from the 5-alarm fire. In recent years, there's been an uptick in the number of diverse night markets in Chengdu that serve up China's greatest hits alongside quick snacks from across Asia and beyond. Yes, there are hamburger stands that we happily ignore.

One of the snacks that we're now seeing frequently is pretty entertaining in both name and culinary spectacle. The *yindu xiangjiao feibing*, or "flying Indian banana pancake"! Though India is referenced, in actuality it's a radically popular street food in Thailand that crossed the border into the Chinese gastronomic canon. One day, it, too will be *very* Chinese, clearly. Our Chengdu buddy Dave Fan, who is well traveled in Southeast Asia, says, "The only thing Indian about these is the name," but the pancake itself resembles a roti quite a bit. They even use ghee in its preparation. Though we're quite sure someone along the way in Delhi put some banana slices in the middle of said roti, we'll still thank the Thai for this morsel.

On spectacle, Chinese street food is full of dishes that exhibit some of the finest in cuisine artistry. A roaring ball of flame engulfs a wok as fried noodles leap as if to escape; a deft set of fingers precisely fold exactly eighteen pleats to seal a stuffed bun with machine-like efficiency; rubber-band-like arms repeatedly whip and twirl noodle dough into filament-thin strands. It can be an adventure to watch Chinese food being made. The feibing is no exception. The first time we saw it being made, we must have watched our pancake mistress expertly craft seven feibing before we ordered our two. She rolled one dough ball translucently thin, then picked up two edges and whirled it about in the air, thereby making it even thinner! Four, five, six whirls, then finally, when just waiting for it to rip got painful, she rested it down like a cloud atop a sizzling griddle, filled it, folded it, served it. Sweet relief.

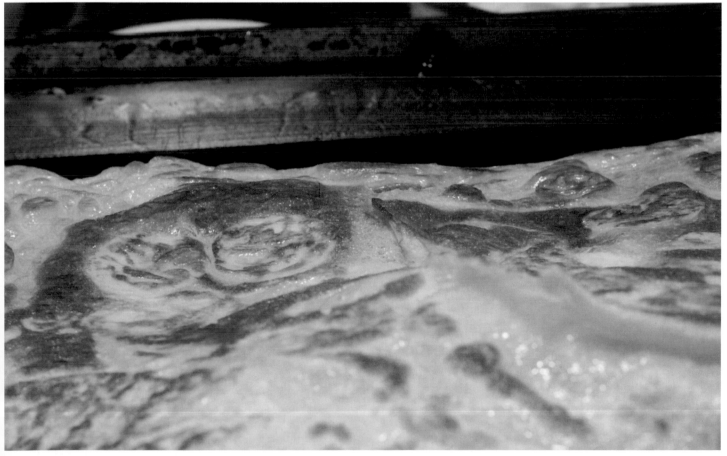

Total Time: 1 hour | Serves: 4–6

½ cup water
½ tsp salt
1 tsp granulated sugar
1 tsp vegetable or canola oil, plus
   more for coating and brushing

2 cups all-purpose flour
3 bananas, peeled, sliced
Butter for frying

In a large mixing bowl or the bowl of a stand mixer, whisk together water, salt, sugar, and oil. Be sure that the salt and sugar dissolve. With the dough hook attached to the stand mixer or with clean hands in the mixing bowl, incorporate 2 cups of flour, ½ cup at a time. When there is no longer visible flour, knead the dough for 3 minutes.

Pour some oil into a bowl for coating. Evenly hand-roll the dough onto a 1-inch-thick log. Cut the dough into 1-inch pieces. Roll each dough piece into a ball, dip into the oil to coat and set aside on a sheet pan. Cover with plastic wrap and let the dough balls rest for 30 minutes.

Uncover one dough ball, then stretch and flatten it as thin as possible, ideally until you can see through it. Do this by hand or rolling pin. Melt a dab of butter in a skillet over medium heat. When the butter is completely melted and begins to bubble, lay the sheet of dough in the skillet. Place a few banana slices in the middle of the dough.

When the bottom of the dough is browned, 1–2 minutes, fold the four edges over the banana, forming a square surrounding the filling. Flip the pancake and cook for an additional 30 seconds. Remove the feibing from the skillet to a paper lined plate and repeat with remaining dough and bananas.

Serve hot.

Wangzi Qisi Malingshu
王子起司馬鈴薯
(Fried Mashed Potato Cheese Balls)

Every once in a while, you run into a dish that is so wild, so outlandish, that you have to ask, "Where the heck did this come from, and why?" *Wangzi qisi malingshu* is one excellent example of such a dish. Taiwanese "fried mashed potato cheese balls" or "Prince cheese potatoes" came out of nowhere, or at least a seemingly heartfelt desire to mimic an Oklahoma-like fully loaded baked potato in a street food context with no rules. It is definitively *not* Chinese by any stretch. By some weird international magic, or perhaps the novelty of it, it's an extremely popular late-night snack in Taipei. Typically, you have the option to smother your large potato croquette with nacho cheese, corn, bacon, broccoli, pineapple, octopus, peanuts, and even dried tuna! Sounds delicious, no? Well, this is one scenario in which we decided to scale *back* just a little bit on a foreign delight.

Just next to the Parkson Hotel in Chengdu, there's a madcap, jam-packed night market at which Mr. Ding proudly hawks his loaded potato balls. He's an enterprising young man of twenty-eight who lived in Taiwan for a spell, made very good friends in the culinary space, and came back to the mainland with dreams of sharing a little bizarre food with the larger populous. Though he is a purist and offers up all the traditional Taiwanese accoutrement, he favors and sells out of the most basic of versions: fried potato ball stuffed with mozzarella and wrapped with ham. Our passports are satisfyingly stamped. Which stamp, we're not quite clear.

2 lb russet or gold potatoes, cut into
   1-inch chunks
½ cup mayonnaise
1 tsp salt
1 Tbsp vegetable or canola oil,
   plus more for frying
8 oz low-moisture mozzarella cheese,
   ½-inch cubes

1 egg
1 Tbsp water
½ cup all-purpose flour
1 cup bread crumbs
¼ lb thinly sliced ham, ½-inch strips
Toothpicks for frying

Preheat the oven to 375°F.

Place potato chunks on a lightly greased sheet pan, wrap tightly with aluminum foil, and roast for 35 minutes. Remove potato from the oven and uncover.

In a large mixing bowl with a potato masher or the bowl of a stand mixer fitted with a paddle, thoroughly mash together roasted potatoes, mayonnaise, salt, and 1 tablespoon of oil. Mash until you have a smooth, consistent mixture that you can form into balls. Allow the potato mash to cool while you prepare the oil for frying.

In a pot over medium heat, add oil to a depth of at least 1 inch, and heat to 360°F. No thermometer? Use the **Handy Trick** within the Doufunao recipe on page 31.

Tear off a golf-ball sized piece of potato mash and form a ball in your hands. Make a large well in the dough ball with a clean finger. Place a cube of cheese into the well and close and reform the ball around the cheese. Repeat with the remaining dough and cheese.

In a bowl, whisk egg and water. Then place flour and bread crumbs into separate rimmed plates. Individually roll the potato balls in flour, then roll in egg wash, then roll in breadcrumbs. Wrap one ham strip around the middle of each ball, secure the ham with a toothpick, and set each ball aside until you've coated all balls. Carefully add potato balls to the oil and fry, flipping occasionally until they are golden brown, about 6–8 minutes. Do not overcrowd the pan; fry in batches.

As the wanzi are done, remove to a paper-lined plate. Serve as a hot, gooey, unique snack.

CHAPTER 8:
CHINESE HOSPITALITY

BACK IN THE LATE 1990s, Howie taught English in China. When his birthday came around, his Chinese friends encouraged him to invite as many people as he could to a big dinner in his honor. So, seeing as how he had fallen in love with the food and more people meant a bigger variety of dishes at the table, Howie set about inviting sixteen of his new buddies to dine together. They all said yes, and when the night finally rolled around everyone ate to their bellies' content. Then, per birthday custom, the bill went directly to . . . Howie. *Huh?* It turns out, the honor of gathering friends to celebrate is larger than the honor of being invited. This was his initiation into the meaning of hospitality among the Chinese. It was an expensive, though delicious, lesson.

The Chinese put being the best host ever front and center. We believe that the three big traditional Chinese philosophies are to blame. The foundations of Confucianism are righteousness and performing one's duties to the best of one's ability. The bases of Daoism are deference and maintaining harmony with all living things. The ideals of Buddhism are selflessness and suffering. When you put all three together, you get an indelible tendency toward acting correctly, bending to the whims of those around you, and dealing with the barbarian in the room with grace.

In addition to deeply rooted rules of hospitality, *foodie* culture is a native aspect of the Chinese mindset. It *defines* China and its populace. They were the original foodies, well before social media made snapping glamour shots of your food a thing. So, when hospitality meets food, things get *extremely* serious. It might be as simple as a meet-up over a corner bowl of noodles, or as lavish as a banquet to cement a new business deal. In all cases, Chinese hospitality dictates that guests have the ultimate of experiences from soup to nuts. The host of a noodle hang-out will undoubtedly find the best slurp in town, and the host of the work dinner will strive to present something downright regal. This is just the norm. So, when you run into what the *Chinese* consider to be a foodie, it's going to be a long night.

Naturally, we've surrounded ourselves with and at times serendipitously bumped into our Chinese counterparts, the cuisine-obsessed. It may be an affable scam-artist who fills us up on Sichuan hot pot, only to insist on a full Chinese barbecue as a nightcap. Or, perhaps it's the owner of a beef company who presents you with a lavish bovine banquet, then takes to the streets to show you how *he* prefers his meat. It could be a top chef who is fascinated by foreigners who love Chinese food, who then whisks us away for late-night guilty pleasures. Over our decades of visits to China, our rule has become: *Whatever happens, just go with it. Buckle up, it's going to be delicious.*

Indeed, while doing our formal research for this book, we scheduled meetings with a few heavy hitters in the Chinese food world. Much to our delight, even we didn't know that what was planned as thirty minute interviews would turn into multi-hour food fests!

When we met with a film director in Beijing, what began as a chat at a duck restaurant evolved into a specifically manicured feast of a fine dining interpretation of street food. When we sat with a social media darling in Chengdu to discuss traditional snacks, out came twelve courses of ancient Sichuan dishes, followed by some treats on the street. In Xi'an, what began as a two-hour food tour extended to a nine-hour snacking maze through back alleys with the off-duty tour guide who was fascinated by our staying power and seemingly bottomless gullets. We're Americans, folks. We had no choice but to be the best, stuffed-to-the-gills guests possible. The examples abound, but trust us, dear readers, it was all necessary.

Sichuan Shaokao
四川烧烤
(Spicy Barbecued Skewers)

In talking about hospitality, we have a rather fitting, though ironic, story about one epic night in Chengdu about fifteen years ago. Early in the day, we had heard rumors about a scam artist working the streets. Reportedly, his tactic was to approach unknowing foreign tourists with an offer to show them the best hot pot restaurant in the city and host them over dinner. The scam was that he would take you to a cheap restaurant, conspire with the owner, and order a ton of food, only to leave you with a price-gouging, oversized tab. He'd then split the proceeds of the night with the restaurant owner.

Lo and behold, about two hours after being warned, we were approached by the kindly Mr. Jiang, along with the promised invitation to dinner. We thought it might be fun to take him up on his invite, in an attempt to con the conman. We insisted on going to *our* favorite hot pot place and stick him with the bill! Well, he pushed back, so that didn't work, so on to plan B. We'd *befriend* him! We had so much fun with Mr. Jiang that he called two of his friends to join us for even more food and laughter. He even called his son to join us, we were such a big hit. Naturally, dinner was only beginning. Mr. Jiang and his friend, "Top Tea," brought us along (um, helmetless on the back of motorcycles) as guest singers for their American top-40 tribute band. If we won them over with our love for food, we sealed the deal with our rendition of "Careless Whisper."

After the show, Mr. Jiang and "Top Tea" ensured that the night was not over and brought us to enjoy, in their words, "an American tribute food," barbecue. This was our first experience with a full *shaokao* onslaught. For an evening that began with a precarious premise and an attempted counter-scam, followed by our impromptu inauguration into the Chinese rock hall of fame, this night was one for the cross-cultural record books.

Total Time: 1 hour | *Serves: 4–6*

20 wooden skewers

GRILLING SEASONING:
3 Tbsp vegetable or canola oil
3 Tbsp red chile oil *or* Lajiao You (Chile Oil) with sediment on page 132

4 tsp salt
1 tsp sugar
1 Tbsp Sichuan peppercorn, ground
1 Tbsp ground white or black pepper
2 tsp ground cumin
1 Tbsp Chinese five-spice powder
2 Tbsp white sesame seeds

SUGGESTED MEATS AND VEGETABLES:

Premium hot dogs or other cured pork sausages, whole or decoratively scored

Pork belly, ¼-inch slices across the grain

Thick-cut bacon slices

Beef rib-eye, ¼-inch slices across the grain

Chicken thighs, 1-inch chunks

Small fish, whole, scaled, cleaned

Larger fish, filleted, 2-inch pieces

Russet potato, peeled, ⅛-inch rounds

Yellow squash, ½-inch rounds

Dry or baked tofu, ½-inch thick squares

Enoki mushrooms, bunch-whole

Hard-boiled eggs of Chadan (Tea-Poached Eggs) on page 167, peeled

Scallions, root cut away

In a baking dish filled halfway with water, soak the wooden skewers for 2 hours. In a large mixing bowl, whisk together all of the grilling sauce ingredients, ensure that the sugar and salt have dissolved, and set aside for 2 hours. Stir occasionally.

Drain the skewers and thread the meat and vegetables onto them, leaving a few inches of "handle." Thread a single ingredient onto each skewer so that they may lay flat on the grill, without too much overhang. Thinly-cut ingredients such as the pork belly or potatoes may be threaded like an accordion.

Light a grill such that the handle of the skewers can remain off of the heat. You want a medium heat so that the ingredients do not scorch or cook too quickly. Grill the food, brushing on the grilling seasoning with a pastry/paint brush and flipping multiple times until cooked through. Serve hot.

Jichi Baofan
鸡翅包饭
(Grilled Filled Chicken Wings)

If you've enjoyed a beer at an American Chinese restaurant, chances are it was a Tsingtao. For decades, it was the only beer exported from China and it's therefore widely known. What's not widely known is that it's named after the east coast city of Qingdao, the location of the first brewery in China. Naturally, it was opened by *Germans*? In the late 19th century, with the Qing royalty in Beijing regularly distracted by foreign demands for trade and the occasional military incursion, the coastal bastion of Qingdao easily fell to the Germans. From 1891 until 1914, the city was rapidly developed under the German flag. In 1916, the brewery was sold to a Japanese company (which eventually split into Asahi and Sapporo). When the Japanese surrendered at the end of World War II, the brewery reverted to nationalized Chinese ownership and it eventually privatized. Anyhow, what goes with beer? Chicken wings!

About a decade ago, we first visited Qingdao. Indeed, it is a beer town. Restaurants all hang the neon signs to woo potential customers, the bigger and brighter, the better. T-shirts from past marketing events seem to be on every other back in the summertime. The beaches and parks are dotted with beer carts selling the ubiquitous large green bottle of liquid gold. Recycled kegs appear everywhere you think recycled kegs *should* appear: topped with wood as alfresco restaurant tables, embellished with a cushion as impromptu stools, stacked up to hold grand-opening banners, converted into street-side ovens. With all this surrounding us, we felt right at home, so how could we *not* be craving some wings? Qingdao did not disappoint. Someone surely got the memo, set up a grill, got all innovative, and started stuffing them with rice and veggies. Today, you see this treat throughout China, and it still pairs best with beer.

Total Time: 1 hour | Serves: 10–12

FILLING:
4 cups water
1 tsp, divided
½ cup fresh green peas
½ cup carrot, diced small

½ cup corn kernels
2½ cups cooked white rice
1 tsp chicken powder or crushed
   bouillon cube

continued on page 234

**20 large chicken wings, wingtip
intact, drumettes removed**

**1 Tbsp salt
1 Tbsp ground cumin
2 Tbsp white or black sesame seeds
1 Tbsp hot chile powder (optional)
1 Tbsp Sichuan peppercorn, ground
(optional)**

Add water and ½ tsp salt to a pot over high heat and bring it to a boil. Add peas, carrots, and corn, and boil for 5 minutes. Drain the vegetables and place in a large mixing bowl. Add rice, chicken powder, and the remaining ½ teaspoon of salt.

To debone the chicken wings, use a cleaver or heavy knife to hack off the end of the bone and skin opposite the wingtip. From the newly opened end, push the skin and meat down, exposing the two parallel bones, toward the wingtip. Once you reach the end of the two bones, and the skin and meat are like an inside-out sock, use a paring knife to cut the bones out. Invert the skin and meat once again, leaving you with a hollowed-out cavity to stuff.

Stuff each chicken wing with 2 tablespoons of filling. It is okay if the filling is exposed at the top of the wing. In a small bowl, mix together salt and other seasonings.

Light a grill and make sure you have an area of the grill that is high heat and an area that is medium-low. Place stuffed wings on the medium-low side of the grill. After 5 minutes, flip the skewers and grill for an additional 5 minutes.

As the meat is cooked for 10 minutes, dust each wing with seasoning and sear on the high heat side of the grill for 2–3 minutes on each side. The skin should be crispy and slightly charred. Serve the Jichi Baofan hot off the grill.

Zha Niurou Wanzi
炸牛肉丸子
(Fried Beef Meatballs)

Hunan cuisine entered the American psyche in the 1980s, or at least the name did. "Hunan" sounded exotic, so it was frequently used throughout the US to distinguish itself from "Szechuan," but frankly, it was all the same stuff, hardly authentic and far from the recipes used in China. For the record, Sichuan uses more dried chiles and numbing prickly ash berries, and Hunan uses more salted chiles. In 2007, we made our first visit to Hunan Province, not to visit the park where they filmed the surreal planet-scapes from the James Cameron film, *Avatar* (though we did), and not to get the low-down on where Chairman Mao was born and raised (we didn't). Rather, we went to eat. You knew where we were going with that.

The day after we *did* visit the incredibly drastic cliffs of *Avatar* fame, we were waylaid in the transit town of Jishou due to torrential rains and the resulting floods that kept busses from driving and trains from running. Tired, wet, and hungry, we sat for a terrific meal at an eatery that advertised the "the most beef dishes in all of Hunan." We happened to be seated at a table next to a bunch of restaurant-supply guys who were also stranded by the floods. Since we are social butterflies and the Chinese are naturally hospitable to foreign guests, of course we struck up conversation and shared some beers with our new food industry friends. One of these dudes, Mr. Liu, strangely enough, was a beef shipper. He had something to say about each and every dish we ordered, some he loved, and some left him scratching his head. "Iron skillet beef is usually overrated, nothing new here," he lamented. "When it's done raining," he continued, "I'll take you for some real beef."

The rain didn't stop, but Mr. Liu and his cadre of truckers escorted us out into the torrent and beneath a hearty awning, under which a guy was stubbornly frying some simple meatballs. Impervious to weather, this guy. Mr. Liu assured us we were about to eat something unique. "Ever since people needed to use the bad parts of meat, they made meatballs," he went on, "but when you use delicious meat, a meatball isn't just a meatball. It's a great meatball." We agreed. The next day, we got dry and went back for more.

MEATBALLS:

1 lb ground beef short rib or chuck
1 Tbsp cold water
¼ bunch cilantro, minced
1 inch fresh ginger, peeled, grated
2 cloves garlic, minced
1 egg white
1 Tbsp cornstarch
1 Tbsp soy sauce
1 tsp sesame oil
½ tsp salt
1 tsp five-spice powder
1 Tbsp white sesame seeds
Vegetable or canola oil for
    deep-frying

DIPPING SAUCE:

½ cup soy sauce
2 Tbsp sesame oil
2 cloves garlic, minced
2 Tbsp cilantro, roughly chopped
2 scallions, thinly sliced
1 Tbsp salted red chiles, red chile
    paste, *or* Lajiao You (Chile Oil) with
    sediment from page 132

In a large mixing bowl, combine all meatball ingredients up to the sesame seeds. Mix thoroughly with clean hands or a wooden spoon, briskly and in one direction. The mixture will lighten in color as air gets incorporated, which ensures a light-textured meatball.

In a pot over medium heat, add oil to a depth of at least 2 inches, and heat to 360°F. No thermometer? Use the **Handy Trick** within the Doufunao recipe on page 31. Prepare a wire rack over a baking sheet and place next to the stove.

Form golf-ball sized balls of the meat mixture and place them on a clean plate. When the oil is heated, reduce the heat to medium-low to maintain the desired heat. Gently place a few balls into the hot oil. Be sure not to overcrowd the pan; work in batches if necessary. While the meatballs are cooking, gently stir the oil around the balls so they cook evenly and do not stick to the bottom. Cook the meatballs for 5–7 minutes, or until the outside is rich and browned. Place finished meatballs on the wire rack. Repeat with the remaining balls.

While the meatballs are cooking or when they are completed, in a small mixing bowl, thoroughly stir together the dipping sauce ingredients. Serve the meatballs warm alongside dipping sauce in individual bowls.

Kao Muli
烤牡蛎
(Roasted Oysters)

Way back in 1888 in southern Guangdong Province, Li Jinshang was cooking up a pot of oysters at a street stall ahead of the lunchtime rush. He fell asleep at the wok. A strong, pleasant aroma woke him from his slumber—the oysters had deeply overcooked and we thank him every day for accidentally inventing oyster sauce. Today, the Li family, though wide awake, still run the *Lee Kum Kee* brand, producers of excellent oyster sauce. Generally, most of us don't associate oysters with Chinese food, but, generally we're wrong. In reality, they cook them every way they cook: stir-fried, steamed, deep-fried, inside of an omelet, over an open flame, you name it!

In the beginning of our love affair with China, we had travelled mainly mountainous areas, so seafood was not on our radar. Sure, we would be drawn toward the occasional sea creature at night markets or specialty restaurants, mostly either farmed or shipped frozen to inland spots. Since oysters are arguably at their best fresh, we'd seldom if ever see them and therefore had never thought about them on the Chinese menu. We were in the same boat as most Americans. Then, during that same beer-and-wing-fueled visit to Qingdao, with its beautiful beaches, bays, and inlets, just like Mr. Li, we suddenly awoke to the aroma of this beautiful bivalve. If there was a street-side grill without a chicken wing, you could bet it was covered in oysters roasting over hardwood charcoal. Not unlike the West, the Chinese also associate the oyster with, er, warm feelings. We've always found those stalls rather congenial.

Total Time: 25 minutes | Serves: 4–6

½ cup soy sauce
1 Tbsp rice vinegar
¼ tsp ground white pepper
1 clove garlic, peeled,
   minced into paste

1 small green or red jalapeño or other
   chile, stemmed, seeded, minced
20 oysters, shucked, on the half-shell,
   rinsed
2 scallions, thinly sliced

Preheat the oven to 375°F, or light a grill to a medium heat. In a small mixing bowl, whisk together soy sauce, vinegar, pepper, garlic, and chiles. Place oysters on a sheet pan and spoon 1 teaspoon of dressing over each. Either transfer the sheet pan to the oven and roast or place oysters, in their shell, onto the grill and close for 10 minutes. Serve hot. Careful—that shell retains some heat!

Cai Wanzi
菜丸子
(Carrot, Celery, and Peanut Fritters)

As we've visited thousands of street stalls over the years, it's fairly typical for us to ponder ingredients and preparation techniques while enjoying whatever snacks are on offer. It's what we do. This can last minutes before we inevitably ask the vendor if they'll tell us their secrets, and end the debate. Some are even willing to give us a rundown of all ingredients they use. Fritters are a terrific vehicle for this kind of dispute, as a lot of the time, deep fried batter can mask the identity of the underlying stars of the show. One notable example of this was in the northeastern city of Shenyang back in the ought years. The aroma of fried dough drew us toward a cai wanzi stall. After the first several bites, the examination began. Howie thought this screamed celery. Greg was on team zucchini. We both agreed on peanuts, and maybe corn or yellow carrot?

Hospitality won that day. Or, perhaps our rather affable vendor, Ms. Qu, got tired of us arguing about what the green bits were? When the line eventually died down, she pulled us aside and not only listed the very basic ingredients that made up her deceivingly simple cai wanzi, but took us through the process from shredding to deep frying. We chatted with her for about an hour as we bought and gobbled up lovely specimens fresh out of the wok. Ms. Qu gave us a history lesson on deep frying in China, why vegetables do much better than meat, and how to do it right, so the food isn't greasy. Her advice was "new oil, every batch." She even let us help by pounding on peanuts to relieve some aggression! We felt honored by her kind treatment of new foreign friends. Howie felt doubly honored since he was right. It was celery.

Total Time: 35 minutes | Serves: 8–10

4 cups water
12 oz carrots, peeled, finely shredded
4 ribs celery with leaves, finely diced
1 cup all-purpose flour
½ tsp salt

⅛ tsp baking soda
¾ cup roasted peanuts, roughly chopped
2–3 cups vegetable or canola oil for frying

Bring water to a boil over high heat. Add carrots and celery and cook for 1 minute. Reserve ¼ cup of the cooking water, and set aside. Drain the vegetables and allow them to cool for ten minutes. In a large mixing bowl, whisk together flour, salt, baking soda, and reserved cooking water. Stir in peanuts. Wring out the carrots and celery in a clean kitchen towel or thoroughly by hand. Stir them into the batter mixture.

In a pot over medium heat, add oil to a depth of at least 1 inch, and heat to 360°F. No thermometer? Use the **Handy Trick** within the Doufunao recipe on page 31.

Prepare a wire rack over a baking sheet and place next to the stove. Carefully place a few spoonfuls of batter into the hot oil at a time, being sure not to overcrowd the skillet. Work in batches. Flip each fritter when the bottom becomes golden brown, about 2–3 minutes. After another 1–2 minutes, when the cai wanzi are golden brown, remove them to the wire rack.

Enjoy this surprisingly delicious combination hot off the rack.

Niurou Tangmian
牛肉汤面
(Beef Noodle Soup)

We've found that it is a rare honor to be invited into a Chinese home for dinner. You might think that this dates back to some Imperial history and custom. But, in fact, it's mostly because Chinese homes are generally really small, and it's tough to fit extra guests around the table, if there's even room for a table. So, we were surprised and honored when Zhang Hao, a food correspondent for Hunan TV, invited us to his family home, which housed an astounding three generations. He was excited to show us the fundamentals of local cuisine. It was an amazing night of culinary exploration. From fiery hot eggplant and smoked tofu to a dish of either pork lung or stomach, depending on who you ask.

As with most Chinese feasts, the evening was capped off by a steaming bowl of soup. In this case, it was an exceptional bowl: deep, rich beef broth with a hint of spice, and smooth, thinly pulled noodles, lightly boiled so as to retain their texture. When we asked *Haohao* (which we could call him, now that we were part of the family) how he had made this amazing soup, in such a small kitchen, with only a few minutes since getting off work, he stared intently at us and then shrugged, a bit embarrassed. He had bought it from a street stand on the way home from work. In a face-saving gesture, we assured him that the soup was mediocre, and that the highlight of the meal had been the prized pork innards. We were lying—the soup was awesome.

Total Time: 7 hours, 45 minutes | Serves: 8–10

BEEF AND BROTH:
1½ gallons water, divided
2 lb beef soup bones, butcher–cut
    into 2-inch segments
1 lb chicken bones or legs
2 lb beef short ribs, bone–in
2 inches ginger, halved lengthwise
2 heads garlic, unpeeled, halved
    lengthwise
2 leeks, rinsed, halved lengthwise
2 cinnamon sticks
3 star anise

1 Tbsp Sichuan peppercorns
1 Tbsp cumin seeds
2 Tbsp salt
3 Tbsp Shaoxing, other Chinese rice
    wine, or dry sherry

NOODLES:
1 lb Chinese wheat noodles, or other
    long, flat or thin pasta

GARNISH:
Red chile oil with sediment *or* Lajiao
    You (Chile Oil) on page 132
1 bunch cilantro, roughly chopped

In a large stock pot, bring ½ gallon of water to a boil and add soup bones and chicken bones. Boil the bones for 5 minutes, then remove, set aside, and discard the water. Rinse out the pot.

In the pot, combine boiled bones, short ribs, ginger, garlic, leeks, cinnamon, star anise, peppercorns, cumin seeds, salt, rice wine, and the remaining 1 gallon of water. Bring to a light simmer over low heat. Simmer, uncovered for 6 hours.

Turn off the heat and allow the contents to rest in the covered pot for one hour. Use a large slotted spoon to transfer the short ribs from the pot to a rimmed plate. Strain the broth into a large pot through cheesecloth or a fine-meshed sieve. Keep the pot of strained broth warm on the stove over low heat. Transfer the short ribs to a chopping board, remove the bone, and cut into ¼-inch thick slices. Set aside.

Cook the noodles according to the package directions.

Evenly distribute broth and beef slices into bowls. Then ladle in simmering broth before topping with Lajiao and cilantro. Serve immediately.

Shengjian Bao
生煎包
(Pan-Fried Buns)

In 2016 we had the rare opportunity to sit down with legendary television director Chen Xiaoqing, the man behind one of China's most popular series of all time, *A Bite of China*. Never before had Chinese cuisine been celebrated on film in such an exquisite manner. Though in the back of our minds, we knew that sitting down for a food chat with a great gastronome such as Chen would undoubtedly lead to hunger, we had no idea what we were about to encounter. We set up a time for the interview and Chen set up the place. In retrospect, it makes sense he is good friends with a Michelin-starred chef, Da Dong. At a flagship location in his empire in Beijing, the dining rooms are opulent, the menu is encyclopedic, and the food is mind-blowing. Not only did we get set up in a private dining room, but on this day, Chen somehow convinced Da Dong's cooks to whip up a fine-dining take on street food. What began as a highly valuable half hour in Chen's day resulted in one heck of a four-hour banquet. Chinese hospitality at its finest.

To think we had access to one of the greatest creative minds in the history of Chinese gastronomy. It still boggles the mind. We asked questions great and small, from historical perspectives on ingredients and minority food culture to Chen's favorite things to film and eat. One of the greatest moments early in the discussion was about the simple *shengjian bao*, or "fried buns." Chen waxed emotional: "When I was a child, my friends and I would run to the street stall after school to spend what little pocket money we had. The idea was to buy some buns and bring them back to my family. But, they were so tempting right out of the pan, the buns never made it home!" Indeed, we've tried to walk away from the pan as well. The buns never get very far.

As shengjian bao are essentially the pan-fried version of Steamed Eggplant or Pork Buns (page 49), they share the same history, including one gruesome origin story. Where the steamed variety has had a long tenure as a street snack, baozi's pan-fried brother had been seen as more refined and for centuries enjoyed a home at the tea table. It's been long held in China that sipping tea while enjoying relatively oily foods helps to cut the grease. Eventually, like most things delicious and quick, it too found its way to the streets. Perhaps the advent of to-go tea cups helped shengjian bao's migration to the streets?

1 uncooked Baozi recipe from
   Qiezi / Zhurou Baozi (Steamed
   Buns) on page 49
2 Tbsp vegetable or canola oil,
   divided
½ cup water, divided

OPTIONAL DIPPING SAUCE:
1 recipe Dipping Sauce from Zhurou
   Jiaozi (Steamed Pork Dumplings) on
   page 53

Prepare stuffed bun pouches from page 49 until all pouches have been sealed. Place pouches on a greased baking sheet, cover with plastic wrap, and allow them to rest for 20 minutes.

In a wide-bottomed skillet with a matching lid, heat 1 tablespoon of oil over medium heat. When the oil begins to shimmer, place dough pouches, pleated-side up, along the bottom of the skillet. It is okay if they touch, but do not overcrowd the skillet. Work in batches if necessary.

Fry the bottom of the pouches until they are golden-brown, about 2–3 minutes. Carefully pour ¼ cup of water into the skillet, cover with a lid, and continue to cook for 7–8 minutes. Turn off the heat and let the bao rest for 2 minutes before removing the lid.

Serve shengjian bao hot and optionally with a dipping sauce.

Roujia Mo
肉加馍
(Stewed Pork Sandwiches)

The first time we visited Xi'an, we had two things on the brain: lamb and bread soup (on page 107), and roujia mo. Arguably, these are the two most famous street foods to come out of central China and we needed to find the best. Enter a friend of a friend of ours who just so happens to guide food tours in his spare time. When you're aiming for the best of the best, it's always a good idea in a new city to enlist those in the know. Jiao Erqiang (English name "Joe") is a star in his own right, the *Energizer Bunny* of food hospitality. It's like there's a button on the back of his head, and when you switch him on, off he goes in the direction of the finest food Xi'an has to offer, repeatedly, until you switch him off.

We had a whole plan for the day: start with the tip-top lamb soup in town, followed by some sloppy sandwiches, then bid adieu to Joe and head off for the Terracotta Warriors. You can't miss those Terracotta Warriors, right? So, we met Joe on a busy corner in the height of tourist season in the Muslim Quarter. We were concerned. But Joe led us down a dizzying maze of tiny alleys and there it was; as Joe said, "This is the best spot in all of the city. Right there is the best paomo and just across the street is the best roujia mo!" We couldn't have planned it any better, or so we thought. Long story short, we had our fill of the city's two culinary gems . . . but the corned beef version of roujia mo, according to Joe, had to be compared with the lamb version, and the chicken version, and the veggie version. But the capper was his next suggestion. "Now we need to head a little bit out of town for the pork version," he insisted, and we couldn't resist. Juicy, unctuous, messy, delicious. Who needs to see a bunch of clay soldiers, anyway?

Before we let you go and make perhaps the best sandwich you've ever made, we need to settle something. This is our official roujia mo *rant*. It seems that whenever you see a roujia mo described in English, including on restaurant signs, it's referred to as a "Chinese hamburger." Some of the smartest culinary minds we know also make this epic blunder. People. It is not a burger! Is it a patty? No. Is it made of ground meat? No. Is it grilled, griddled, or roasted? No. Is it served on a soft bun? No. Lettuce, tomato? Nope and nope. What, then, is the relation to a burger? If anything, it's the Chinese cousin of a pulled pork sandwich from your local barbecue joint. But, even then, the meat is stewed and not smoked. Sheesh. It's *roujia mo*! Rant over. Go cook.

Total time: 5 hours | Serves: 6–8

4 qts water, divided
1 (3-lb) piece pork belly or
    shoulder, boneless
5 scallions, halved lengthwise
10 cloves garlic, unpeeled
2 inches ginger, peeled,
    halved lengthwise
2 Tbsp five-spice powder

1 Tbsp salt
½ cup Shaoxing, other Chinese rice
    wine, or dry sherry
3 Tbsp dark brown sugar
½ cup soy sauce
1 recipe Baiji Mo (Baked Sandwich
    Buns) from page 105
1 bunch cilantro, roughly chopped

In a stock pot or Dutch oven over high heat, bring 2 quarts of water to a boil. Add the pork and cook for 1 minute, rolling it over so that each side is in contact with boiling water for at least 30 seconds. Carefully transfer the pork from the water to a plate, and set aside while you prepare the remaining ingredients.

Wipe out the pot and form a bed on the bottom using scallions, garlic, and ginger. Completely cover the aromatic bed with the pork. Into the pot, add five-spice powder, salt, rice wine or sherry, sugar, soy sauce, and the remaining 2 quarts of water. Bring the mixture to a light simmer over medium heat. Reduce the heat to low, cover, and continue to simmer for 3½ hours.

Turn off the heat and allow the pork to rest in the covered pot for one hour. Use a large slotted spoon to transfer the pork from the pot to a rimmed plate. Strain the broth into a large mixing bowl through cheesecloth or a fine-meshed sieve.

Transfer the pork to a chopping board and using a knife or two forks, shred the meat. Try to leave some larger pieces for variety. Cut Baiji Mo buns, place some of the pork, a spoonful of the broth, top with cilantro, close up the sandwiches, and serve immediately.

Tudou Bing
土豆饼
(Fried Potato Cake)

In the late 1990s, for some really odd reason, most hole-in-the-wall restaurants displayed a large photo, like a glamour shot, of a stereotypical Western breakfast. We'd enjoy it whenever we saw it, as garish and out of place as it was, and would always ask the server the reasons behind it. We've been asking people for years why that trend came and went, and to this day, nobody can tell us. Perhaps like many things from the 90s, it was all the rage, and then just gone. Sort of like grunge. There may be a beautifully sunny-side up egg, a cuppa joe, a bright red tomato quartered and salted, two pieces of buttered toast, and in many cases, some crispy bacon! You'd think it would make us pine for home, but it didn't.

Once we were in Lüchun County, at the very south end of Yunnan Province, soaking up the sun and looking at terraced rice fields with our American buddy Ray. This was his first trip to China and we'd been telling him about this breakfast photo thing. He said, jokingly, "You should go into that restaurant and ask them to make you a Western breakfast, just like in the photo." As this was Yunnan and it was fairly common practice to choose from the bounty of local ingredients and tell them how you'd like them cooked, this was a realistic yet hilarious plan. So we pointed at some steamed bread we'd ask them to grill, chose some eggs to fry, a tomato to season up, some pork belly to slice thin and brown up on the flat top, and finally some Yunnan coffee, black, which is actually a thing.

Mr. Yan, the cook, watched on as the dishes were brought to our table and we laughed and high-fived like we were school kids. It was delicious. When we were done eating, Yan came over and told us that he figured we were aiming for the breakfast in the photo, he hoped we liked it, but then urged us out of our seats to follow him down the street. Were we too loud? Did our antics come off as being offensive? Did he think we were poking fun at him? Chinese hospitality being what it is, Yan stopped us in front of a street food stall and happily said, "I saw that you were trying to create an American breakfast. Why not try some of our local hashbrowns!" Such thoughtful hosts.

POTATOES:

1½ lb Yukon Gold potato, peeled, shredded

2 tsp salt

1 tsp ground white pepper

2 tsp Chinese five-spice powder

½ cup vegetable or canola oil, divided

DIPPING SAUCE:

½ cup soy sauce

2 Tbsp red chile oil with sediment *or* Lajiao You (Chile Oil) on page 132

1 Tbsp sesame oil

2 tsp rice vinegar

2 cloves garlic, minced

1 tsp ground cumin (optional)

1 tsp Sichuan peppercorn, ground (optional)

In a large mixing bowl, combine potatoes, salt, pepper, and five-spice powder. Let the mixture sit for ten minutes. In a small mixing bowl, whisk together the dipping sauce ingredients. Set aside.

Heat ¼ cup of oil in a skillet over medium. When the oil begins to shimmer, drop ¼ of the seasoned potato shreds evenly across the bottom of the skillet. With a rubber spatula, gently form the shredded potato into an even disc. Try not to overly compress the potato; you're not looking for a solid mass.

After 5–5½ minutes, gently lift up one side of the hash brown to check that the bottom is golden brown and releases easily from the bottom of the skillet. Flip the pancake.

After 4–5 more minutes, the potato cake should be brown and crispy on both sides. Remove the potato cake from the skillet onto a paper towel-lined plate. Repeat the process with the remainder of the seasoned potato shreds, ¼ at a time, adding oil if necessary between pancakes.

When they're all done, serve hot as a side dish or as a stand-alone snack, along with the dipping sauce.

CHAPTER 9: NOW THAT'S ONE EXPRESS PANDA

IN THE US, WE GENERALLY accept that most of the Chinese food to which we have easy access is highly Americanized. However, there are some brilliantly simple examples of dishes we enjoy in the US that can be found throughout the Chinese streets as well. Whenever we're traveling and are presented with something that we grew up on from Hunan Dynasty down the block, we think it's pretty cool. "Hey, it's actually real," is a typical first reaction! But, before we launch into the beauty of pot-stickers, spring rolls, and Peking duck, the history of Americanized Chinese food is worth a look.

Chinese laborers brought to the US to pan for gold and build the transcontinental railways in the 1800s were men. Back home in China, women did the majority of the cooking. So, not only did you have a bunch of men trying to figure out how their wives, mothers, and sisters *made* this or that, they were also presented with a largely different set of ingredients from which to start.

From 1882 until 1943, the Chinese Exclusion Act limited immigration and the industries in which the Chinese were able to work, namely, the service realm, hence Chinese laundries and restaurants mostly operated by the men who were already engaged in a makeshift cuisine.

From the rise of Communist power in mainland China after World War II, through the Reform and Opening policies of the late 1970s, professional culinary training was seen as bourgeois and elitist. So, the generation that *could* bring real recipes to the US either trickled in from Taiwan or Hong Kong, or simply didn't exist.

The *chop suey* craze of the 1930s, 40s, and 50s, if you can call it a craze, did a lot to define, or undermine, how Americans saw the *exotica* of Chinese cuisine. Thought to be originally served to a Chinese statesman visiting San Francisco in the late 1800s, chop suey, or *za sui* in Mandarin, literally means "broken miscellany." It was unfortunately a stir-fried collection of whatever the cook had left over when the emissary stopped in, hungry and unannounced. Well, it took off.

Considering this set of circumstances, the menu that developed was mostly a hodgepodge of delicious replication, adaptations from Cantonese and Taiwanese cooking, and above all, things that appealed to the paying American customer. Still, no matter the origin stories, we happen to believe American Chinese food has blossomed into a cuisine in its own right. The old standbys—broccoli beef, shrimp in lobster sauce, and that crunchy, deep fried goodness that is the classic egg roll—can be made with panache and delivered in under thirty minutes. But, can authentic Chinese cuisine still find its place in America?

Howie was once on an Asia Society panel with Chef Martin Yan, of *Yan Can Cook* fame, and Ian Cheney, director of the film *The Search for General Tso*. Facilitated by Monica Eng from WBEZ in Chicago, they discussed Chinese food as a "cultural ambassador." Howie contended and all agreed that Chinese food in the US is currently undergoing a renaissance. Deeply authentic regional Chinese restaurants are popping up all over. Though mostly in the expected urban areas, we're still thankful. Finally, we save the thirteen-hour commute for a good Chinese meal! Dishes that we had only seen in China are making their way to our shores. Spicy and numbing Sichuan hot pot, Chinese-Muslim street snacks, and quick, satisfying Beijing-style crêpes are now just a drive away, with more to surely come. Definitely a step in the right direction for cross-cultural understanding!

If we hosted a second panel, it would be entitled "The foods that we already have in common, and where to find them." As we note above, there are several examples of real Chinese street foods that we have unknowingly been consuming since childhood, and usually from the appetizer list, or in our parents' day, the pu-pu platter. As Mike Wong, a Beijing restaurant manager with whom we're friendly, put it, "When an American comes to China, they always buy fried noodles, barbecue pork, pot stickers, and scallion pancakes. That's all they know, but when they leave, they can appreciate how it should really taste!" Mike was right, it is better in China, but we'll give you a leg up with the following recipes.

Tudou Loubo Chunjuan
土豆萝卜春卷
(Pan-Fried Potato and Carrot Spring Rolls)

According to Andrew Coe, author of *Chop Suey: A Cultural History of Chinese Food in the United States*, the "egg roll" was inducted into American Chinese canon in New York City in the 1930s. The format and the common ingredients (cabbage, pork, carrots, herbs, and seasoning) were concocted by an enterprising Chinese cook who knew that Americans go crazy for deep fried, crunchy, meaty things. As time marched on, the egg roll became more and more complex, various fillings abounded, and it finally burst out of the American Chinese restaurant and onto the gastropub scene. Ever try a Tex-Mex egg roll? You should; they're delicious.

Enter the *chunjuan*, literally "spring roll," so named to celebrate the season when you're wrapping up fresh vegetables, or to evoke the memory of the season when you're wrapping up pickled vegetables. Eventually, this lighter-sounding, vegetable-centric snack started to appear as an American Chinese appetizer. It may have reflected a concerted effort to introduce more authentic dishes to the American diner, but it's more likely that the 1980s diet craze saw deep-fried sales plummet. Said every Chinese chef, "We have just what you're looking for!" Ironic that it took 100 years and an American desire to eat healthier to get a real Chinese dish on the menu of a cuisine that most folks see as take-out junk food, eh?

It's presence in this book also tells you that in China, spring rolls are indeed a street food snack. During our first trip to Chengdu twenty years ago, we passed by an eclectic street stand that was selling "San Francisco Chicken Nuggets," whatever that meant, and some permutation of a Chicago-style hotdog, loaded up with the works. We thought it would be funny to try these China-fied delights. Luckily, we noticed that the guy was also selling spring rolls. We thought, "What are the chances this guy is making an Americanized version of the roll, stuffed with no fewer than twelve vegetables that all lose their individual character?" We're cynics, what can we say? One bite, blissfully incorrect. Simple magic. Delicately seasoned potatoes, carrots, and chiles. Believe it or not, the hot dog wasn't half bad either.

DRESSING:
2 Tbsp rice vinegar
2 Tbsp soy sauce
1 tsp toasted sesame oil
1 Tbsp red chile oil *or* Lajiao You
   (Chile Oil) with sediment on
   page 132
½ tsp salt
½ tsp white pepper
¼ tsp sugar

FILLING:
8 cups water
1 lb russet or gold potatoes, peeled,
   julienned
1 lb carrots, peeled, julienned
2 green jalapeño peppers, julienned

ROLLS:
1 egg
1 Tbsp water
12–16 spring roll wrappers
4 tsp vegetable or canola oil

In a large mixing bowl, whisk together all dressing ingredients. Be sure that the salt and sugar dissolve.

Add water to a large pot and bring to a boil over high heat. Add potatoes and carrots to the boiling water and cook for 2 minutes. Remove, drain, and rinse the vegetables with cold water. Add the vegetables and peppers to the bowl and combine thoroughly. Cover and refrigerate overnight.

In a small mixing bowl, whisk together egg and water. Remove the dressed vegetables from the refrigerator and toss to redistribute the seasoning. Drain the vegetables. Brush the inside of two stacked wrappers with a thin layer of egg wash. Place a small handful of vegetables along the center of one spring roll wrapper, and roll up like a burrito, so that both ends are closed and sealed. Place aside, seam-side down, and continue filling wrappers.

Add 2 teaspoons of oil to a skillet over medium heat. When the oil begins to shimmer, add wrapped parcels, seam-side down, to the skillet. Work in batches, don't overcrowd the pan. Cook the parcels on one side for 2 minutes before rolling ¼ of the way over and cooking the next side for 2 minutes. Continue rolling and cooking until the entire rolls have turned golden brown, 8–10 minutes. As the spring rolls are done, remove to a paper towel-lined plate. Serve hot.

Jianjiao
煎饺
(Pot-Stickers)

Jianjiao, or "fried dumplings," are often mislabeled as "pot-stickers" on American menus. In China, they are two different snacks entirely, and it all has to do with the shape. Pot-stickers, or *guotie*, are long, flattened cylinders whose ends have been sealed shut. *Jianjiao*, on the other hand, are the same shape as a steamed dumpling, with pleats pinched at the top. More importantly, jianjiao is just a better name for a food. A dish can only be called a *pot-sticker* if something has gone horribly wrong, right? So, to both relate this dish to something you've had in an American Chinese restaurant and to face our fears of a dish being named after a cooking catastrophe, we stuck with the English name we hate and the much more elegant Chinese name.

Back in 2008, through our archaeologist friend, Qu Feng, we met Wang Rexiang, an anthropologist who specializes in everything culinary. When Mr. Wang talked about the origins of cooking in China, he waxed poetic about steam. "Steam is the foundation. Steam is the root and everything branches from it. In China, it all begins with steam. Bread, dumplings, vegetables, even fish!" he excitedly listed. He went on, "In the West, you bake everything. Carbon. That hurts both the environment and your health!" On that bit of hyperbole, we interrupted his poetry, "Hey, what about fried dumplings? That can't be any healthier than a bagel!" "Yeah, they are delicious . . . but remember they are fried *and* steamed. That changes everything." Let's all walk away with that in mind.

Total Time: 45 minutes | Serves: 6–8

JIAOZI:
1 uncooked Jiaozi recipe from Zhurou / Baicai Jiaozi (Steamed Dumplings) on page 53
2 Tbsp vegetable or canola oil, divided
½ cup water, divded

OPTIONAL DIPPING SAUCE:
1 recipe Dipping Sauce from Zhurou Jiaozi (Steamed Pork Dumplings) on page 53

Prepare filled pouches from page 53 until all pouches have been sealed.

In a wide-bottomed skillet with a matching lid, heat 1 teaspoon of oil over medium heat. When the oil begins to shimmer, place dumpling pouches, sealed or pleated-side up, along the bottom of the skillet. It is okay if they touch, but do not overcrowd the skillet. Work in batches if necessary.

Fry the bottom of the pouches until they are golden-brown, about 2–3 minutes. Carefully pour ¼ cup of water into the skillet, cover with a lid, reduce the heat to medium-low, and continue to cook for 5–6 minutes. Turn off the heat. When the audible sputtering of oil has ceased, carefully remove the lid.

Serve jianjiao hot, optionally with a dipping sauce.

Shaomai
烧卖
(Steamed Open-Faced Dumplings)

Shaomai could easily fit into the "What's in a Name?" chapter of this book. You see, *shaomai*, as it is commonly translated, literally means "cook and sell." *This could be the name for every food ever sold on earth*! Wow, that's a lot of power in one little dumpling: the chosen bun, if you will. Our good archaeologist friend clearly had something to say about this most generic of naming conventions. According to Qu Feng, "The name was originally *shao*, meaning little, and *mai*, meaning wheat. The skin was thinner than other dumplings. At some point, the pronunciation of those characters changed, but salesmen didn't want to change the name of the snack, so they went with words that sounded like the original and would sell well." Makes perfect sense. Since "cook and sell" is now commonly seen on American Chinese appetizer menus, and even is in the freezer aisle at Trader Joe's, it's happy in this chapter as well.

The first mentions in literature of shaomai came about 700 years ago, along with the Yuan Dynasty. They appeared from the north along with China's new barbarian overlords. They were quite lamb-centric and rough around the edges, just like the Mongols with whom they arrived. Around that same time, there are tales of shaomai originating in Hunan Province (heavy on the chiles), in Guangdong Province (heavy on the seafood) and in Shanghai (heavy on the high fashion). So, in our scientific estimation, we believe the true origin of shaomai to be any cook who thought it too complex to seal a darned dumpling. You see, the one thing they all have in common is that they are all open-topped, which points to no actual origin for the shaomai, aside from the lazy-man's dumpling house. License to chill, granted.

FILLING:
½ lb ground pork
½ lb shrimp, peeled, deveined, minced
1 inch ginger, peeled, grated
2 water chestnuts, minced
1 Tbsp soy sauce
1 tsp toasted sesame oil
½ tsp salt
½ tsp ground white pepper
1 Tbsp cornstarch
¼ tsp baking soda

WRAPPERS:
1 egg, beaten
1 Tbsp water
1 16-oz package wonton, shaomai, or gyoza skins, square preferred
Water for steaming

OPTIONAL DIPPING SAUCE:
1 recipe Dipping Sauce from Zhurou Jiaozi (Steamed Pork Dumplings) on page 53

In a large mixing bowl, thoroughly combine all filling ingredients.

In a small mixing bowl, whisk together 1 egg and 1 tablespoon of water. Lightly brush one whole side of one wrapper with egg wash. Place the wrapper egg-side up in a cupped palm. In the middle, place 2 teaspoons of filling. Raise up the sides of the wrapper, making a cup around the filling, pleating onto itself and leaving the top of the filling exposed. Gently press the sides of the cup to ensure none of the wrapper falls away. Repeat with the remaining filling and wrappers.

Prepare steamer baskets by lining them with cheesecloth or parchment paper. Place the filled dough parcels atop the lining in a single layer. If you have stackable steamer baskets, continue to fill baskets. Otherwise, steam dumplings in batches. Cover the steamer basket(s) with their matching lid(s).

Place a skillet or pot over medium heat, fill with 2 inches of water, and bring to a boil. Carefully place the steamer baskets atop the pot of boiling water, cover, and steam the dumplings for 12 minutes.

In a mixing bowl, whisk together the dipping sauce ingredients. Serve shaomai along with a bit of dipping sauce.

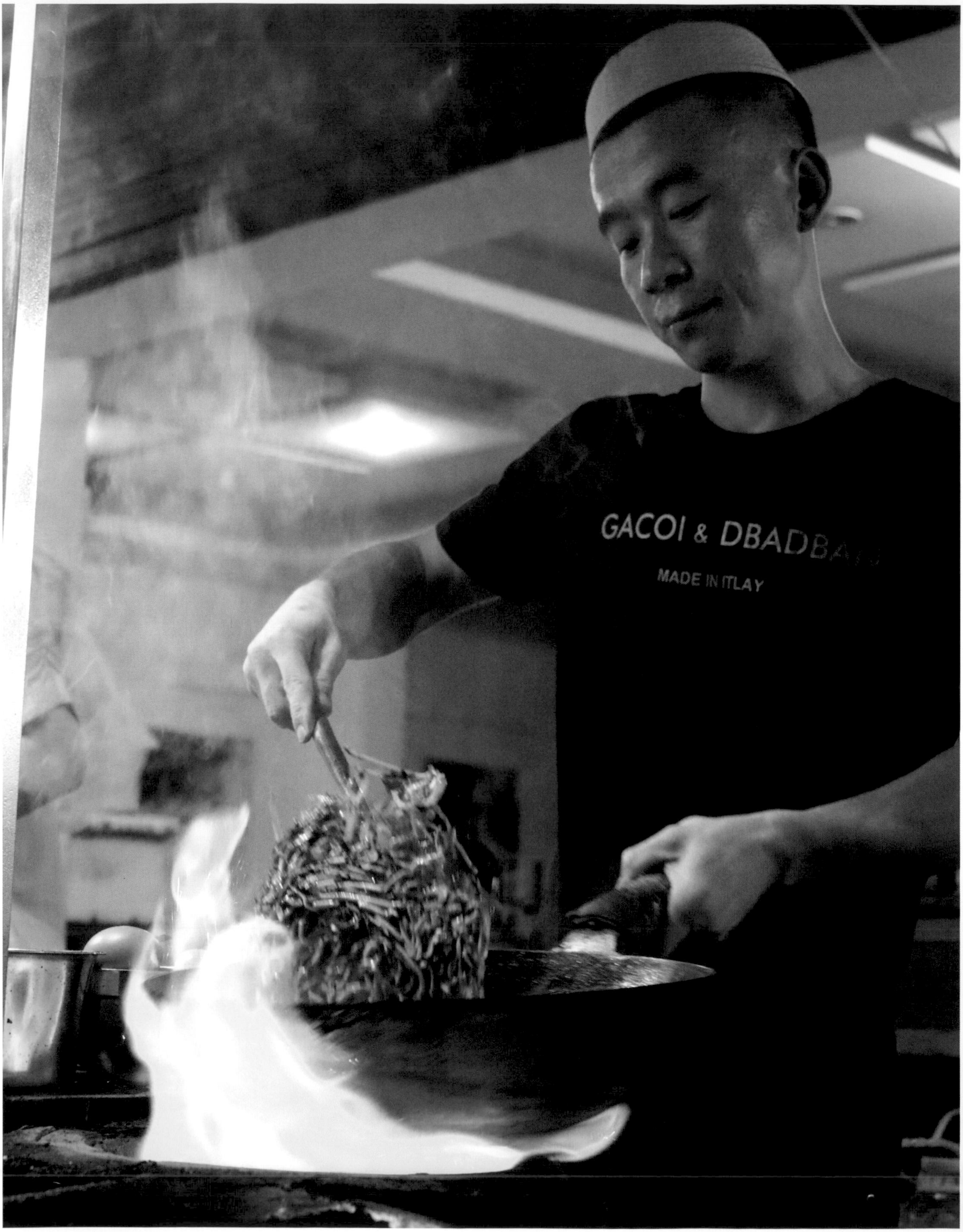
MADE IN ITLAY

Zasui Chaofan / Zasui Chaomian
杂碎炒饭 / 杂碎炒面
(Fried "Miscellany" Rice) or (Fried "Miscellany" Noodles)

When you eat out at a restaurant in China, fried rice is a fairly staid affair, seldom seen as a highlight, and reserved as the filler near the end of a meal. Frankly, it's a great way to liven up leftover rice just enough to forget that it was yesterday's miscalculation: day-old rice, scallions, scrambled eggs, and some salt. There are some notable exceptions, namely the famous fried rice from the east coast city of Yangzhou: The standard recipe, plus shrimp, ham, peas, ginger, garlic, and if the chef is feeling particularly adventurous, some kind of nut. This comparatively rich permutation is the great-grandmother of what we see in US restaurants.

On the street food scene, if you're lucky enough to see a big ball of flame from afar while on a nighttime stroll, run to it. Someone is undoubtedly wok-ing up some crazy fried rice concoction for a lucky passerby. Even for the non-Chinese speaker or casual traveler, it's a point-and-eat pleasure. Street stall fried rice may still be a safe way of using up leftovers, typically acquired from surrounding restaurants, but it's also a cross between a visit to Chipotle and a circus performance. This type of stir-fry acrobatics, usually kept behind closed kitchen doors, offers an open-air spectacle, which makes the resulting snack even more of a tale for the folks back home.

Speaking of tales, fried rice once saved an evening. Guilin, the familiar China of landscape paintings, tall karst peaks plummeting down to placid rivers, can sometimes be a terrific setting for an episode of *Bizarre Foods*. In some neighborhoods, it can be easier to be offered exotica from cages outside of a restaurant than it is to find some Chinese comfort staples. On a particularly challenging food night in 1999, we were hungry and pleasantly surprised, after passing a *literal* zoo of choices, to wander into a kindly Muslim street cook whipping up halal fried rice and noodles. The choose-your-own adventure selection you see below was the welcome antithesis to the fresh guinea pig a few blocks back. Homemade fried rice or noodles can be equally delicious if you approach this meal as a fridge clean-out and swap out ingredients at will. But, to us, this will always be Guilin in a bowl.

2 Tbsp vegetable or canola oil

½ red onion, or whole shallot, thinly
sliced

1 large bell pepper, diced

2 scallions, white and green parts
divided, thinly sliced

2 cloves garlic, finely minced

¼ head green cabbage, thinly sliced

4 oz bean sprouts

1 tsp salt

½ tsp ground white pepper

4 eggs, beaten

4 cups cooked white rice, cool, ideally
day-old *or*

½ lb thin rice noodles, cooked, cooled

OPTIONAL SEASONINGS:

Red chile oil with sediment *or* Lajiao
You (Chile Oil) on page 132

Toasted sesame oil

Soy sauce

Heat a skillet over high heat and add the oil. When the oil begins to lightly smoke, add
red onion and bell pepper, and quickly sauté until softened, 1–2 minutes. Add scallions and
garlic and quickly sauté until fragrant, about 30 seconds. Add cabbage, bean sprouts, salt, and
pepper, and continue to sauté for 3-4 minutes, or until the cabbage has completely wilted.

Push the vegetables to one side of the skillet and add beaten eggs, and quickly scramble
them, then sauté along with the vegetables. Add the rice or noodles to the skillet. Stir the
rice or noodles around to mix everything in the skillet evenly. Every 30–45 seconds, stir the
rice or noodles to mix it up again, but leaving it to cook on the bottom. This will create bits
of slightly crispy rice or noodle in the end. After 3–5 minutes of cooking, the zasui is done.

Top with sliced scallion greens and optional seasonings, and serve hot.

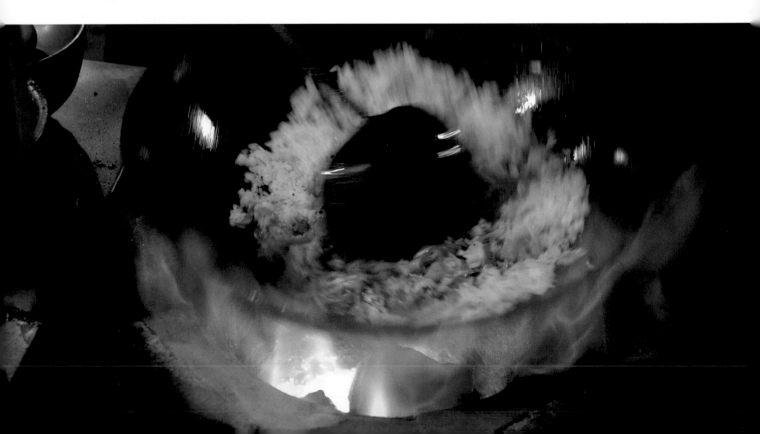

Chashao
叉烧
(Basic Roasted Pork)

Historically, China, with its vast treeless plains, has had a shortage of cooking fuel. Slow-cooked dishes, for centuries, were reserved for the elite. So, it makes sense that most traditional cooking methods seek the biggest bang from their scant heat source, resulting in quick, efficient, and generally high-heat affairs. You have your ingredients cut into small bits. You have your stir-fries. You have your open-fire grill. You have your steam. What then of big, relatively fatty meats? You let chemistry do some of the work ahead of any heat. Enter, the partial cure. Perhaps the most famous of these dishes is *chashao*, or the "fork-roast," named for the traditional method of hanging strips of pork over a fire.

Whether or not you've known it, you've been familiar with chashao all of your life. Those little maroon bits of succulent pork in your fried rice? Those long strips of crimson meat hanging in Chinatown windows next to the Beijing-style roasted duck (page 275)? Those slightly charred ruby ribs your dad regularly ordered on Friday nights and dipped into spicy yellow mustard for some reason? Those are all chashao, and it's even more popular in China. Though it's typically sold at street markets for home use, seldom is it a stand-alone street snack. We offer this recipe to accompany some others in the book. Then again, we won't judge you if you wish to cook some up, slice it, and just munch. We do it, too.

Total Time: 48 hours, plus 3 hours, 45 minutes | Serves: 4–6

¼ cup soy sauce
2 Tbsp mushroom or dark soy sauce
2 Tbsp Chinese rice wine or dry sherry
2 Tbsp red chile oil *or* Lajiao You (Chile Oil) on page 132
⅓ cup honey
1 tsp red food coloring (optional)

1 inch ginger, peeled, finely minced
2 cloves garlic, finely minced
½ tsp Chinese five-spice powder
½ tsp ground white pepper
¼ cup white sesame seeds
2 lb pork shoulder, boneless, 2 x 2-inch strips
1 cup water

In a mixing bowl, whisk together soy sauce, dark soy sauce, rice wine, chile oil, honey, red food coloring if using, ginger, garlic, five-spice powder, white pepper, and sesame seeds. Transfer ¼ of the mixture to a separate container, cover, and refrigerate. This is the basting mixture. Place pork in a sealable container, snugly at the bottom, or in a ziplock bag. Pour the remaining marinade over the pork, and massage the meat until thoroughly coated. Cover and transfer the container to the refrigerator for 48 hours. Every 12 hours or so, turn the meat to redistribute the marinade.

Remove the pork from the refrigerator, discard the marinade, and place the pork on a roasting rack above a roasting pan. Allow the meat to rest at room temperature for 30 minutes. Preheat the oven to 325°F. Remove the basting mixture from the refrigerator.

Carefully pour water into the roasting pan below the pork and transfer the pan to the oven. Roast the pork for 3 hours, turning over half way through. Every ½ hour, brush the pork with the basting mixture. Remove the pork from the oven and allow to rest at room temperature for 15 minutes before carving and serving, or reserve for other recipes. Chashao would be a good addition to dishes such as Xianggu Zhou (Mushroom Rice Porridge) on page 65 or as a filling for Baiji Mo (Baked Sandwich Buns) on page 105. If you're feeling adventurous, diced chashao would also be a great replacement filling for the Zhurou Baozi (Steamed Pork Buns) on page 49.

Cong Youbing
葱油饼
(Scallion Pancakes)

Like a lot of Chinese flatbreads, *cong youbing*, or "scallion pancakes," likely belongs in the "What Came with the Camels" chapter just as easily as it fits into this one. You see, it's darn-near close to the Indian paratha in method, taste, and texture, and despite its pervasiveness across China, nobody can pinpoint when it begins to appear in literature. So, it's safe to assume that it's a centuries-old import from attempted conquests to the West of China. But, since 1) we're big fans of ordering these in *every* Chinese restaurant we visit in America, and 2) it's the one true example of a flaky-layered snack that is most likely to be as delicious outside of China as it is within, this chapter is the perfect home.

One of the main reasons we believe that cong youbing can be deliciously found wherever Chinese have settled is that it's one of those super-basic recipes that's typically taught from older generation to the next. You would be hard pressed to find a Chinese cook around the globe who didn't learn how to craft these pancakes as a child. A buddy of ours, Kaiser Kuo, is the host of the *Sinica Podcast* and a gastronome of epic proportions. Kaiser remembers, "It was one of the things my grandmother made constantly when we were young. The main thing that I learned from her was the right dough consistency: I've never measured. I'd tried to make it a couple of times before my big brother, who had watched more carefully, taught me the trick." Where we do recommend Kaiser's cooking-by-touch, and honing the texture of a perfect dough, here's a solid place to start.

Total Time: 1 hour, 30 minutes | Serves: 6–8

3 cups all-purpose flour, plus more
   for dusting
½ tsp salt
1 cup hot water

1 tsp vegetable or canola oil, plus more
   for brushing and frying
10 scallions, thinly sliced

Whisk together flour and salt in a large mixing bowl or the bowl of stand mixer. Using clean hands in a mixing bowl or the dough hook in a stand mixer, slowly incorporate the water and 1 teaspoon of oil and knead until a single mass of dough forms.

continued on page 274

NOW THAT'S ONE EXPRESS PANDA

Dust the work surface with flour and transfer the dough on top. Knead and form the dough into a smooth ball. Transfer the dough to a lightly oiled, clean bowl, and cover with plastic wrap. Allow the dough to rest for 30 minutes.

Divide the dough into four equal parts, and cover the others with plastic wrap while you work with the first. Dust your work surface with flour. Form the dough into a ball, then use a rolling pin to form a large ⅛-inch-thick rectangle. Leaving ½-inch gap at the edges, brush a thin layer of oil, sprinkle ¼ of the scallions across the top.

Starting at the bottom (long edge), tightly roll the dough forward onto itself, as you would a poster. Then, starting at one end, coil the tube into a tight spiral. Once you reach the other end, fold the tip underneath the spiral of dough. Using a rolling pin, evenly flatten the coil to a 6–7-inch disc. Set aside and create more discs with the remaining dough.

Add 1 teaspoon of oil into a skillet over medium-high heat. When the oil begins to shimmer, place one dough disc into the skillet. Fry for 2–3 minutes or until the bottom is golden brown. Flip the pancake and fry for another 2–3 minutes. Remove the pancake to a paper towel-lined plate and repeat for the remaining dough discs.

Cut the scallion pancakes into wedges and serve immediately as a stand-alone snack or as the starch component of a meal. Optionally, for dipping, provide some soy sauce or perhaps Lajiao You (Chile Oil) on page 132.

Beijing Kaoya
北京烤鸭
(Beijing-Style Roasted Duck Breasts)

Beijing kaoya or "Peking" roasted duck is a dish that was first created by royal chefs during the Ming Dynasty while the capital was in Nanjing. So, technically, shouldn't it be Nanjing Duck? Anyhow, it's morphed from a questionably complicated roast, cooked inside of the stomachs of larger creatures, to a single-animal affair—sugar, syrup, and spices coating the dried-out skin of the bird, hanging from a hook over wood. Rumors abound that royally refined recipes used dozens of secret spices, à la Colonel Sanders. When a small number of *Emperor-approved* restaurants started popping up outside the royal compound in the 1500s in Beijing, chefs stiffly guarded their modified recipes from one another, so the rumors of high complexity remained.

The truth is much less exciting. Howie once had a rare opportunity to chat with Li Shanlin, proprietor of the Li Family Restaurant in Beijing. Li's grandfather, Li Shunqing, was a palace guard in the Forbidden City during the final days of the Qing Dynasty. His charge was the royal kitchens and roughly 100 troops who watched over as cooks prepared meals, assuring that VIPs were never poisoned. As the dynasty was collapsing around him, Li Shunqing committed recipes to memory, and surreptitiously recorded them. Flash forward to today, Li Shanlin is the keeper of the imperial kitchen's flame, including their duck. Mr. Li agrees, based upon his grandfather's notes, real Beijing duck is simple, and it should taste like duck. If a spice or two help the meat and skin retain their flavor, texture, and quality, then that should be that.

In our experience, when you go out for "Peking Duck" in Beijing, it's a whole big thing. You go with a crowd. You order a whole duck. You get duck bone broth soup, fried duck tongues, duck blood-infused tofu, and all manner of duck offal prepared in creative ways. On principle, we appreciate that the whole bird is being put to use, with little if any waste. That being said, we'd prefer to avoid the nasty bits. Over the past decade, we've happily witnessed a steady increase in street food vendors selling just the crispy duck breast in traditional thin pancakes, adorned with the usual restaurant-style accoutrement. Finally, a place to fulfill our love for Peking duck in a non-guilt-inducing fashion.

DUCK:
2 Tbsp soy sauce
1 Tbsp Chinese rice wine
1 Tbsp honey
½ tsp five-spice powder
20 oz duck breasts, skin-on, boneless

PANCAKES:
1 (16-oz) package "Peking Duck" wrappers
3 Tbsp hoisin sauce
1 cucumber, julienned
4 scallions, julienned
½ cantaloupe, julienned
2 Tbsp granulated sugar

In a small bowl, whisk together soy sauce, rice wine, honey, and five-spice powder. Add duck breasts and coat thoroughly with the marinade. Place duck breasts skin-side up in a rimmed plate or baking dish, so that the duck fits snugly at the bottom. If there is marinade left in the bowl, pour it over the duck. Place the plate in the refrigerator, uncovered. For the first 6 hours of marinating, every hour, use a pastry brush to paint the marinade from the bottom of the dish on top of the duck skins. Then, allow the skin to dry out for the duration.

After at least 18 hours, remove the duck from the refrigerator, score the skin in a grid pattern and allow it to rest at room temperature for 30 minutes. Preheat the oven to 400°F. Place the duck skin-side down in a skillet and press it flat, so that the skin has complete contact with the bottom of the skillet. Heat the skillet over medium-low. You will notice duck fat begin to render out from beneath the skin. After about 7–8 minutes, the fat will have melted away, and the skin will be crispy.

Transfer the duck from the skillet to a sheet pan, skin-side up. Transfer the sheet pan to the oven and roast until the duck is just cooked through, about 7–10 minutes. Remove the duck from the oven and allow it to rest for 10 minutes before carving into thin slivers that include skin and meat.

Prepare a wrapper by brushing it with hoisin sauce, placing some cucumber, scallion, and cantaloupe, sprinkling it with sugar, and finally adding some slivers of duck. Roll it up like a burrito and indulge.

Danhua Tang
蛋花汤
(Egg-Drop Soup)

Let's get something out of the way first. In Chinese, the name of this dish is incredibly elegant. *Danhua tang*, or "egg flower soup," totally beats "egg-drop soup" in the *appetizing* contest, every time. One connotes delicate, wispy petals floating like a cloud, and the other, something that ends in catastrophe. Crack, sploosh. Sometimes it's a real head-scratcher to consider who thinks—or doesn't think—this stuff up! Maybe we'll start a campaign.

Now then, this is yet another soup that is on every Chinese menu in the US. It typically sits alongside its two compatriots, wonton soup and hot and sour soup. All three are authentic and all three can be found in some permutation or another across China. But, here's where the American Chinese and Chinese food cultures diverge: these elixirs, and most notably, egg flower soup, are popular *breakfast* street snacks! During our first China adventures, we'd always keep our eyes peeled for any foods with which we were already familiar as Americans, just to make some connection points. Most lunch and dinner dishes in restaurants looked over-the-top and just different enough to not ring many bells, and the soups certainly appeared new. But, once we ventured beyond our normal baozi buns for breakfast and took a look behind the steamer stack, there it was, a simmering cauldron of hearty stock and a bowl of beaten eggs, awaiting the next hungry guest before joining forces.

In fact, danhua tang is seldom eaten on its own and is nearly always coupled with whatever is coming out of those very steamers, likely a starchy best friend. After this early discovery some twenty years ago, our choice has always been baozi, since they're filled with delicious meat and/or vegetables, thereby standing up on their own, and have a pillow-like wrapper, great for soaking up soup. Not only does this type of pairing comply with the traditional Chinese gastronomic ideal of balance in flavors and textures, but it also checks the box of Chinese nutrition. In lore, soup should be a part of every meal to aid in digestion. But, at the very least, soup during breakfast gets the body going in the right direction. It turns out, the idea of breakfast being the most important meal of the day is universal!

10–12 cups chicken broth *or*
   broth from Jirou Tang
   (Chicken Soup) on
   page 189

1 lb baby spinach
8 eggs, beaten
½ tsp salt
4 scallions, thinly sliced

Bring broth to a boil over medium heat, then reduce the heat to low. Stir spinach into the pot and simmer for 5 minutes. In a mixing bowl, whisk together eggs and salt.

Stir the broth to create a current, then slowly drizzle the beaten eggs into the pot. Continue to slowly stir and simmer for 2–3 minutes, until the eggs are fully cooked.

Evenly distribute the soup into bowls. Top with scallions and serve hot. Danhua tang goes well with Youtiao (Fried Dough Sticks) on page 67, Baozi (Steamed Filled Buns) on page 49, and Mantou (Steamed Buns) on page 11.

CHAPTER 10: SWEET STREET

GIFT-GIVING IN CHINA IS A big deal. Especially when being hosted or helped out by a local, it is imperative that one brings something special from the home country to offer the receiver some good will, sort of a pre-thank-you for being willing guides. In our early days of visiting China and re-visiting friends we've met along the way, we've presented all sorts of gifts from the US: keychains, pens, I ♥ NY t-shirts, etc. Eventually, our trips became so food-centric that it felt most appropriate to give back a little by bringing along edible gifts from home. So, we would figure out some Western snack that would transport well and make an impression on our hosts. It didn't go so well.

When we were cutting the proverbial ribbon on our ill-fated Chinese art import business some years back, we had a big set of meetings scheduled with the director of an art school who was going to be our main supplier, Mr. Wang. We had to make a big splash with this guy, and thoroughly considered the perfect gift. We knew a few things about Chinese culture that may help us choose a meaningful, *let's-be-successful-partners* token. All good things in China start with the color red, symbolizing joy, luck, and happiness. If you want to promote wealth, treasure, and prosperity, you go with gold. Painstakingly, we lap-carried a beautiful rose bouquet dotted with those Ferrero Rocher balls in gold foil. It was gorgeous and the gift was a hit with Mr. Wang.

Flash forward one year, while giving the art import business one last college try, we made a quick visit to check in with Mr. Wang. There it was, in all of its sun-dried glory, our beautiful bouquet dotted with those Ferrero Rocher balls in gold foil. Though it was indeed still picturesque in its own special way, we couldn't help but to think, *what gives*? Mr. Wang explained, "The arrangement just looked so perfect, I couldn't bear to think of unwrapping any of the gold balls. Is that chocolate inside? Yeah, that's a little too exotic for me." We were confounded.

Time to dig a little deeper. When you dine at a restaurant in China, you will undoubtedly notice the lack of a dessert menu. If you've spent a good penny on a big banquet, "compliments of the chef" may come in the form of an elaborate fruit plate. That's about the extent to which a meal capper would involve sweets. But still, no lava cake? No brownie sundae? No key lime pie? The Chinese view on sweets is simply different. Though they learned about granulated sugar from the Indians while Europe was still sucking on the cane, their confections tend to rely on the natural sweetness of primary ingredients such as sweet potato, nuts, glutinous rice, sweet peas, seeds, bean paste, squash, etc., with sugar as a *nice-to-have* enhancer.

As such, it's a challenge to find a Chinese treat that is as sweet as Western desserts. Texture and subtlety are just as important as a sweet flavor, if not more. From the surprising springiness of Fried Sesame Balls (page 303) to the delightful crispiness of Peanut Candies (page 282), even in what we will stubbornly still call *dessert*, they somehow find their way to balance.

(P.S. If you feel like devouring some Rocher balls after you enjoy some Chinese pastries, we won't blame you. We also may join you.)

Huasheng Tang
花生糖
(Peanut Candies)

Our archaeologist friend, Qu Feng, is one of those guys who will argue, faced with a shadow of doubt, that many things commonly thought of as "New World" were originally found in ancient China. We once challenged him with the history of the peanut, which science overwhelmingly places somewhere in South America. Qu Feng debates the point, "We have found traces of peanuts on pottery that is over two thousand years old. So, if you are correct, then traders arrived here way before you think. But, if you're wrong, then we perhaps cultivated it ourselves." Then, his most controversial alternative hypothesis yet, "Or, maybe the Chinese discovered the Americas first and brought them back." We love that guy. Don't get him started on pizza and spaghetti.

One thing is for sure, no matter how peanuts got to China, they were fully embraced as a culinary friend, from savory to sweet. One of the more entertaining street snacks involving peanuts is *huasheng tang*, or "peanut candies." If you visit a touristy street in China, typically fabricated to look like an ancient road ("Chinatown" right there in the middle of China?), you will undoubtedly hear the thumps of sledge hammers pounding peanuts into oblivion. It's fun to watch on as the inevitable crowd gathers to witness two percussively synced yet competing pounders go to town. It's a fantastic sales technique, unless someone gets dinged by shrapnel . . . or a giant mallet. We would classify this as *don't try this at home*.

Most everyday huasheng tang vendors make a safer, vastly more accessible version, one that is very close to traditional brittle with a Chinese accent. If we were to ask Qu Feng, you can bet that it was the Chinese who came up with brittle in the first place.

Total Time: 30 minutes | Serves: 4–6

1 lb raw peanuts, shelled, skinless
1½ cup granulated sugar
½ cup water

½ tsp salt
3 Tbsp toasted sesame seeds

Add peanuts to a skillet over medium-low heat. Stir continuously for 10 minutes. Remove from the heat, transfer to a bowl. Once cool to the touch, lightly crush the nuts in a ziplock bag with a rolling pin, or other blunt object. Wipe out the skillet.

continued on page 284

Line a rimmed sheet pan with parchment paper. Sprinkle half of the sesame seeds across the parchment.

Add sugar, water, and salt to the skillet over medium-high heat. Stir and cook until the mixture begins to darken slightly, about 8–10 minutes. Reduce the heat to low, add the nuts, and quickly stir until they are well coated.

Immediately pour the skillet contents across the parchment in the sheet pan and use a spatula to spread an even layer. Sprinkle the top with remaining sesame seeds. After a few minutes, while warm, use a knife to shape individual bars of brittle. Separate the bars and allow them to cool completely before getting nutty with it.

Huasheng Jiang Danhong Gao
花生酱蛋烘糕
(Peanut Butter Pancakes)

Danhong gao, or "baked egg cakes," should be familiar to the Western palate. Our guess is that it was indeed influenced by New World recipes, as it's younger than the earliest known missionaries to visit Sichuan Province. It's also a departure from the typical Chinese pastry ethic. It's essentially a cross between a flapjack and a crêpe, but with a fermented dough. So, we'll modify the comparison to most accurately describe it as a sourdough flapjack crêpe. The Chinese mostly top them with savory and/or spicy spreads, occasionally meat, or pickled vegetables. If they go sweet at all, it's macerated fruit or jam. To further cement it as Chinese, of course there is no maple syrup, Nutella, or even ham and cheese inside these guys. Right? Not so fast.

Last year in Chengdu, we ran into a guy selling danhong gao with the options of whipped cream, condensed milk, peanut butter, chocolate sauce, and even ham! With danhong gao! Can you believe it? We stuck around, ate a ton, and got to the bottom of his story. We naturally introduced ourselves to the gao master, Mr. Guo, as the queue faded toward the end of his night. We jumped right to it, "Peanut butter and whipped cream? That's so un-Chinese. How are you selling out of these?" He told us the story of a few years back when a tour group from Hong Kong descended on his stall since they recognized what they thought to be Western-style pancakes and wondered why he didn't have toppings to which they've grown accustomed. By the next night, Mr. Guo had gone shopping for *exotica*, so he was prepared to cook up a storm for his new Hong Kong friends. That crowd drew more crowds and these relatively un-Chinese pancake adornments eventually spread to all corners of Chengdu.

Of all the extraordinary toppings at Mr. Guo's snack stall, we've been most intrigued by the peanut butter. As noted in the previous recipe, peanuts have been around China for a long time and they are used in soups, stir fries, candies, and even crushed up as a crunchy garnish. Heck, even peanut oil is the preferred fat for most Chinese chefs. So, if this humble groundnut is consumed in literally every other format, why is its creamy descendent considered alien? We've eaten a lot of peanut butter danhong gao ever since.

PANCAKES:
1 cup all-purpose flour
1 tsp rapid-rise yeast
1 cup soy or cow's milk,
   warm to the touch
2 tsp granulated sugar
1 tsp brown sugar
½ tsp salt

¼ tsp baking soda
2 eggs
6 tsp vegetable or canola oil, divided

PEANUT BUTTER SAUCE:
¾ cup creamy peanut butter
1 Tbsp soy sauce
1 Tbsp sugar

In a large mixing bowl, whisk together flour, yeast, and milk. In a smaller mixing bowl, whisk together sugars, salt, baking soda, and eggs. Ensure that the sugar and salt dissolve. Cover bowls with plastic wrap and allow them to rest at room temperature for 90 minutes.

In a small mixing bowl, whisk together peanut butter, soy sauce, and sugar. Set aside.

Add the egg mixture to the flour mixture and whisk thoroughly into a smooth batter. Add 1 tsp of oil to a small skillet (with a matching lid) over medium heat. When the oil begins to shimmer, add a thin layer of batter and swirl the pan to reach the edges. Add a bit of additional batter to fill any gaps. Allow the pancake to cook for 1½-2 minutes, or until the bottom begins to brown. Cover the skillet and allow the pancake to cook for 1 additional minute.

Remove the cover, gently shake the skillet to ensure the pancake freely moves. Smear a good dollop of peanut butter sauce across the middle of the pancake, fold it into a half-moon, and slide out of the skillet onto a plate. Repeat with remaining batter and sauce.

Tangyou Guozi
糖油果子
(Fried Sweet Dough Balls)

Traditionally, *tangyou guozi*, or "sweet oil fruit," are served several to a stick. There are many examples of sweet, round confections presented in a batch to represent family. Like other sweet treats in this chapter, they were originally only prepared during festivals to conjure up some family unity and happiness. Well, as with most food traditions in China, if something is truly delicious, all-year-long anticipation of limited-edition enjoyment and the timings of old get tossed out the window. Today, if you're in the right place at any time of the year and see what appear to be golden donut holes on a stick, you've found tangyou guozi. Eat them and have your own momentary festival.

In the early days of our China adventures, we were like two walking festivals. Nothing was off the table. New Years' dumplings in July? Count us in. Harvest moon cakes in February? Hold our beers. Tangyou guozi in May? We got dibs. So, one May, we decide on a hike up one of the four sacred Buddhist mountains in China, Mount Emei in Sichuan Province. Emei town sits at the base of the trail and that's where we began our journey. As is our morning custom, we had already carbo-loaded on baozi and hot tea to get some walkin' fuel in the old tank. As we strolled closer to the trail, sweets stalls became more frequent, as if someone was trying to tell us to throw a personal festival in the woods.

Greg insisted on devouring a stick of tangyou guozi while they were still warm from the wok and they were gone within 100 feet of the stall. Howie, on the other hand, was determined to enjoy the snack amidst the conifers and mist of Emeishan, so he managed to wrap the stick of sticky balls in paper and gently placed it into his backpack. (Greg once insisted on toting a *plastic bag* of noodles up the Great Wall to slurp with some ambience, so he owed Howie one silly indulgence.) About two hours into a postcard-perfect valley, dotted with temples among thick pine and fog, Howie unleashed his inner festival, brandished his stick of fried goodness, went in for his highly anticipated first bite . . . when a *monkey* swooped in, snatched the skewer, and fled back to the trees, to the wild cheers of his fellow mischievous macaques. Friends, never invite monkeys to a festival.

Total Time: 30 minutes | Serves: 4–6

BALLS:
1 cup glutinous rice flour, plus
   more for dusting
3½ Tbsp rice flour
3 Tbsp granulated sugar
½ cup water, warm from the tap

2 cups vegetable or canola oil for
   frying

COATING:
1 cup granulated sugar
¼ cup water
1 Tbsp white or black sesame seeds

In a large mixing bowl, whisk together glutinous rice flour, rice flour, and sugar. Add warm water and mix with chopsticks or a spoon until a smooth dough forms. Hand-shape 16–20 ping-pong-sized balls out of the dough, and set aside on sheet of parchment paper or cheesecloth.

In a pot over medium heat, add oil to a depth of at least 1 inch, and heat to 360°F. No thermometer? Use the **Handy Trick** within the Doufunao recipe on page 31.

Prepare a wire rack over a sheet pan next to the stove. Carefully add balls to the oil and fry, rolling occasionally until they are golden brown, about 6–8 minutes. Do not overcrowd the pan; fry in batches. As the guozi are done, remove to the wire rack.

Add sugar, water, and sesame seeds to a separate pot over medium heat. Stir until the sugar dissolves, about 3–4 minutes. Turn off the heat and add the fried balls, in batches, coating them in the mixture and removing them to a wire rack. Serve with toothpicks for easy grabbing. They won't last long.

Hongshu Bing
红薯饼
(Baked Sweet Potato Pastry)

Huguosi is one of the oldest surviving snack streets in Beijing. The street is named after the Buddhist Huguo temple, originally constructed during the 1300s. Though the temple had undergone a number of name changes over the centuries, *Huguosi*, or "temple to protect the country," stuck around. Unfortunately, the physical temple did not. Beginning during the Ming Dynasty in the 1300s, it was common for the local temples to hold a monthly street fair to raise funds and keep their doors open to the public. The fairs would teem with devout and hungry locals and dozens of snack vendors to feed them. Long after the temple was no more, the street on which it sat is still a foodie draw.

In recent years, the Beijing government has been shutting down street-side vendors and encouraging them to take their operations inside. So, looking down Huguosi street is much different today than it was twenty years ago. No hustle, no bustling crowds, no collective sigh of gastronomic pleasure. Sure, you can still enjoy the hundreds of traditional snacks, but these days, you have to walk into a sterile, air-conditioned cafeteria for *street* food. But, we digress. About a year ago, we were strolling through Huguosi, to see if we'd missed any *must-have* morsels the last eight times we'd visited. We were famished. We got very excited to see a tiny steel and wood housing attached to the front of a larger building, jutting out into the sidewalk.

This rather creative entrepreneur had successfully bucked the new system by identifying a little piece of unaccounted for sidewalk in which to sell his *hongshu bing*, or "sweet potato pastries." We were so excited that we ended up talking with Mr. Zhang for an hour before we realized that we had also consumed about a dozen pastries between us. They're that good and, frankly, addictive. Of course, we chatted about his history, why we love to visit China, and naturally, good food. But, we spent the most time talking about his ingredients. We had never seen this particular shade of purple anywhere in China. His secret: friends in the Philippines who give him seeds to grow this uniquely bright sweet potato (well, actually, it's a yam, *shhh*). It was an hour well spent eating delicious snacks, *on the street*.

1 lb orange or purple sweet
    potatoes, peeled, cut into
    1-inch chunks
⅓ cup water, cold, plus 1 Tbsp,
    divided
5 tsp sugar, divided
½ tsp salt

2 tsp vegetable or canola oil,
    plus more for brushing
1½ cups all-purpose flour, plus
    more for dusting
½ cup glutinous rice flour
1 tsp baking powder
1 egg white

Preheat the oven to 350°F. Place sweet potato chunks on a lightly greased sheet pan, wrap tightly with aluminum foil, and roast for 35 minutes. Remove sweet potato from the oven and uncover.

In a large mixing bowl with a potato masher or the bowl of a stand mixer fitted with a paddle, thoroughly mash together roasted sweet potato, ⅓ cup water, 4 teaspoons of sugar, salt, and 2 teaspoons of oil. In a separate mixing bowl, whisk together all-purpose flour, rice flour, and baking powder. With clean hands or the dough hook of the stand mixer, slowly add rice flour mixture until a dough forms that is not sticky to the touch.

Dust the countertop or work surface with additional all-purpose flour and transfer the dough onto the flour. Dust the top of the dough, knead, and form the dough into a ball. Dust the top of the dough ball and cover with a clean dish towel or plastic wrap. Allow the dough to rest for 30 minutes.

Uncover the dough and evenly hand-roll it onto a 2-inch-thick log. Cut the dough into 2-inch pieces. Knead and roll each of the dough pieces into a ball. Preheat the oven to 400°F.

Hand-roll one ball into a 1-inch log. Using a rolling pin, roll the dough into a long oval, about ⅛-inch thick. Using a clean finger, dipped in oil, rub the top surface of the dough, leaving a small gap at the edges. Starting from one narrow end, roll it up as you would a poster. Stand the roll on its end and gently flatten and roll it into a 3-inch disc. If an outer edge sticks out, fold it under the bottom of the disc as you flatten it. Place the disc on a lightly greased baking sheet and continue to make discs with the remaining dough balls.

In a small mixing bowl, whisk together egg white, 1 tablespoon of water, and 1 teaspoon of sugar. Brush the top of the buns with the egg wash. Transfer the sheet pan to the oven and bake for 10–15 minutes, or until the pastries are crispy and risen. Serve hot or warm as a quick sweet treat.

Heimi Gao / Nuomi Gao
黑米糕 / 糯米糕
(Black or White Sticky Rice Fritters)

We love Chinese walls. We've scrambled up the oldest crumbling remains of the Great Wall outside of Beijing, stood atop an 11th century Manchurian wall and waved "hi" to North Korea, gleefully bicycled along the entirely refurbished wall that surrounds the ancient town of Pingyao, and sipped Shaoxing rice wine, watching the sunset over the city after which the booze is named. But, let's tell you about our *favorite* wall of all time. One day, we revisited Howie's old 'hood in the countryside of Liaoning Province with our archaeologist buddy, Qu Feng. He said this area had great history, and we believed him. We hiked through corn fields, stone-hopped across rivers, gave our regards to the occasional village, and ended up climbing up a steep hill that Howie could see from his house, back in the day.

We soon realized that this hill was much farther than it appeared from Howie's balcony. After three meal-less hours (really?) we finally made it to the initial slope and climbed up to the eerily flat hilltop. Qu Feng was right about the history, as he excitedly pointed out ruins of old building foundations, a drainage system, even some broken pottery about six inches into the crusty soil. What was surrounding us, as we pushed away some overgrown brush? Remnants of a wall. Qu Feng busts out a chisel and a little hammer and starts to whack away at the wall. Astonished, we tried to stop him. "It's okay, I'm allowed. I'm an archaeologist," he laughed with an Indiana Jones swagger, then continued, "Look, this was a Korean fort, not Chinese. This part of the province must have been fought over, hundreds of years ago!" How in the world could he tell? "There was no sticky rice in the mortar!"

That's a long story to make a point, but it was worth it, right? The Chinese have been cultivating and cooking with glutinous rice for over 2000 years, and when they began to put up walls around themselves, they found that it also held bricks together really, really well. Though momentarily distracted by cool history and construction uses notwithstanding, the mere mention of sticky rice reminded us of how hungry we were. As the sun was setting and visions of navigating cornfields in the dark scared us, we hurriedly descended the hill, stopped in the first village, and serendipitously came across a guy frying sticky rice fritters for the neighbors. As if by some ancient magic, we were able to raise an appropriate toast to the builders of our new favorite wall. Then, with full bellies, hitched a ride the rest of the way.

2½ cups black or white glutinous rice flour, divided	¼ cup granulated sugar
6 oz Chinese sweet red bean paste	1 tsp vegetable or canola oil, plus more for frying
3 Tbsp dark brown sugar	1 cup water, hot from the tap, divided
	¼ cup all-purpose flour

Place ½ cup of rice flour in a rimmed plate. In a small mixing bowl, combine bean paste and brown sugar. Form the mixture into marble-sized balls and roll them in the rice flour. Set aside.

In a separate small mixing bowl, whisk together granulated sugar, 1 teaspoon oil, and ½ cup of water.

In a large mixing bowl or the bowl of a stand mixer, whisk together all-purpose flour and 2 cups of rice flour. With clean hands or the dough hook of the stand mixer, slowly add the water mixture until a dough forms that is not sticky to the touch. If the dough is still too stiff, add more water, 1 tablespoon at a time.

Tear off a golf-ball sized piece of dough and form a ball in your hands. Make a large well in the dough ball with a clean finger. Place a ball of bean and brown sugar paste into the well and close the ball around the paste. Reform a smooth ball. Slightly flatten the ball and set aside. Repeat with the remaining dough and paste.

In a pot over medium heat, add oil to a depth of at least 1 inch, and heat to 360°F. No thermometer? Use the **Handy Trick** within the Doufunao recipe on page 31.

Carefully add dough balls to the oil and fry, flipping occasionally until they are golden brown, about 7–9 minutes. Do not overcrowd the pan, fry in batches. As the gao are done, remove to a paper lined plate. Serve hot or warm as a quick, sweet treat.

Mahua
麻花
(Fried Dough Twists)

We love traveling on Chinese trains, so much so that we pad our trips to allow for extra time between points A and B. Typically, we will dip into a convenience store near the station to grab some snacks for the journey and walk away with crackers, cookies, knock-off Oreos (they were terrible), and bottles of tea. Back in 2013, we were on a trip around northeastern China to film a special winter episode of *Sauced in Translation*, spent some bitterly cold days in Harbin, and were headed out of town for some R&R. When we arrived at the station, we spotted a woman with a cart, frying *mahua*, or "sesame twists," in the freezing cold. As it was about -9°F, we thought it would be nice to hang around a fryer long enough to thaw and grab some mahua for the train. It's always nice to linger around food being prepared. The aroma, the warmth, the anticipation of eating these crunchy, piping hot confections fresh out of the wok. But then Howie looked at the tickets as we stood; we were at the *wrong train station.*

No time to waste, bag up the mahua, hot, hot, run for a taxi, get to the right station! Bang! One of the wheels of the equipment case pops off. No time! Drag the case on one wheel, get to the taxi stand! We know Chinese drivers to be a bit on the crazy side, but this once, we were glad for the high-speed zigging and zagging through traffic. When we arrived at the right station with fifteen minutes to spare, we thought we were in the clear. Then we noticed that the main entrance was closed off for repairs, and guards were routing *thousands* of folks to a badly marked detour that circumnavigated the entire building, just to get inside. So, off we went through scaffolding and tunnels, up staircases, and down staircases. *Bam!* The other wheel popped off the equipment case, so then we were lugging the 60 pounds instead of dragging. *Run! Time's running out!* All was for naught; as we arrived, panting, beads of sweat now frozen on our brows, adrenaline coursing through our veins, our jaws dropped as the train pulled out of the station. Like we were in a sad movie. Well, we thought, at least we got our mahua. They were great.

Total Time: 45 minutes | Serves: 4–6

PASTRY:
½ cup water, warm from the tap
⅓ cup sugar
½ tsp salt
1 Tbsp vegetable or canola oil,
   plus more for deep frying
1 egg, beaten
2½ cups all-purpose flour

COATING:
1 cup granulated sugar
¼ cup water
1 Tbsp white or black sesame seeds
1 Tbsp chile powder (optional)

In a mixing bowl, whisk together water, sugar, and salt. Be sure that the sugar and salt dissolve. Then, whisk in the oil and egg.

Place the flour in a large mixing bowl or the bowl of stand mixer, using clean hands or a dough hook, incorporate the liquid mixture until a smooth dough forms.

Dust the work surface with additional flour and knead the dough into a ball, then hand-roll into a 1-inch-thick log. Cut the dough into 1-inch pieces. Hand-roll one piece into a pencil-thin snake. Pinch to seal the two ends of the snake, then twist the snake 2–3 times, forming an appealing design. Set aside and repeat with the remaining dough.

In a pot over medium heat, add oil to a depth of at least 1 inch, and heat to 360°F. No thermometer? Use the **Handy Trick** within the Doufunao recipe on page 31.

Prepare a wire rack over a sheet pan next to the stove.

Carefully add dough twists to the oil and fry, turning occasionally until they are golden brown, about 4–6 minutes. Do not overcrowd the pan, fry in batches if necessary. As the mahua are done, remove to the wire rack.

Add sugar, water, sesame seeds, and (optionally) chile powder to a separate pot over medium heat. Stir until the sugar dissolves, about 3–4 minutes. Turn off the heat and add the fried dough, in batches, coating them in the mixture and removing them to the wire rack to cool. Once the mahua are cool to the touch, enjoy the crunch.

Nangua Bing
南瓜饼
(Pumpkin Fritters)

The Chinese have long been fans of the gourd. The flesh is sweet, and the seeds plentiful, so of course this unique fruit has been the perfect gift to send wishes of fertility and plenty of offspring. As if that wasn't enough, the hard shell is perfect for carving out a carrying vessel for everything from water and booze to the occasional magic potion. The latter, combined with the gourd's figure-eight shape, was so prominent in folklore that it came to represent the meeting of heaven and earth, the universe, right there in the produce aisle. Beats the heck out of a jack-o-lantern, eh? So, when its cousin, the pumpkin, was introduced by a group of Mexican tourists in the 1200s (okay, we don't really know the origin story), it was an instant hit.

Some years back, we were hanging out in Qujing, Yunnan Province, with Tanghao, a friend with a government job. Whenever we come to visit, he knows that we'll cure his boredom over several great meals. Despite being in Yunnan, we took him out for Sichuan hot pot. After a couple of hours of palate-burning fun, we suggested that we needed something sweet to counter the lingering tingling in our mouths. Tanghao took us down the block to a stall selling pumpkin fritters, and said, "You Americans love pumpkin pie. This is the pumpkin pie of China." We both despise pumpkin pie, but we're polite guests. One bite and we were sold. These things were nothing like pumpkin pie in all the right ways. Crispy on the outside, creamy and gently sweet on the inside. Perhaps most importantly, no cloves. Ah, *that's* why we hate pumpkin pie.

Total Time: 1 hour | Serves: 8–10

2½ cups glutinous rice flour, divided
8 oz Chinese sweet red bean paste
1 lb pumpkin, or acorn or butternut squash, peeled, seeded, cut into 1-inch chunks

2 tsp vegetable or canola oil, plus more for brushing and frying
4 tsp sugar
¼ tsp salt
2 Tbsp water

Preheat the oven to 350°F. Place ½ cup of rice flour in a rimmed plate. Roll the bean paste into marble-sized balls and roll them in the rice flour. Set aside.

Place squash chunks on a lightly greased sheet pan, wrap tightly with aluminum foil, and roast for 35 minutes. Remove squash from the oven and uncover.

In a large mixing bowl with a potato masher or the bowl of a stand mixer fitted with a paddle, thoroughly mash together roasted squash, 2 teaspoons of oil, sugar, salt, and water. With clean hands or the dough hook of the stand mixer, slowly add remaining rice flour until a dough forms that is not sticky to the touch. If the dough is still sticky, add additional rice flour, 1 tablespoon at a time.

Tear off a golf-ball sized piece of dough and form a ball in your hands. Make a large well in the dough ball with a clean finger. Place a ball of bean paste into the well and close the ball around the bean paste. Reform the ball, and gently flatten it into a 2½-inch puck. Repeat with the remaining dough and bean paste.

In a pot over medium heat, add oil to a depth of at least 1 inch, and heat to 360°F. No thermometer? Use the **Handy Trick** within the Doufunao recipe on page 31.

Carefully add squash pucks to the oil and fry, flipping occasionally until they are golden brown, about 7–9 minutes. Do not overcrowd the pan, fry in batches. As the nangua bing are done, remove to a paper-lined plate. Serve hot or warm as a quick, sweet treat.

Zhima Qiu

芝麻球

(Fried Sesame Balls)

Zhima qiu, or "sesame balls," are also known as *jiandui*, or "fried heaps." We're food guys, so we lean away from tragically descriptive names and toward happily descriptive names. *Heaps*? Who calls a food *heaps*? Anyhow, we've eaten zhima qiu all over China, and despite all looking the same on the outside, there are vast differences on the inside. Some are filled with coconut, some with nuts, some with sweetened egg yolk, but most have a sweetened bean paste core. The chewy sticky rice layer beneath the sesame seeds can also vary. In the South of China, you will find zhima qiu that are sweet, sweet, sweet all the way through, as it's preferred to mix *a lot* of sugar in with the rice flour. We, on the other hand, are honorary Northerners, so we lean toward the version we offer below, which mixes potato and a bit of sugar in, creating a more diverse array of layers and tastes.

You may remember our *hula tang* story (page 151) and our adopted Chinese mother, Mrs. Liu, who wouldn't let us go hungry, not even for a minute, whenever we visit Xi'an. Well, her husband, the eminently affable Mr. Ma, after spending the night crafting the perfect beef broth, spends his days out on the sidewalk frying sesame balls. In his words, "Let the missus feed people what they *need* to eat. I'm in charge of what they *want* to eat." The first time we chatted with him, we asked him about when he learned to make sesame balls, thinking that he would say twenty years ago, or something. Instead, he insisted on speaking for the city of Xi'an. "We've been making sesame balls longer than any other Chinese," he says. "We invented it. Every other city in China can claim any other snack, but if someone in Shanghai tells you that they created the first sesame balls, you tell them about me." We're spreading the word, Mr. Ma.

Total Time: 45 minutes | Serves: 8–10

2½ cups glutinous rice flour, divided
8 oz Chinese sweet red bean paste
½ lb russet or gold potato, cut into 1-inch chunks
1 cup water, boiling

2 tsp vegetable or canola oil, plus more for brushing and frying
2 Tbsp granulated sugar
¼ tsp salt
⅔ cup white sesame seeds

Preheat the oven to 350°F. Place ½ cup of rice flour in a rimmed plate. Form the bean paste into marble-sized balls and roll them in the rice flour. Set aside.

Place potato chunks on a lightly greased sheet pan, wrap tightly with aluminum foil, and roast for 35 minutes. Remove potato from the oven and uncover.

In a large mixing bowl with a potato masher or the bowl of a stand mixer fitted with a paddle, thoroughly mash together roasted potato, hot water, 2 teaspoons of oil, sugar, and salt. With clean hands or the dough hook of the stand mixer, slowly add remaining rice flour until a dough forms that is not sticky to the touch. If the dough is still sticky, add additional rice flour, 1 tablespoon at a time.

Place sesame seeds in a rimmed plate. Tear off a golf-ball sized piece of dough and form a ball in your hands. Make a large well in the dough ball with a clean finger. Place a ball of bean paste into the well and close the ball around the bean paste. With wet hands, reform a smooth ball. Roll the ball in sesame seeds and set aside. Repeat with the remaining dough and bean paste.

In a pot over medium heat, add oil to a depth of at least 1½ inch, and heat to 360°F. No thermometer? Use the **Handy Trick** within the Doufunao recipe on page 31.

Carefully add dough balls to the oil and fry, flipping occasionally until they are golden brown, about 7–9 minutes. Do not overcrowd the pan, fry in batches. As the zhima qiu are done, remove to a paper lined plate. Serve hot or warm as a quick, sweet treat.

Wandou Bing
豌豆饼
(Fried Sweet Pea Crackers)

Sweet peas arrived in China around the 600s and instantly grew in popularity. But, according to a notable Sichuan blogger friend of ours, Jimmy He, "The Chinese weren't patient enough to wait for the peas to fully ripen, so they cultivated a fast-growing version, and enjoy the pod and all." You won't see too many fully matured green peas in Chinese cooking that aren't pureed. Jimmy then got snarky: "These full pods, I think you Americans call them snow peas, and we can't figure out why. There is no snow involved." We *could* have taken the bait, and challenged Jimmy to a food-naming duel. *Dare we mention barbarian heads? Really, Jimmy?* But, we opted for the gentler route of simply allowing Jimmy to take us out for dinner, and forgave him his English-dissing ways. By the way, notable that green peas were originally called *hudou*, or "barbarian beans." What is it with Chinese food and barbarians?

So, when we got to the restaurant that Jimmy suggested, he revealed that he had planned ahead with the owner to present us with a full Sichuan banquet of ancient recipes. We were so pleased and honored. On the way into the dining room, the entrance was lined with cooks preparing classic Sichuan street snacks. Of course, we were curious and stopped to ask Jimmy a bunch of questions and sample the treats. There were Fried Sweet Dough Balls (page 288), Fried "Pan-Helmet" Beef Pastries (page 27), and one that we had never even seen before, let alone tasted. Deep-fried *wandou bing*, or "sweet pea crackers," totally took us by surprise. We're used to crispy Chinese crackers of all flavors, but whole sweet peas? In China? We had to try. Their secret: freeze-dried peas. Already crispy, very smart, and very good. We couldn't stop ourselves. Jimmy chimes in to our overindulgence, "Hey guys, go easy, we have about three hours of dishes ahead of us." *Uh oh.*

Total Time: 1 hour | Serves: 4–6

2 cups all-purpose flour
1 tsp baking powder
1 egg
½ tsp sugar
½ tsp salt

2 cups water
¼ cup vegetable or canola oil, plus
  more for coating and frying
1 cup freeze-dried peas

Preheat the oven to 400°F.

In a large mixing bowl, whisk all ingredients together, aside from the additional oil and peas. Stir in the peas. Allow the batter to rest for 15 minutes. Coat a sheet pan fitted with ring molds or a muffin tin with a thin layer of oil. Ladle enough batter into the molds or muffin tin to cover the bottom of a mold or muffin cup. Transfer the pan into the oven and bake for 15 minutes. Remove the pan from the oven, transfer the pea cakes to a cooling rack, and allow them to cool for 20 minutes.

In a pot over medium heat, add oil to a depth of at least 1 inch, and heat to 360°F. No thermometer? Use the **Handy Trick** within the Doufunao recipe on page 31.

Carefully add pea cakes to the oil and fry, flipping occasionally until they are golden brown, about 3–4 minutes. Do not overcrowd the pan, fry in batches. As the wandou bing are done, remove to a paper lined plate and allow them to cool completely. Crunch away.

ABOUT THE AUTHORS

Greg Matza and Howie Southworth are the bestselling authors behind *One Pan to Rule Them All: 100 Cast-Iron Skillet Recipes for Indoors and Out*, and *Kiss My Casserole: 100 Mouthwatering Recipes Inspired By Ovens Around the World*.

They first formed their creative partnership over twenty-five years ago. This dynamic duo first met during college, working at a summer camp on the University of California campus in Santa Barbara. Be jealous. They became fast friends over Sammy Davis Jr. tunes, Freebirds burritos, and cans of Cactus Cooler.

Their early collaborations included amateur theater productions, ill-fated double-dates, harrowing road trips, and epic dinner parties. These soirees were the seed of their culinary partnership, and continue to this day. Weeks are spent devising and preparing themed parties, which have ranged from A Pirate Feast to a 20-Course Chinese Banquet. Their dress code simply reads, "elastic."

When not near their stoves, Howie and Greg can likely be found eating their way across China. For this insatiable pair, going out for some Sichuan usually involves a trans-Pacific flight. Want to share in their culinary adventures? Visit them on 📷 @HowieAndGreg.

CONVERSION CHARTS

METRIC AND IMPERIAL CONVERSIONS
(These conversions are rounded for convenience)

Ingredient	Cups/Tablespoons/Teaspoons	Ounces	Grams/Milliliters
Butter	1 cup = 16 tablespoons = 2 sticks	8 ounces	230 grams
Cheese, shredded	1 cup	4 ounces	110 grams
Cream cheese	1 tablespoon	0.5 ounce	14.5 grams
Cornstarch	1 tablespoon	0.3 ounce	8 grams
Flour, all-purpose	1 cup/1 tablespoon	4.5 ounces/0.3 ounce	125 grams/8 grams
Flour, whole wheat	1 cup	4 ounces	120 grams
Fruit, dried	1 cup	4 ounces	120 grams
Fruits or veggies, chopped	1 cup	5 to 7 ounces	145 to 200 grams
Fruits or veggies, pureed	1 cup	8.5 ounces	245 grams
Honey, maple syrup, or corn syrup	1 tablespoon	0.75 ounce	20 grams
Liquids: cream, milk, water, or juice	1 cup	8 fluid ounces	240 milliliters
Oats	1 cup	5.5 ounces	150 grams
Salt	1 teaspoon	0.2 ounce	6 grams
Spices: cinnamon, cloves, ginger, or nutmeg (ground)	1 teaspoon	0.2 ounce	5 milliliters
Sugar, brown, firmly packed	1 cup	7 ounces	200 grams
Sugar, white	1 cup/1 tablespoon	7 ounces/0.5 ounce	200 grams/12.5 grams
Vanilla extract	1 teaspoon	0.2 ounce	4 grams

OVEN TEMPERATURES

Fahrenheit	Celsius	Gas Mark
225°	110°	¼
250°	120°	½
275°	140°	1
300°	150°	2
325°	160°	3
350°	180°	4
375°	190°	5
400°	200°	6
425°	220°	7
450°	230°	8

INDEX

Roujia Mo, 248–250

S

sausage
  Hand-Rolled Sausage Pancake, 73–75
  Spicy Barbecued Skewers, 229–231
Scallion Pancakes, 272–274
Sesame Millet Porridge, 149–150
sesame paste
  Baked Sesame Buns, 197–198
  Dandan Mian, 32–34
  Fried Tofu, 183
  Spicy Buckwheat Noodles, 143–145
  "Strange Flavored" Chicken, 16
  Sweet or Spicy Bread, 209–211
  "Sweet Water" Noodles, 41
sesame seeds
  Baked Flatbread, 113–115
  Basic Roasted Pork, 269–271
  Chicken Sandwiches, 203–205
  Fried Beef Meatballs, 235–237
  Fried Dough Twists, 297–299
  Fried Sesame Balls, 303–304
  Fried Sweet Dough Balls, 288–290
  Mushroom Rice Porridge, 65–66
  Peanut Candies, 282–284
  Roasted Chicken, 191–193
  Sesame Millet Porridge, 149–150
  Spicy Barbecued Skewers, 229–231
  Spicy Buckwheat Noodles, 143–145
  Spicy Cured Beef Salad, 141–142
  "Strange Flavored" Chicken, 16
  Sweet or Spicy Bread, 209–211
  "Sweet Water" Noodles, 41
  Tianjin-Style Pancake Wraps, 59–60
Shandong Jianbing, 61–63
Shandong-Style Pancake Wraps, 61–63
Shaomai, 263–265
Shengjian Bao, 245–247
Shouzhua Fan, 118–119
shrimp
  Steamed Open-Faced Dumplings, 263–265
Sichuan Shaokao, 229–231
soup
  Beef Bone Soup, 101–103
  Beef Noodle Soup, 242–244
  Black Pepper Beef Soup, 151–153

Chicken Soup, 189–190
  Cornmeal Porridge in Sour Soup, 155–156
  Egg-Drop Soup, 278–279
  Green Fish Ball Soup, 161–162
  Lamb and Bread Soup, 107–109
  Mushroom Rice Porridge, 65–66
  Sesame Millet Porridge, 149–150
  "Swallowing Clouds" Soup, 25
  Tomato and Egg Noodle Soup, 91–93
soybeans, yellow
  Dandan Mian, 32–34
Spicy Barbecued Skewers, 229–231
Spicy Buckwheat Noodles, 143–145
Spicy Cured Beef Salad, 141–142
spinach
  Egg-Drop Soup, 278–279
spring rolls
  Pan-Fried Potato and Carrot Spring Rolls,
    257–259
squash
  Spicy Barbecued Skewers, 229–231
Steamed "Barbarian Head" Buns, 11–12
  Pickled Vegetables on Grilled Buns, 79–81
Steamed Brown Sugar-Filled Triangle Buns,
  55–57
Steamed Cabbage Dumplings, 53
Steamed Corn Beef Rolls, 126–127
Steamed Eggplant Buns, 49–51
Steamed Open-Faced Dumplings, 263–265
Steamed Pork Buns, 49–51
Steamed Pork Dumplings, 53
Steamed Rice and Beef Cups, 214–216
Steamed Soup Dumplings, 123–125
Stewed Pork Sandwiches, 248–250
Sticky Rice Fritters, 294–296
Stinky Tofu
  Chou Doufu, 157–159
"Strange Flavored" Chicken, 16
Suannai, 213
Suantang Shuijiao, 120–122
sugar, brown
  Fried Brown Sugar Dough, 71–72
  Steamed Brown Sugar-Filled Triangle Buns,
    55–57
  Sticky Rice Fritters, 294–296
Sunflower Seed Brittle, 175–176
"Swallowing Clouds" Soup, 25
sweet bean paste
  Pumpkin Fritters, 300–301